The Economics of US Health Care Policy

In this book, Phelps and Parente explore the US health care system and set out the case for its reform. They trace the foundations of today's system, and show how distortions in the incentives facing participants in the health care market could be corrected in order to achieve lower costs, a higher quality of care, a higher level of patient safety, and a more efficient allocation of health care resources.

Phelps and Parente propose novel yet economically robust changes to US tax law affecting health insurance coverage and related issues. They also discuss a series of specific improvements to Medicare and Medicaid, and assess potential innovations that affect all of health care, including chronic disease management, fraud and abuse detection, information technology, and other key issues.

The Economics of US Health Care Policy will be illuminating reading for anyone with an interest in health policy, and will be a valuable supplementary text for courses in health economics and health policy, including for students without advanced training in economics.

Charles E. Phelps was elected to the Institute of Medicine (now the National Academy of Medicine) in 1991. From 1984 to 2010 he was on the faculty of the University of Rochester (NY), in the departments of economics, political science, and public health sciences, and he served for 13 years as Provost (Chief Academic Officer) and is University Professor and Provost Emeritus at the University of Rochester, USA.

Stephen T. Parente is Professor of Finance at Carlson School of Management, University of Minnesota, Minneapolis, USA. In Washington DC, he has served as Governing Chair of the Health Care Cost Institute, a US Congressional Budget Office health advisor, a senior health policy advisor to Senator John McCain (R-AZ) and a legislative fellow for Senator John D. Rockefeller IV (D-WV).

The Economics of US Health Care Policy

Charles E. Phelps and
Stephen T. Parente

Routledge
Taylor & Francis Group
LONDON AND NEW YORK

First published 2018
by Routledge
2 Park Square, Milton Park, Abingdon, Oxon, OX14 4RN

and by Routledge
605 Third Avenue, New York, NY 10017

Routledge is an imprint of the Taylor & Francis Group, an informa business

British Library Cataloguing-in-Publication Data
A catalogue record for this book is available from the British Library

Library of Congress Cataloging-in-Publication Data
Names: Phelps, Charles E., editor. | Parente, Stephen T. (Stephen Thomas), 1965- editor.
Title: The economics of US health care policy / Charles E. Phelps and Stephen T. Parente.
Description: Abingdon, Oxon ; New York, NY : Routledge, 2018. | Includes bibliographical references and index.
Identifiers: LCCN 2017031429 | ISBN 9780415784313 (hardback) | ISBN 9780415784320 (pbk.) | ISBN 9781315228518 (ebook)
Subjects: | MESH: Delivery of Health Care--economics | Health Care Reform--economics | Insurance, Health--economics | Health Policy--economics | United States
Classification: LCC HG9396 | NLM W 74 AA1 | DDC 368.38/200973--dc23
LC record available at https://lccn.loc.gov/2017031429

ISBN: 978-0-415-78431-3 (hbk)
ISBN: 978-0-415-78432-0 (pbk)
ISBN: 978-1-315-22851-8 (ebk)

Typeset in Goudy
by Sunrise Setting Ltd, Brixham, UK

To Dale and Carrie—they light up our lives in every season and in every way

Contents

Figures

Tables

Foreword

The Economics of US Health Care Policy is not a general survey of Health Care Economics. Rather it is a brilliant laser-like exposition of the distortive incentives that negatively alter behavior in the American health care financing and delivery system and a set of well-conceived proposals for how to fix them. The distortive incentives are largely the result of public policies that were enacted without any or adequate consideration of the economic incentives they created or their long-term consequences. The analytical tools are classical economics, but the book is written for the general (non-economist) reader who is interested in understanding our present health-economic predicament. The book is not about the current debate over the proposed repeal and replacement of the Affordable Care Act. The issues pre-dated the Affordable Care Act and are likely to remain after enactment of any replacement.

The National Academies of Sciences estimated that some 30 to 40% of US health expenditures are waste, that is they do not contribute to the better health of patients. Passing laws against waste doesn't work. The only things that can work are strong incentives that reward economical behavior.

As the authors observe, "The major problem comes with the reliance of our health care financing system on a tax-subsidized system of employer-provided health insurance." And indeed, this system is "the original sin of American health care finance." And the authors were absolutely right in attacking it first and starting with a sensible proposal to correct it. Their novel and constructive proposal is to abolish the tax exclusion of employer contributions from the taxable incomes of employees, and to return all the savings to taxpayers in the form of reduced personal and payroll tax rates. Then people would come to realize that health insurance and health services cost a great deal, and they and their doctors (acting in their patients' best interests) would choose services wisely. The lower tax rates would encourage work and economic growth.

Separating health insurance from jobs would have many benefits. Some people would like to leave their employer either to a better job or to start their own business. But they have been inhibited by the loss of tax subsidized health insurance, known in the trade as "job lock."

The incentives in the current system are cost-increasing. The first incentive is to cover in the tax-free premium everything that might be described as health care—deductibles, copayments, dental care, eye glasses, hearing aids, etc. to take advantage of the tax break—to leave employees unconscious of what these things cost and therefore uninterested in shopping for value-for-money or using these resources wisely. Employers don't mind because they just take the cost out of what otherwise would be wages and salaries.

If I had been writing a book on this general subject, I probably would have started by attacking our dominant model of open-ended, uncoordinated, third-party-paid fee for service, because that too is filled with perverse incentives. ("Open ended" refers to the lack of any prior budget or resource constraint, "uncoordinated" refers to physician autonomy and the lack of teamwork or information sharing, third-party payment refers to the fact that the entity that pays the bills is not the one that makes the expenditure decisions.) The incentives are to resolve all doubts about value to the patient in favor of doing more services, whether or not more are beneficial for the patient. This model was not the consequence of the workings of the free market. Rather, it came about as a consequence of the coercive political power of organized medicine (that is the American Medical Association and the affiliated county medical societies that, for example, could and did expel doctors who wanted to develop alternative forms of organization and payment). Employers, for their own reasons, have chosen to use their control over employee health care, not to offer employees cost-conscious choices, but to lock them into the uncoordinated, open-ended fee for service model. Where employees are offered such a responsible choice of health plan (e.g., Federal Employees, California and Wisconsin state employees) most choose economical Health Maintenance Organizations (HMOs) or High-Deductible Health Plans (HDHPs).

But I would grant the authors that the "original sin" contributed to and enabled these perverse incentives. The authors achieve clarity, coherence, and conciseness by sticking to their self-chosen assignment "to find and correct perverse incentives," and I would be reluctant to suggest messing it up with politics. (This is a non-political book.)

The alternative to job-based health insurance might be exchanges like Covered California.

The authors go on to Medicare and Medicaid, both with their own distorting incentives. For Medicare, they suggest re-setting the deductibles to appropriate levels. And they would adjust the premiums Part B (physician services) and payroll taxes for differences in regional costs so that in more costly regions, people pay more and thus might be more interested in measures to bring down the costs. These are just two of a list of ten Medicare- and Medicaid-specific proposals. Another is to create mechanisms to bypass deductibles and coinsurance for treatments that are reasonably demonstrated to lower the overall cost of care. Yet another concerns that many Medicare beneficiaries have supplemental insurance, called "Medigap" whose effect is to reduce the cost of services to patients. The effect of this is to increase use of services which raises the cost of Medicare, so Medicare is subsidizing Medigap. The proposal is to tax Medigap plans sufficiently so that the tax receipts recoup the extra costs to Medicare.

Medicaid has always had the problem that because it is intended for poor people, it is thought to be inappropriate to charge beneficiaries for use of services. The authors develop innovations that reward cost conscious behavior such as how to reward adhering to prescription drug regimens that prevent the onset of more costly illness, and how to discourage patients from going to expensive emergency rooms in cases in which a primary care visit to their doctors would be better and cheaper.

Waste, fraud, and abuse have been costing Medicare and Medicaid tens of billions per year for many years. I remember this being cited as a major problem in the early 1970s. Politicians love to criticize it, and for a time were blaming the rapidly rising cost on that. Yet, a truly effective solution has eluded the government for all these years. In what I find to be one of the most original of proposals, the authors recommend bringing waste, fraud, and abuse prevention technology into the 21st century by a new prevention system that is transaction-based and assesses claims on a real-time basis and before payment is made and that is based on what the Financial Services industry does. Have you ever been called by your credit card company to ask about the validity of an unusual charge to your card? I have, and the conversation has often ended with "thank you for catching a fraudulent use of my card."

The authors go on to describe the frightening consequences for public finances of an ageing population with increasing prevalence of chronic conditions and the very steep curves relating more cost to more chronic conditions, and also the rising ratio of retirees to workers who pay the taxes to support Medicare and Social Security. They discuss many constructive innovations, including the urgent need to move health care to more coordinated integrated systems with more teamwork and information sharing among providers, and the need to address the lifestyles that generate the costly conditions.

I would have appreciated more discussion of the potential of the "legacy HMOs" Kaiser Permanente, Intermountain Health System, and Partners in Minnesota and what might be done to open the market to more of them. In California where Kaiser's market share among commercially sponsored health insurance now exceeds 42%, more than twice that of BlueCross, other providers are creating their own HMOs and Blue Cross has announced a large program for the capitation financing of some prominent provider systems, all frankly to compete with Kaiser; the transformation to coordinated integrated systems could move much more quickly, and more extensively, if only every employed person were offered a cost-conscious choice of insurance plan in which they could personally benefit by choosing wisely. People often ask me "if these systems are such a good idea, why have they not taken over America?" I suggest they ask employers why they have not opened their markets to them. The likely answers will not do credit to the idea that employers should have such control of health insurance. And this brings us back to where we started with the perverse incentives inherent in tax-subsidized employer-sponsored health insurance.

Alain Enthoven, PhD
Stanford, CA
June 2017

Preface

As this book goes to press in mid-2017, the world of US health policy faces an almost unprecedented time of uncertainty and potential disruption. When we began this project, the Affordable Care Act (ACA) had become law, but implementation was just beginning. In the intervening years, much has happened, some for better, some for worse. Health insurance coverage increased greatly, as did health insurance costs. Many puzzles remain about how best to balance between the many competing goals of such a large piece of legislation. Yet as we go to press, the Trump administration and the Republican-controlled House and Senate have promised to repeal or "repair" the ACA and replace it with a yet-to-be finalized alternative, with the House version—the American Health Care Act (AHCA) passed along strict party lines, and a select group of Senate GOP members crafting a separate version in closed session with no public hearings. Both that effort and a straight "repeal" effort failed in the Senate.

When we began this book, we decided to focus on a key idea—find and fix distortive incentives that negatively alter behavior in the health care system. Much—but not all—of our effort focuses on things that lie completely outside the domain of the ACA and, as such, remain key issues with or without the ACA and with or without any successor "replace" legislation. Thus, we ask our readers to make a quick mental substitution: whenever you read "the ACA" or "the Affordable Care Act," please mentally substitute "the ACA as modified or replaced."

The area of our work most specifically aimed at the ACA centers on the health insurance exchanges. As things appear at this writing, the federal marketplace will likely continue for at least several years and perhaps survive under Republican repair or replacement plans for ACA (if and when they become law). The state-based exchanges will also likely survive as long as their individual insurance markets remain robust, otherwise the states will revert back to the federal marketplace. Many states may choose to get a waiver from the federal government to try their own attempt at reform, which would largely be based on prior success. It is important to keep in mind that the exchange concept has origins with Republican Governors (for example Minnesota's former Governor Tim Pawlenty and Massachusetts' former Governor Mitt Romney) and will likely survive since it is bipartisan in origin and as well as execution. As a result, we believe that our recommendations for "fixing" the health insurance exchanges still pertain.

Similarly, we urge that the "precious metal" standard for rating insurance plans be revised, an issue that preceded the current situation and will likely continue into the future. The idea that more health insurance coverage is always better—the heart and soul of the Platinum, Gold, Silver, and Bronze rating system—is fundamentally flawed. So this issue, although framed in the specific language of the ACA, will also persist in the future.

Thus, our book goes to press the same as would have occurred with a different outcome from the electoral process. We seek to find and fix distorting incentives in our health care system. The biggest of these remains the "original sin" of an income tax-based subsidy to private health insurance. Our Part I deals with these and related issues. Similarly, as before the ACA was enacted, and after it is repealed, modified, or replaced, major issues remain within the structure of Medicare and Medicaid, a program now over half a century old. Our Part II deals with these issues. And some issues in the future—electronic health records, fraud and abuse, finding the best ways to deal with chronic diseases, and related issues—affect both private health insurance markets and public plans (Medicare and Medicaid). Our Part III deals with these issues.

We acknowledge here that we have not addressed some potentially important health policy issues. These would include (among others) questions of medical liability and malpractice reform, and issues of intellectual property rights that (at least in part) affect both the rate of development of new drugs and medical devices and also the prices charged for them by their inventors and manufacturers. Our focus, for better or for worse, has aimed more narrowly at the world of health care finance and related topics. We leave for others these remaining issues.

Finally, we note that (unlike many complex health care legislative packages such as the ACA and the "GOP Replace") most of our proposed reforms can be enacted one at a time or in small packages. This is not a Swiss clock, where removing a single gear brings things to a standstill. In general, legislation can proceed on single components of our proposals without fear that the entire package must rise or fall together. We hope that our efforts herein will lead to subsequent legislation that—we sincerely believe—will improve our health care system across all "seasons" and efforts at health care reform.

Acknowledgments

As with any major work such as this, our intellectual debts literally span the duration of our professional lives, encompassing colleagues (shared by one or both of us) at the RAND Corporation, the University of Rochester (across the fields of economics, political science, business, history, community and preventive medicine, and others), Project Hope, Johns Hopkins University, and the University of Minnesota, as well as numerous contacts throughout the world of health policy in Washington, DC and elsewhere. We could not possibly enumerate a proper list to thank individually, so instead we offer our gratitude to our past and present colleagues who have taught us, challenged us, and hopefully sharpened our abilities to think and write clearly.

We also wish to express our appreciation to the editorial staff of Routledge Press both for carrying our project forward and for their excellent editorial assistance and advice, beginning with Emily Kindleysides, our Corresponding Editor, and Laura Johnson, Senior Editorial Assistant and copyeditor Andrea Ashworth. We also add our appreciation for excellent typesetting work by those at Sunrise Setting Ltd., led by Sharon Nickels.

Executive summary

Our analysis of the US health care system contains three parts—somewhat discrete, but all interacting together. In each case, we focus on distorted incentives that unfavorably alter the behavior of people and organizations engaging each other in the various markets for health insurance and health care. In order, we focus on three distinct segments—private health insurance markets, Medicare and Medicaid, and things that affect everybody.

This summary does not develop the logic behind our proposals in any meaningful detail, but rather summarizes them into a single setting. We ask readers to view this summary as "stage-setting" and, where possible, to defer reaching agreement with or opposition to our proposals until they have read the full set of arguments presented in the main manuscript. Those who do not find such a summary useful should proceed directly to the main text.

Part I: The market for private health insurance

The major problem comes with the reliance of our health care financing system on a tax-subsidized system of employer-provided health insurance. That system arose almost by chance during World War II as a way for employers to attract workers in an era of strict wage and price controls, and grew after rapidly after the war. The World War II wage controls exempted employer-paid health (and term-life) insurance both from the measure of wages paid and hence from the definition of taxable income. This created a subsidy to employer-paid insurance that expanded rapidly when the subsidy was made permanent and uncapped in 1954 tax legislation. With that simple legislative step, a series of unintended consequences emerged that now entangle our entire health care financing system. Because of that 1954 legislative action, we have a health care financing system with the following set of adverse characteristics:

- Too much insurance for those with strong work force connections, leading in turn to too much health care spending.
- Diminished availability, affordability, and variety of non-employer-based insurance.

- Too little attention to cost control among existing insurance plans.
- Too many new technologies flowing into our health care system, a major source of cost growth over time.
- A systematic and large flow of wealth from the poor to the rich.
- More labor disputes, disruptions and work stoppage than would otherwise occur.
- Impaired job mobility, dampening the economy's performance.
- In combination with minimum wage laws, permanent dampening of employment among lower-skilled workers when employer-based coverage is mandated.
- Diminished formation of new and creative startups—the growth engine of the future.
- And finally, a personal income tax and payroll tax system that has higher marginal tax rates than would otherwise exist, hence penalizing productive work, and thus harming economic productivity and growth.

Thus, we state with assurance the following:

> *The most important health care law ever passed in the United States was not the Medicare/Medicaid Act of 1965 or the Affordable Care Act of 2010, but rather a simple provision of the 1954 tax code stating that employer-paid health insurance premiums are excluded from the definition of taxable income (and hence both personal income and payroll taxes).*

We propose to reverse this distortive 1954 segment of the tax code. We are not the first to do so—indeed, a long string of prominent health and labor economists have urged the same thing. But none have created a viable political means to do so. We propose a simple solution to do this that we believe can achieve the goal of eliminating this distortion in health care financing and at the same time provide a permanent stimulus to the US economy. Thus, our first and most important proposal:

> **Proposal 1:** *We propose complete elimination of the favored tax treatment for employer-paid health insurance premiums, coupled with proportionate across-the-board reductions in the marginal income tax structure for personal income taxes, Social Security taxes and Medicare taxes paid by all US workers and their employers as a marginal tax on labor.*

This would add more than $600 billion to the taxable income base in 2016. Simultaneously, we would reduce all marginal tax rates—personal income, employers' and employees' shares of Social Security and Medicare payroll taxes—by the same percentage change as the tax base increases through the addition of employer-paid premiums to the taxable income base.

If nothing else changed, tax revenues would remain unchanged—the taxable income base would expand by more than $600 billion in 2016 (growing annually), representing 5.7% to 8.6% of the current taxable income base (varying by personal income and payroll taxes). In a key part of our proposal, with the expansion in the taxable income base, marginal tax rates would fall by comparable proportions.

Because this combination of changes would be revenue-neutral without any changes in labor force participation, and because we can be assured that the lower marginal tax rates will unambiguously increase the amount of labor provided to the economy, we can thus also say with assurance that the lower taxes on wage income (both income and payroll taxes) would permanently expand employment in the US economy by reducing both the cost of hiring workers and increasing the returns to working in the labor force.

The extent of such expansion is the subject of numerous and contentious discussions among members of the economic profession, but the concept that lower tax rates would lead to an expansion in employment is agreed upon essentially universally. We have estimated the magnitude of the increase in economic activity in three ways, the results spanning estimates of increases in the annual size of the economy from 0.3% to 2.4%, depending on the economic model employed. We estimate that increased tax receipts (federal income taxes, Social Security taxes, Medicare taxes and state income taxes) would increase by $35 billion—certainly not large enough to eliminate the federal deficit, but nevertheless an economic bonus on top of the benefits of removing the distortion in our health care financing system.

Some groups would predictably benefit and some would predictably become worse off financially under our proposal. Those who would benefit most would include people with no (or less than average) employer-paid insurance benefits and those with weak or no connection to the labor force, since all of these groups would see their marginal tax rates (both for income taxes and payroll taxes) decline, with any offsetting increases in taxable income small enough (or nil) to assure positive net changes in after-tax income.

Employers would almost universally benefit in two ways. First, they would see lower marginal payroll tax rates on all workers. Although the taxable income base would rise for workers currently paid below the Social Security tax income cutoff ($118,500 in 2016), our proposed approach assures that the reductions in tax rates would wholly offset the increased taxable income base. Further, any expansion in hours worked—either with new hires or extended work time by existing workers—would come with lower marginal payroll taxes associated with hours worked. Self-employed individuals would receive a triple benefit through reduction of personal income taxes and all Social Security and Medicare taxes (both employer and employee shares).

Employers would also see (as the health insurance market reshaped itself) elimination of labor disruptions and disputes over the magnitude of health insurance benefits. Since workers would pay income and payroll taxes on all forms of compensation—income and any employer-paid premiums—they would have no reason to segment health insurance as a separate bargaining issue. Indeed, we would expect current employer payments towards health insurance to be shifted directly to wage income, allowing workers to take their (increased) wages and shop for health insurance at multiple sources without being tied to employer offerings (which we believe will persist).

Any person relying on something other than employer groups for health insurance would benefit, since the quality, variety, and prices of non-group insurance can only expand once the favored tax treatment of employer group insurance vanishes. We view the current non-group market as having essentially been squeezed out by the subsidized employer-based market. With that subsidy removed, we expect the non-employer-based market to blossom. This will most primarily affect low income workers and those without any health insurance through their workplace, prominently including the self-employed, family owned businesses, and persons working for small firms, both startups and long-time enterprises.

We have a good model of how the employer-based health insurance market would look once our proposal is enacted. Before the 1954 tax law codified the special tax status of employer-paid health insurance, life insurance and health insurance operated as a parallel and equal offering by employers. In both cases, employer-paid premiums were exempt from taxation, so long as the total did not exceed 5% of wage income. The 1954 law capped tax-exempt employer-paid premiums for life insurance at the premium of a $50,000 term life policy. Since then, employers have continued to offer a rich array of life insurance plans to their employees, but the employees pay for the entire cost (except for the premiums for $50,000 of term life, in some cases) with post-tax dollars. Employers offer these plans to their employees because the group purchase arrangement provides a valuable benefit to their employees—life insurance sold at low-cost group rates rather than at more-expensive individual policy rates. So it would continue to be with health insurance, but the decisions would be made without the tax subsidy that now exists.

In life insurance markets, an enormously rich market exists beyond the employer-group market. Individuals can buy a very wide array of term life, whole life (with embedded savings plans), and a wide array of variants to these basic policies. The life insurance market is much richer in its offerings than the parallel non-group health insurance market. The over-65 market in the US provides a similar glimpse of such possibilities for health insurance, with a wide array of group offerings for Medicare Advantage (MA) (Part C) and non-employer-group Medigap plans. With the tax subsidy gone, health insurance markets would similarly flourish.

Indirectly, and in the long run (as the health care system reshapes itself in response to the altered incentives to purchase health insurance), demand for all forms of health care would fall (other things held equal), some more so than others. Health care providers who focus solely on profitability of their enterprises could oppose our proposed change, since the presence of the tax subsidy has unambiguously increased the amount of insurance coverage in force for their services, and hence (because of the way health insurance works) increased aggregate demand for their services. But for those (many) health care providers who also seek to rationalize the health care system, our proposal offers some welcome improvements.

Health insurance plans may divide on this issue. The first response of some will likely reflect high anxiety, as the favored tax status of their main product evaporates. However, those insurers with the foresight to understand the new health insurance market and who can create products that people will more wish to have when the tax incentives change may well have a different view. If one views our taxation proposal as a disruptive technology, then those who can flourish in such an environment should applaud our proposal and thrive upon its enactment. We anticipate, for example, significant additional growth in markets for novel cost-controlling plans, including (but not limited to) Health Maintenance Organizations (HMOs) and High-Deductible Health Plans (HDHPs).

Who would see a negative effect? The most direct answer is simple: Those with higher-than-average levels of employer-paid health insurance relative to their wage incomes. A common group in this condition will be members of labor unions that have negotiated high levels of health insurance coverage. On average, workers in state and local government also have a higher ratio of health insurance premiums to total compensation. We need not conjecture about this—these are the very groups who vigorously opposed the "Cadillac tax" on high-premium health plans within the Affordable Care Act (ACA). With our proposed change to tax all health insurance premiums, the "Cadillac tax" would be repealed, offsetting some (or perhaps all, in some cases) of the increased income and payroll tax levels that would emerge under our proposal.

Proposal 2: *Eliminate the employer mandate.*

While it should be obvious, once the favored tax status of employer-paid insurance is gone, the logic for using employer-paid insurance as a key component to reach universal coverage no longer exists, and hence the logic for continuing the employer mandate evaporates. Many employers will continue to offer employer-sponsored plans (and may continue to pay for some portion of them, at least in transition), but with the favored tax treatment of such plans gone, the market for non-employer plans (both individual and group plans) will grow and flourish in ways that are impossible when facing the tax-subsidized competition of employer-based plans. The mandate forces some firms (most notably those with small work forces and those with many employees at or near the minimum wage) to undertake something that is uneconomic and unnatural, and (because of the ways group insurance is priced) puts them at an economic disadvantage since they have to pay more to gain the same insurance coverage for their workers. We would dissolve the employer mandate immediately upon completion of our Proposal 1.

As we discussed previously, this does not mean that all employers would drop their health insurance offerings. As with life insurance, they would likely continue to offer health insurance options to their employees, but those offerings would likely change to reflect the preferences of workers who no longer purchased health insurance with a major subsidy. Indeed, once it became manifestly clear who was paying for the health insurance (the workers), it is possible that a wider array of smaller firms which (until the employer mandate) did not offer health insurance would happily and voluntarily do so under our proposal. But whether they did or not, we can confidently expect a much richer and more diverse non-employer-based market that will widen the choices of all under-65 US citizens.

Proposal 3: *Eliminate the "precious metals" ranking system.*

The Platinum... Bronze ranking system focuses on the wrong thing—the percentage of medical bills covered by health insurance. Indeed, the presence of too much coverage (and shaped in the wrong ways) sits at the center of many of the problems our health care system faces. Better ranking systems would focus on the extent to which the plans reduced financial risk, increased access to health care providers for enrollees, and carried out their insurance functions efficiently. Better ranking systems will incorporate the extent of coverage, risk protection, quality of care, provider access, and other attributes.

Proposal 4: *Fix the insurance exchanges.*

The Health Insurance Exchanges (HIX) created in the ACA were a major source of embarrassment to the Obama administration, and for good reason—the "rollout" was an operational disaster from any perspective. While the mechanisms were slowly improved, and functioned reasonably well (but far from perfectly) in 2014 and subsequently, we have five specific suggestions to improve the operation of the insurance exchanges, all designed to lead to more efficient operation and more intense competition among insurers. These specific suggestions involve:

A. *Franchise the Exchanges*. Put simply, there is no logical basis for restricting the operation of the HIX to federal or state governments. Allowing states or the federal government to bid out the operational aspects of the HIX operations would provide an increased efficiency. They could be operated under contract with the various states, or even to compete with the federal healthcare.gov operation.

   This would not be a novel step in governmental policy. The Centers for Medicare and Medicaid Services (CMS) already use private firms known as Medicare Administrative Contractors (MACs) to manage the actual claims processing of Medicare Parts A and B and, of course, private companies not only administer but bear the risk in MA (Part C) plans and for Prescription Drug coverage (Part D).

B. *Use Dynamic Bidding*. Dynamic bidding has an active market where insurance carriers bid for the right to provide health insurance. It could readily be used in the HIX environment. As early as 1999, private auctions to provide health insurance were created by Hewitt Associates, to secure competitive bids for a consortium of corporations seeking to lower their health insurance premium costs. The results demonstrate the value of dynamic bidding, and we encourage its use in HIX.

C. *Allow and Encourage National Bidding and Competition*. This capability may actually already exist, but remains hidden. Insurance carriers already bid on national markets in the federal HIX. We simply would allow insurance firms to bid nationally rather than on a state-by-state basis. Allowing this simple step would create economies of scale for insurance companies and increase choice to consumers.
D. *Allow Insurance Sales Across State Lines*. The key idea here, quite simply, is to increase the number of participants in markets that are sometimes narrow and thin (where relatively few insurers operate within the state). Competition from out-of-state firms will increase the competitive pressures on premium costs and will also enhance the variety of plan offerings available to consumers.
E. *Passive Management*. Active management of markets places up-front barriers to entry as the government either prevents entry or forces modification of premiums if regulators think that the plan (or company) is not viable. Passive management lets firms post prices (after an auction, preferably, as discussed above), and lets the market then determine viability. Bids that are too high will fail to attract business. Bids that are too low will cause firms to go out of business or readjust, burning their reserves along the way. Mandatory reserve levels will generally protect consumers even with massive under-pricing of insurance contracts.

Part II: Medicare and Medicaid

Since 1965, the US government has been a major (and in most cases, the largest) single force in the US health insurance "world." Medicare and Medicaid directly account for almost 40% of all health care spending, far larger than any single private insurer. But the effects spread more broadly. Private insurance plans can learn from Medicare and Medicaid successes and failures, and embrace the successes as part of their own efforts. They have done so on numerous occasions, including the widespread adoption of the ways in which hospitals and physicians are paid and determinations of what specific treatments to cover (or not).

Since its inception in 1965, Medicare and Medicaid have evolved hugely, sometimes in beneficial ways, often to the contrary. In all cases (as in the private-insurance markets), we focus our attention on distortions in the incentives confronting people (both patients and providers) in Medicare and Medicaid. We find a series of issues that need repair. In particular, we offer 10 specific proposals (each with a brief statement of the underlying logic supporting our proposal):

Proposal 1: *Reset the annual Part B deductible to something between $350 and $400, and then annually adjust it using the Consumer Price Index (CPI).*

Logic: The Part B deductible per year was originally set at a reasonable level, but over time, increases have not kept pace with inflation. A full CPI adjustment would bring the annual deductible to approximately $375 in 2016. This step will help control Medicare costs for all years into the future, thus extending the time frame where the Medicare Trust Fund can assuredly fulfill its promises to the citizens of the nation.

Proposal 2: *Using parallel logic, reset the Part A deductible to something near $700, instead of the current $1316 per hospital admission deductible, and remove the higher cost-sharing parts of Medicare Part A (for hospitalizations exceeding 60 days in length). Index the Part A deducible annually using annual changes in the CPI to adjust for inflation.*

Logic: The current Part A structure imposes great financial risk on enrollees without achieving any meaningful reduction in hospitalization. The incentives on providers (the Prospective Payment System (PPS) using Diagnosis-Related Groups (DRGs)) assure that providers carefully monitor hospital lengths of stay, obviating the need for consumer-based incentives.

Combined Effect: Increasing the Part B deductible will likely reduce hospitalization rates such that the combined effect of these two changes will likely lead to a lower total Part A program cost, even with elimination of much of the enrollees' cost sharing in Part A. On net, enrollees' financial risk will fall, and the incentives for over-utilization will have been curbed. But one cannot responsibly undertake Proposal 2 without also achieving Proposal 1.

The average out-of-pocket charges to Medicare enrollees will remain nearly unchanged with these two proposals, but will spread the burden across almost all Medicare enrollees instead of concentrating it upon those who are hospitalized—a group that by definition is less well off than the average Medicare recipient.

Proposal 3: *Using a phased-in approach, alter Part B premiums and the Medicare payroll taxes levied on both employers and employees to adjust for regional costs of treating Medicare patients.*

Logic: The current system does not recognize the well-documented differences in the cost of providing health care for enrollees, differences that have nothing to do with the age or health status of the enrollee, and which have no measurable effect on health outcomes of the enrollees. As a consequence, the current payment structure creates a steady flow of income from cost-conscious areas to high-spending areas, a subsidy paid by the thrifty to the profligate, and (with less specificity) from sickly low-income people to higher-income people. The pricing of Part D, Medigap, and Medicare Advantage (MA) plans already follows this path, so this change merely brings original Medicare A+B into line with these more modern programs.

The phase-in would allow time for communities (through discussions involving employers, employees, Medicare enrollees, and—most importantly—health care providers) to adjust treatment styles and modes of care. Those communities wishing to maintain lavish treatment styles could do so, but would do so without the cross-subsidy currently embedded in the law.

Proposal 4: *Remove the shackles from Medicare Advantage (MA) (Part C) High-Deductible Health Plans (HDHPs) so they compete evenly with other plans. The key changes would: (a) allow coverage for prescription drugs within HDHPs; and (b) allow Medicare enrollees to personally add funds into a Medical Savings Account (MSA). In addition, to encourage low-income Medicare enrollees to opt for HDHP coverage, we would have a system where Medical Savings Accounts are appropriately seeded with public funds (such seeding diminishing as income rises).*

Logic: Two barriers exist for enrollees considering otherwise-desirable HDHPs within the MA structure. First, enrollees must purchase separate Part D coverage, whereas other MA plans can and often do incorporate prescription drug coverage comparable to Part D coverage. This limitation on HDHP plans should be removed entirely. Second, associated MSA plans for MA-HDHP enrollees may only receive funds from the MA plan—the difference between the cost of the plan and the benchmark payment from the Centers for Medicare and Medicaid Services (CMS) (using Medicare Parts A+B funds). Removing this limitation would allow not only enrollees themselves but also relatives and others to add funds to enrollees' MSA accounts, allowing further smoothing of the cash flow over time associated with an HDHP plan. In the case of dually-eligible enrollees, state Medicaid Programs should also be allowed to seed MSA accounts (see Proposal 5, next).

Proposal 5: *Require (as a condition of Federal support) that states offer HDHP plans to Medicaid enrollees with appropriately seeded MSA accounts matching the HDHP plans, the amount of "seeding" taking Medicaid enrollees' income into account.*

Logic: Standard Medicaid plans, while differing greatly from state to state, have a common feature—only a limited subset of providers accept Medicaid payment as payment in full, since it typically covers only a fraction of providers' actual costs. As a consequence, Medicaid enrollees often have great difficulty in finding providers who will treat them. Offering an HDHP plan with an associated MSA provides Medicaid enrollees a pathway to attaining care in a reasonable and humane way, while appropriately sharing in the costs of such treatment through their own contributions to their MSAs and payments for treatments until they meet their HDHP deductible. This approach has been successfully tested in Indiana and elsewhere.

Proposal 6: *In Medicare Part B, Part D and all MA programs (Part C), create mechanisms to bypass deductibles and coinsurance for treatments that are reasonably demonstrated to lower overall cost of care and/or create health improvements at relatively low cost. To achieve this in Part D and MA plans, CMS must mandate the appropriate structure of coverage across all plans.*

Logic: Particularly for people with chronic conditions, daily use of prescription drugs and regular monitoring of health status by physicians or other appropriate providers can improve health at far lower cost than awaiting exacerbation of the chronic conditions, and in many cases will actually reduce the total cost of care. When such circumstances are reasonably demonstrated, such treatments should be exempted from Part B and Part D deductibles and copayments. These "bypass" rules would be particularly important in HDHPs.

CMS must mandate this change, since the Part D formulary composition and choice of drug pricing tiers do not normally account for effects on total cost of care, and hence provide too-little insurance coverage for these types of drugs in Part D plans.

Proposal 7: *Alter the legislative mandate controlling CMS National Coverage Determinations (NCDs). The original Medicare legislation required that Medicare cover services that are "necessary and reasonable" without providing guidance on the meaning of this important pair of words. We would instead propose that CMS coverage determinations be made on the basis of safety, efficacy, cost-effectiveness, and other relevant attributes.*

Logic: Health economists have long understood that the introduction of new technologies into our health care system has been a major driver of cost increases over time, and that Medicare's approach to authorizing new treatments (with no formal consideration of cost) has led to the inclusion of some technologies that have very little health benefit compared to their added costs (very high cost-effectiveness ratios).

Proposal 8: *Tax Medigap plans sufficiently so that the tax receipts recoup the extra costs paid by Medicare when these Medigap plans remove deductible and copayments, which serve important purposes in controlling utilization.*

Logic: The original program structure of Medicare left important financial risk-facing enrollees, the result of which was a blossoming of various "Medigap" plans, designed to reduce or remove that risk. But in so doing, particularly in those plans removing Part B deductible and copayments, the Medigap plans increased utilization of the basic Medicare A+B programs excessively, thereby adding to Medicare's program costs. In effect, they allow people to buy full coverage insurance without having to pay the full added costs that such coverage creates, thereby shifting those costs to the primary sources of Medicare financing—the Medicare payroll tax, general revenues, and Part B deductibles. This proposal will eliminate this market distortion.

> **Proposal 9:** *Within the structure of the Center for Medicare and Medicaid Innovation (CMMI), allow Medicare MA plans to offer insurance with a set of covered services (scope of benefits) that is not required to match those covered by standard Medicare. Part D prescription drug coverage allows plan-specific coverages of drugs. This proposal would extend this option to MA plans for all medical services.*

Logic: The current CMS mechanism for deciding about treatment coverage (National Coverage Determinations (NCDs)) operates under restricted rules (see Proposal 7). If they err in one direction (by disallowing valuable treatments), MA plans can always add those to their coverage, but at the risk of increasing their premiums. However, if Medicare chooses to cover a treatment that is very costly, used by only a few, and has poor cost-effectiveness (or other) characteristics, MA plans are required to include those treatments in their coverage. This proposal would allow insurers to offer plans that did not necessarily match the exact services covered by "standard" Medicare.

> **Proposal 10:** *Within the structure of the CMMI, accelerate research and innovation in physician payment reform, moving away from fee for service (FFS) towards value-based payment methods, and increase research on the consequences and effectiveness of various payment methods, including understanding of how physician ownership of ancillary resources affects health care pricing and utilization.*

Logic: It is well-understood that FFS payment leads to over use of health care as physicians alter the advice they give patients about treatment choices. It is also well understood that pure capitation payments can have incentives in the reverse direction. Thus, using and analyzing alternative approaches within Medicare (and Medicaid) and providing more research to assist the decisions of private insurers about the effects and effectiveness of various payment protocols has great potential value. This research should include an understanding of the effects of physician ownership on use of resources (e.g., imaging and therapy) and (as necessary) modify payment plans or operational rules accordingly.

Combined effects of our Medicare and Medicaid proposals

These proposals have some common themes. First, they correct distortions in the incentives facing participants in the health care market, most notably those affecting plan choice among Medicare enrollees and the options available for

Medicaid recipients. Correcting these distortions will generally lead to acceleration of a shift that is already underway among Medicare enrollees—the *voluntary* shift to MA from Original Medicare coverage. We would also envision a shift towards HDHPs once the biases against them are removed, since those plans represent by far the fastest growing segment of the pre-Medicare private health insurance market.

Introduction of MA programs in 1997 greatly enhanced the value of the Medicare program by widening the choice set available to Medicare enrollees; our proposals expand that choice set even wider, and put all choices on an even economic footing.

Second, our proposals also eliminate some important inequities built into the current financing system, most notably where low-cost regions of the country pay more than their share for the excesses of high-cost regions.

Our proposals would also provide a choice for Medicaid enrollees to obtain health coverage that will markedly expand their access to wider provider markets, since adding the option of HDHP plans with MSA would not carry with it the overly-low provider payment levels that reduce providers' Medicaid participation in current arrangements.

Overall, our proposals would all combine to lower the cost of the Medicare and Medicaid programs and make them more efficient providers of both health care and risk protection. Current research does not allow precise quantification of the full effect of our proposals, but the direction of change is both clear and favorable for the physical and financial health of the people of the United States of America.

Part III: Things that affect everybody

Chronic health conditions

The US faces a growing health care cost from its aging population that cannot be dealt with well using current public policy and approaches to preventing and treating chronic conditions. The problem arises from a confluence of factors:

- The US population is aging rapidly and the ratio of workers to retirees is falling even more rapidly. Thus, the payroll tax financing of Medicare becomes an accelerating tax burden to workers.
- The frequency of chronic conditions grows with age.
- Annual costs of care grow exponentially with the number of chronic conditions. Medicare enrollees with five or more chronic conditions cost almost 14 times as much every year as those with no chronic conditions.
- Most chronic conditions occur with greatly enhanced frequency in people with unhealthy lifestyle choices, most notably tobacco use and obesity, followed (distantly) by alcohol abuse and (even more distantly) other substance abuse.

- Our public policy has generally under-utilized interventions that would reduce these chronic conditions and in some cases prohibited such interventions. These issues arise in numerous areas of public policy, including three important "I" areas:

  - Information—creation and dissemination of relevant knowledge.
  - Incentives—in private and public health insurance.
  - Investment—inappropriate focus of National Institutes of Health (NIH)-sponsored research.

- Treating chronic conditions (once they occur) takes place in a health care financing environment that seems designed to minimize coordination of care, leading to duplicative testing, numerous drug–drug interactions, and overall increase of costs and degradation of health outcomes for affected individuals.

While we do not have specific "fixes" for most of these issues, we emphasize the importance of dealing with them in both public and private health care financing settings, which lead to the following general proposals:

Proposal 1: *In both private health insurance and Medicare and Medicaid, strengthen rewards for people adopting and maintaining healthy lifestyle choices that reduce the risk of chronic illness, including introducing health insurance discounts for non-smokers and non-obese people.*

Proposal 2: *Shift the NIH research priorities to better reflect the true causes of health burden and premature death—tobacco, obesity, and lack of exercise, with a much stronger emphasis on prevention through medical intervention, education, and provision of information.*

Proposal 3: *In both private health insurance and Medicare and Medicaid, shift the financial incentives for providers to emphasize coordinated care for people with chronic conditions, particularly those with multiple chronic conditions.*

Proposal 4: *In both private insurance and Medicare and Medicaid, shift to full coverage for maintenance drugs for people with chronic conditions, particularly when generic drugs adequately reduce or eliminate consequences of the condition.*

Fraud detection and prevention

Much has been written, and more spoken, about eliminating waste, fraud, and abuse to solve the Medicare budget problems. There is much to be done, for sure, but in many ways, the legislative requirement to do it correctly already exists. Three keys to this problem come to the forefront:

A. To most effectively solve the problem, CMS and private insurers must cooperate in data sharing and analysis. Methods to do this have been done and widely proven as both safe and valuable in the context of banks sharing data about credit risk and fraud. Pooling of data across all participants in the health insurance market—private and public—allows creation of "behavior engine" models that identify fraudulent activity early and often, and with much better success than any single insurer's results allow.

B. Both CMS and most private insurers use a "pay and chase" strategy, wherein they pay claims and then retroactively attempt to catch fraudulent claims. The credit card industry long ago moved to a dynamic "real time" model to detect credit card theft and fraud, and has proven the value of these approaches. They would be readily adaptable to the world of health insurance.
C. The methods adopted must speed up rather than slow down payments for legitimate claims, and hence must not impact access to health care by consumers.

The legal mandate exists for CMS to undertake most of what is needed, but they have proceeded at a snail's pace to accomplish this task (which has been given to them legislatively). To get maximal gain from the fraud and abuse detection system, CMS and private insurers must fully pool their data. This leads to a specific proposal:

> **Proposal 5:** *Create new legislation requiring CMS and all private insurers to place all claims data (in a common format) into a central data bank that can be used for active detection of fraud and abuse, following the model of the financial services sector in detecting credit card fraud. In the same legislation, strengthen the existing requirements for CMS to follow through on currently enabled fraud detection efforts.*

Electronic health records (EHRs)

EHRs offer great promise to assist not only in improving treatment of chronic conditions (see previous discussion) but in all health care in general.

The hidden—but perhaps the most important—benefit from universal use of EHRs will come later, as these data allow new approaches to finding which medical interventions work best for which subsets of patients.

The old paper-based medical record system actually contains most of what we need to get to a comprehensive EHR system. When a patient has a primary care provider (PCP), that PCP comes as close as we have to a comprehensive medical record for the patient, but it is incomplete in content, incompletely available to providers and patients, and (at best) only partially legible in most cases. But patients can and do trust their PCP doctors to assemble, maintain, and (sometimes reluctantly) share those records with others (including the patients themselves). We envision the PCP's record keeping becoming replaced by an active market of "trusted third party" providers who would (at the patients' request) place an up-to-date digital copy of the medical record (in its entirety—notes, lab results, images,... everything) into the Trusted Third Party vault, where it would then be available for viewing by health care providers and others as designated by the patient.

The current status of the nation's EHRs gets us most of the way towards achieving these goals. The most important step to complete the journey is the passage of legislation requiring that all health care providers who use EHRs make available (after patient approval) a full, up-to-date copy to a "trusted third party" specified by the patient. Without this legislation, some providers will refuse to place copies of the record into the trusted-third-party vault, and hence the records will become incomplete. We also envision a second potentially necessary law protecting providers against certain legal damages, modeled, perhaps, after the nation's laws protecting vaccine manufacturers against liability against standard vaccine-induced illnesses and injuries. This leads to our specific proposal:

> **Proposal 6:** *Create legislation requiring (within appropriate time lines) that all health care providers with sufficient EHRs provide and maintain a current copy of all of the records with any Trusted Third Party named by any patient to assemble and maintain a complete EHR for that patient.*

This "trusted third party" presence represents a major conceptual shift from the current world where each health care provider "owns" the data and often restricts consumer access to data about their own health and treatments. Credit bureaus provide an analogy of the "trusted third party," but they currently primarily serve the financial sector (and charge consumers for access to their own credit information). But nothing in concept prevents third-party aggregation of medical and health data.

The "trusted third party" market should be vigorous and diverse. These organizations—much like "wealth-portals" that widely exist in the financial services sector—would aggregate health records from all health care providers specified by the patient/customer, distribute them to approved providers upon request, and also make the information available to the consumers themselves. We anticipate a robust market of advisers to help people interpret and understand their medical records. These trusted-third-party organizations would replace the paper-based assembly of medical records that now occurs (somewhat sporadically) in the offices of patients' primary care providers.

The promise of accountable care organizations

Health care in the US has—from the very beginning—been anchored in a fee-for-service (FFS) model. The doctor (or hospital or pharmacy or therapist or...) provides some service (or product) for you, and you (or your insurance company) pays for it, piece by piece. That model works well in most markets. When you buy a pound of T-bone steak, you know what you are getting, and can tell right away if it's spoiled. If spoiled, you can take it back to the butcher and get a refund or exchange. The same is essentially true of haircuts, restaurant meals, clothing, guitars, and most other things we buy. The same is approximately true with automobiles and trucks, with the additional thought that there may be hidden product defects that can sometimes be lethal. Our liability laws deal with these issues, along with regulatory mechanisms that help to assure auto safety.

Health care is often the same as a restaurant meal or haircut. If things work, fine. If not, you seek out another doctor (or hospital or pharmacist or...). But—like the hidden defect in cars—sometimes things can go very poorly also in health care, leaving permanent impairment or death. Doctors call this iatrogenic disease—"healer-caused disease." The more often these issues arise, the less well an FFS payment system works because it emphasizes volume of treatment, not quality.

HMOs and FFS operate at the ends of a spectrum of care. With FFS, you pay for each intervention, and the provider(s) have (aside from medical legal liability) no particular obligation to guarantee good results. HMOs operate at the opposite end of the spectrum. You pay the same amount no matter how much (or little) treatment you receive, but if you are sick, they have a legal obligation to care for you. But these are polar ends of a spectrum. The question basically is who bears the risk for illnesses and restoration to health. In the FFS case, the risk is borne by the individual person (who can purchase health insurance to deal with that risk). In the HMO, the treating organization bears the risk.

Accountable Care Organizations—ACOs—lie somewhere in the middle of this spectrum. The idea—still weakly formed in most cases—aims to find ways to move away from pure FFS to have some risk bearing by the treating organization. The most common name for payments like this is "service bundles" (SBs). In Medicare Part A, service bundles center around hospitalizations, easy to administer because the time frame is fixed (by admission to and discharge from the hospital) and only one provider is involved (the hospital). CMS calls this system the Prospective Payment System (PPS), and it pays fixed amounts to hospitals for caring for patients classified into about 500 categories called DRGs. More general SBs will involve chronic care conditions that have no specific time boundaries and involve many health care providers. Therein lies the complication.

ACOs will take on the role taking lump sums of money for SB activities and dispersing them among a diverse set of providers. Unlike the PPS world of Medicare Part A, each ACO can choose their own methods for dispersing the lump sums to providers. This will create a rich set of experiments to learn regularities about which payment mechanisms work best, allowing ACOs to learn from each other over time, thereby improving their overall performance.

One major emphasis appearing in ACO discussions centers on quality of care. In ACOs, payments to providers will depend importantly on quality.

The issue centers on what quality measures get included in the evaluation, how they get measured and how they are adjusted for existing co-morbidities.

The key to achieving success in ACOs will come from identifying who is at risk for various outcomes, setting the incentives right for all participants, and managing treatment at the boundaries of care where it seems as if "everybody" is in charge, in which case nobody will be in charge.

To gain maximally from the emerging ACO models that will emerge around the country, two things are necessary, leading to our specific proposal for this issue:

> **Proposal 7**: *CMS should establish specific (and fund generously) resources to analyze the outcomes in various ACOs, including the early creation of a common vocabulary to describe ACO structures and mandating that ACOs (as a condition of operation) gather common information about not only their outcomes but also the organizational structures and financial incentives they employ to achieve those outcomes.*

Getting rid of hyper-inflated medical bills

This may seem like a small annoyance, barely worth our attention, yet the issue begs for a solution. Everybody who has looked at medical bills in recent years knows that they bear no resemblance to real costs of care. Yet the problem has existed at least since the dawn of Medicare, when the (then) Health Care Finance Administration set about paying hospitals based not on their billed charges but instead adjusting billed charges by the ratio of charges to cost (the latter determined from accounting information from the hospitals). They were worried about hyper-inflated bills even then—50 years ago.

Hospitals, doctors, pharmacies—everybody in the system—has an incentive to post absurdly high prices for their services, even though almost nobody actually pays them. They do have a purpose, albeit not socially useful—to provide a basis for the amounts claimed by the providers as charity care and/or bad debt. For-profit organizations can use these as expenses to offset revenues and hence to bolster their profits. Not for profit hospitals (and nursing homes and clinics and others) do not automatically receive their tax-exempt status as Section 501.c.3 charitable organizations by way of their mere existence. They must demonstrate sufficient charitable activity to pass a set of Internal Revenue Service (IRS) rules in order to qualify as "tax exempt." Thus, they too create "list prices" that have no resemblance to anything they ever get paid by private insurance plans, Medicare, Medicaid, or any other third-party payer. But the "list prices" continue to exist, because they help justify the charitable organization status of the hospitals and clinics.

These artificial list prices do have real consequences. Some patients actually try to pay them, often failing. Others negotiate them down. But many people lose their credit standing, and some even file bankruptcy because of bills with these inflated charges embedded in them. This need not and should not happen.

We believe that one simple administrative change by the IRS will cause these list prices to vanish (since their fundamental purpose would vanish). Thus, we offer a specific proposal:

> **Proposal 8:** *Pass legislation specifying that the charitable deduction or bad debt expense taken by any health care provider is limited to the greater of: (a) the amount that Medicare would pay for the same service; or (b) the amount that their state's Medicaid program would pay.*

With that change, the incentives to post hyper-inflated prices would essentially vanish and so (we believe) would the hyper-inflated price lists themselves.

Concluding remarks

Much of what we propose requires legislative action. Without new laws to remove the distortions in our health economy, we are doomed to continue along on the current roadway, caught in a traffic jam of higher costs, lower quality of care, less patient safety, and inefficient use of our scarce health care resources than is possible to achieve. Changing the incentives faced by every participant in the health economy—patients, providers, and insurers (private and public) is necessary. The time is now.

Part I

The market for private health insurance

1 The pivotal role of employer-paid health insurance

Prologue and proposition

Our health care system has numerous issues awaiting improvement; this will always be true. But until we fix the most fundamental flaw of all, other attempts at improving our health care system cannot achieve their full beneficial effects. The core problem is that our health care financing system, and with it, the entire health economy, are distorted and overly large due to the presence of a large and widespread subsidy to health insurance through the income tax system. Because of this, we have an insurance system that ironically is overly generous for many and overly stingy for others. Until we fix this distortion, all other reforms can—at best—have limited effect. Thus, we make the following proposition (which we defend in detail below):

> *The most important health care policy law ever passing the United States was not the Medicare legislation of 1965 or the Patient Protection and Affordable Care Act*[1] *of 2010, but rather a simple provision of the 1954 tax code*[2] *stating that employer-paid health insurance premiums are excluded from the definition of taxable income (and hence from both personal income and payroll taxes).*

This single piece of legislation led to significant distortions in the private health insurance market, leading to over-insurance among those with employer-based coverage and squeezing out the non-employer-based (individual) market. Further, without this subsidy, we would not have had (in the early 1960s) a large pipeline of workers reaching mandatory retirement at the age of 65 who suddenly lost their employer-paid health insurance coverage. Without that, we would likely not have Medicare as we know it—albeit perhaps we would have something else, perhaps quite different. All of this would look very different but for the growth of employer-paid health insurance and all that came with it, and the size and spread of those plans is irrefutably linked to the tax treatment of employer-paid premiums.

To understand how this happened and its consequences, we must go back to the beginning—how it all began. Let us now begin that journey.

How World War II still haunts us

Looking back about eight decades, almost nobody in the United States had employer-paid health insurance. Indeed, there was very little health insurance of any sort at the time, and when it first began (as Blue Cross hospitalization plans and companion Blue Shield medical/surgical plans in the 1930s) it was quite limited coverage compared with what we now know. For example, hospital coverage typically had a limit of 30 days of hospitalization, and in some sense provided better protection for hospitals against bad debts than it did against the risks of long-term hospitalization for serious illness that confronted the insured people.[3]

Then came World War II. With that war (among other things) came wage and price controls that limited not only the prices that firms could set to sell their products, but also the wages they could pay their workers. Some firms began to realize that to attract high-quality workers, they could increase total compensation by providing life insurance and health insurance to their workers, since the wage and price controls did not include such "fringe benefits" in the limits on payments to workers, so long as they did not exceed 5% of wages. Thus began the movement to have employers responsible for our health insurance coverage, a process that was actually designed more to circumvent the World War II wage controls than anything else.

By the end of World War II, a good number of workers had become quite familiar with and happy to have the employers paying some or all of their health insurance premiums, particularly since those payments were not counted as taxable income. So not only did the workers get the insurance, but they avoided paying income taxes on those health and life insurance premiums paid by the employer.

By keeping employer-paid premiums out of the income tax base, this system initiated what has since become a very large and counter-productive subsidy to the purchase of health insurance, a subsidy that (as we shall detail shortly) has completely reshaped our health insurance and health care systems. It has led to too much insurance for those blessed by the employment benefit, and crowded out non-employer markets that others might have relied upon. Thus, we have the persistent irony that we both have people with too much and others with too little health insurance at the same time. The tax subsidy increased the amounts of coverage for people with access to such insurance, and the subsidized insurance squeezed the viability of the non-group market (crowding out).[4]

How the tax subsidy became permanent

All this became codified into federal law in 1954, but with an odd twist.[5] That law made permanent the total exclusion of employer-paid health insurance premiums from the income tax base, but it set a limit on the amount of life insurance premiums that an employer could pay under the tax-exempt umbrella—the costs of providing a term life insurance policy with $50,000 in death benefits, which represented about 20 times the per capita income of that era. That $50,000 cap remains as such today—unchanged despite almost a nine-fold increase in the Consumer Price Index (CPI). Thus, employers commonly pay (if anything) the premiums for $50,000 worth of term insurance (about the same as annual per-capita income today), and no more. If the $50,000 limit had merely tracked with the CPI, it would now be approximately $435,000. And this seemingly minor wrinkle in the 1954 tax law provides a very useful natural experiment to help us understand what happens to insurance markets with and without the tax subsidy.

Had there been no limit placed on employer-paid life insurance premiums, we would almost certainly see a very different market for life insurance than the one we now see; one that would be dominated by employer-paid premium arrangements. But it did not happen with life insurance, so we currently find that employer-paid life insurance premiums represent only 2.3% of the amount paid by employers for health insurance premiums,[6] and well under 3% of the total life insurance premiums paid annually in the US.[7] Thus, we see that in health insurance, employer-provided and employer-paid insurance dominate the industry. In life insurance, employer payment of premiums is barely relevant. The difference comes from the differential tax treatment of these two types of insurance created in 1954.

With the 1954 law, the exclusion of employer-paid health insurance premiums became not only permanent, but uncapped. As noted before, the World War II era controls had capped the total of health and life insurance fringe benefit value at 5% of wages. This uncapping set the stage for rapid growth in the role of employer payments in the world of health insurance, altered labor-management bargaining in unfortunate ways (consider how many strikes have occurred simply over the issue of health benefits), and led many people to believe that our employer-paid premium system puts the US at a disadvantage in international trade.[8]

The exclusion of employer-paid health insurance premiums from the taxable income base creates a subsidy for people who have part or all of their health insurance premiums paid by their employer. The subsidy reduces the price of health insurance that people think about when they decide how much to purchase. Just like any other normal good, when people see a lower price for something, they usually buy more of it. Or they buy a higher quality of the good than they would otherwise buy. If the prices of automobiles fall, that does not necessarily lead people to buy two of them, but they might choose a fancier one, more luxurious, safer, faster, sleeker looking, and certainly more expensive. Sometimes people both upgrade the quality and also buy two vehicles: one for commuting to work, the other for general family activity, or even a third vehicle for taking off-road excursions in the mountains, the beach, or the desert.

With health insurance, it works slightly differently. People expand the scope of coverage so that it covers not only hospital care and physician and surgeon treatments within the hospital (as the original Blue Cross and Blue Shield plans did) but it might also begin to cover visits to the emergency room, visits to doctors' offices, and then (as the price of insurance got lower and lower) things like dental care and prescription drugs. And consumers might also shrink down the deductibles and coinsurance or copayments per physician visit, and they might begin to select managed care plans (as they later emerged) that were less restrictive in their access to the medical care they wanted. After all, freedom to choose is desirable, if affordable.

How the subsidy changed through time

How did the subsidy to health insurance change year to year? The answer comes by understanding the effect of the tax treatment on the real price of insurance. Economists define the price of insurance as the markup paid above and beyond the statistically expected benefits (the "actuarial value") that the plan will pay. If—on average—the insurance plan would pay $1000 in benefits, and they charge $1100 a year for the premium, then the price of insurance is the extra $100, usually specified as a percent of the expected benefit payments; so in this example the price of insurance would be 10%.

This is what happens before you look at the effect of the exclusion of employer-paid premiums from the income tax system. Once the tax law says "you don't have to pay income taxes on employer-paid premiums," you have a subsidy to the health insurance premiums, the size of which depends upon the applicable marginal tax rate (MTR). If the MTR is defined as t ($0 < t < 1$) then the worker saves t times the employer premium payment, and the tax system pays the other portion. So if t = 0.2 workers face a premium of $1100, then they actually really only pay $880, and the 20% subsidy pays the remaining $220. And if the marginal tax rate is 40% instead of 20%, the $1100 premium gets split as $660 paid by the worker and $440 paid by the income tax system as a subsidy. As we shall expand upon momentarily, the people with the bigger subsidies in our health economy are those with the highest incomes. This part of the tax system systematically benefits wealthier people more than it does lower income people.

As we look across the years, we see two trends running in close parallel approximately through 1980—increasing coverage via employer-paid health insurance premiums and also (on average) increasing MTRs for workers. Figure 1.1 shows the time path of typical MTRs for median income families and those with twice median income from 1955 through 2009.[9] The higher the MTR, the bigger the subsidy. In the pre-1980s era, the tax subsidy steadily increased in magnitude, and the proportion of the under-65 population covered by employer-related plans increased essentially in parallel. This went on unchecked until the 1980s tax reforms in the Reagan administration, which systematically reduced MTRs across the board, and thereby reduced the subsidy to health insurance. As Figure 1.1 shows, for median income families, the typical MTR peaked at about 38%. For families at twice the median family

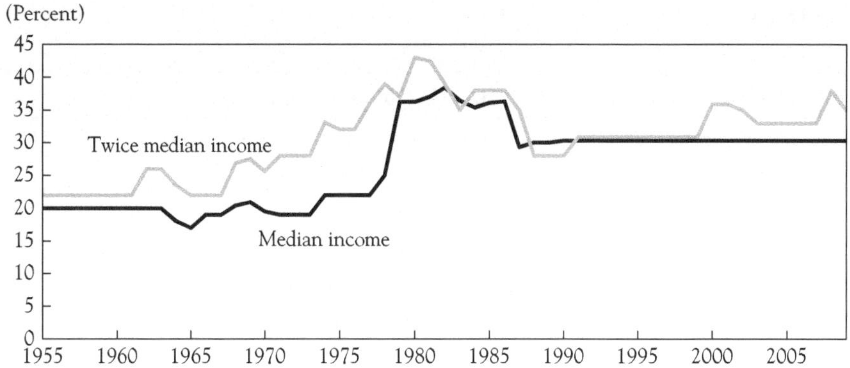

Figure 1.1

The time path of marginal tax rates on earnings for a family of four with a single earner, 1955 to 2009, for a family with median income (dark line) and twice the median income (light line). The marginal tax rates include both personal income tax and payroll taxes
Source: US Department of the Treasury

income, it peaked at about 43%. It is no coincidence that 1980 was the year in which proportion of under-65 persons covered by employer paid health insurance peaked at 71.4%.[10]

How big is the subsidy now? The MTR in 2016 is actually quite large—much more so than most people understand. Begin with the federal income tax structure. For a person making the average per capita income of $50,000, filing as a single person, the income MTR is 25%. Table 1.1 shows precisely how the MTR—and hence the health insurance subsidy—systematically increases as individual or family income grows. For people earning over $400,000, the marginal income tax rate—and hence the rate of subsidy to their health insurance policies—reaches 39.6%.[11]

However, federal income taxes are only part of the story. We must also include payroll taxes from the Social Security system, where both the employer and the employee pay 6.2% of wage earnings up to a maximum of $127,200 in 2017. In addition, both employer and employee pay a 1.45% wage tax to support the Medicare program.[12]

Many economists—in the "long run"—would normally attribute both the employer and employee share to the worker; the presumption being that employers would adjust the amount of wages to offset their share of the Social Security and Medicare taxes. If so, one would also add the employer's share of Federal Insurance Contributions Act (FICA—the formal name for the Social Security System payroll taxes) and Medicare taxes to the MTR (and hence the subsidy). This becomes most obvious for self-employed persons who pay both the worker's and employers' shares. The Self-Employment rate is 12.4% FICA plus 2.9% Medicare (15.3% total) for incomes up to the $127,200 limit, and 2.9% thereafter.

Table 1.1 Marginal income tax rates from federal income tax structure, 2015. Does not include payroll taxes or state taxes

2015 Tax rates					
Tax rate		Single	Head of household	Married filing separately	Married filing jointly/ qualifying widow or widower
Ordinary income	Long-term capital gains and qualified dividends	Taxable to income over ($)	Taxable to income over ($)	Taxable to income over ($)	Taxable to income over ($)
10%	0%	0	0	0	0
		9225	13,150	9225	18,450
15%	0%	9225	13,150	9225	18,450
		37,450	50,200	37,450	74,900
25%	15%	37,450	50,200	37,450	74,900
		90,750	129,600	75,600	151,200
28%	15%	90,750	129,600	75,600	151,200
		189,300	209,850	115,225	230,450
33%	15%	189,300	209,850	115,225	230,450
		411,500	411,500	205,750	411,500
35%	15%	411,500	411,500	205,750	411,500
		413,200	439,000	232,425	464,850
39.6%	20%	413,200	439,000	232,425	464,850
		—	—	—	—

Source: www.irs.com/articles/2015-federal-tax-rates-personal-exemptions-and-standard-deductions

Most people with incomes below the FICA "cutoff" income face a 25–28% MTR on their income (depending on how they file and other deductions). Adding to that the 12.4% from Social Security brings the total to just over a 37–40% MTR. In addition, we must add the 1.45% Medicare tax paid by both the employer and the employee—another 2.9%, but this time without any income limitation. This brings the total for people just under the Social Security income limit (i.e., below $127,200 in 2017) to as high as 43%. That is almost the highest federal MTR for any income group, but for most workers under the FICA income limit, the de facto MTR is well over 35%. Only for those workers with incomes in the 10% marginal tax brackets does the subsidy fall below 30%, once one attributes the 12.4% FICA tax and the 2.9% Medicare taxes to the worker, ignoring any state or local income taxes.

In addition, for those who live in states (or the occasional city) with income taxes, we also must add the marginal state taxes, the measurement of which is still further complicated for the 35% of tax-filers who itemize on their federal returns, hence allowing the deduction of state income taxes in their federal income tax calculation.

Of course, as John Maynard Keynes once famously observed, "In the long run, we are all dead."[13] At the other extreme, one might assume that at least in the short run, none of the FICA and Medicare tax burdens on the employer are passed through in terms of lower wages to employees. Even if so, the magnitude of the tax subsidy shows the same features—it is large, and it grows with income. Assuming no shifting of the employer's share, the average of all federal marginal income tax rate in 2011 was 17.6%,[14] so adding to that the Medicare tax (1.45%) and 6.2% for FICA taxes on about 85% of workers, the subsidy sits at just under 25%, even ignoring state income taxes. Adding in the average state income tax rate of 4.5% gives an easy and valuable number to remember—almost 30% of all employer-paid health insurance premiums are offset by reductions in income and wage taxes on average—even when ignoring the employers' share of wage taxes (FICA and Medicare).

Why it matters: how the subsidy expands health insurance and health care use

A current snapshot

Let us now take a closer look at how this matters, first by assessing the effect of the subsidy on the choice of health insurance, and then looking at how the changes in health insurance affect decisions about using health care itself.

How the tax subsidy changes health insurance

Consider the following: if somebody else was paying for one-third or more of a person's food bills, would their food-buying habits change? If somebody else was paying for one-third of their automobile purchases, would they change their vehicle purchasing and driving habits? If somebody else was paying for one-third of their clothing, would you expect them to have a finer array of clothing? The answer is almost surely "Yes" for any rational person for these and most other purchases. And so it is with health insurance. The exact magnitude of the effect has not been determined with high precision, and the literature on demand for health insurance has a wide variety of estimates of the magnitude of the tax-subsidy effect, but there is little dispute in the literature about the direction of the effect—lower prices increase the amount of health insurance coverage.[15]

A snapshot of the current health insurance coverage in the US can be taken from many angles. We recommend to the interested reader annual summaries from the Kaiser Family Foundation and the Health Research and Educational Trust (HRET), which provide highly detailed analyses of the nature of current coverage.[16] In brief summary, we note the following facets of this complex structure, reflecting 2015 data that do not yet show the full effects of the Affordable Care Act's (ACA) individual mandate.[17]

- About 60% of the under-65 population had health insurance coverage through work-related groups. Note how much lower this is than the peak of 71% before the Reagan tax reforms that reduced the subsidy to employer-paid health insurance. Another 14% had Medicaid or similar coverage, 5% had other private (non-group) coverage, and 20% had no health insurance coverage.

- Almost all of those with any employer-related coverage had extensive coverage for hospital, physician, and emergency care, and now, also prescription drugs.
- Preferred Provider Organization (PPO) plans have the highest market share (52%), followed by High-Deductible Health Plans (HDHPs) with savings options (SOs) (24%), Health Maintenance Organizations (HMOs) (14%,) and Point of Service Plans (10%).[18] The PPO share dropped from a high of 58% in 2014 to 52% in 2015 as more enrollment took place through health insurance exchanges.
- Traditional health insurance coverage has essentially vanished.[19] Twenty-five years ago these plans had 73% of the employer-paid market. Now they have less than 1%.
- HDHP/SO plans are rapidly gaining market share. They have grown from no market presence in 2005 to 24% of the employer-group market in 2015.
- Pure HMO plans have slowly lost market share over the years, now with half the market share (14%) they held in 2000.
- On average, employers pay for over 80% of the premiums for single workers, and over 70% of the premiums for family coverage.
- The average total cost for single-worker plans in 2015 was $6251 per year (a bit over $500 per member per month). The 80% average employer share is $416 per month.
- The average total cost for family coverage was $17,545. At the national average of 70% employer payment, this represents a per-worker payment of $12,280 per year, just over $1000 per month.

What about those without employer-based coverage? A small handful (about 5% of the under-65 population) had bought non-group insurance before the ACA's "individual mandate" began to take hold. As of the end of the ACA enrollment period on February 1, 2017, 12.2 million people had enrolled through state and federal health insurance exchanges, but not all of these represent additions to the total number of people with health insurance, since some of this will be replacement of other coverage. How this might change in the future as Republican efforts to repeal and replace the ACA emerge remains to be seen, since the individual mandate has been a key element of Republicans' ire over the ACA.

What about the remainder? The answer depends upon many factors, but most prominently upon age. Those in the under-18 category have widespread access to a special program known as the Children's Health Insurance Program (CHIP), so that 30% of this age group has governmental coverage through Medicaid or CHIP. The under-65 adult population has much lower Medicaid coverage, leaving (in round numbers) one-quarter of them without health insurance. (These levels will also change with the insurance exchange enrollment and enhanced Medicaid eligibility that's part of the ACA.) But the bottom line is this: before the ACA, about a fifth of the under-65 adults had no insurance, while well under 5% of the under-18 age group were similarly "bare" of insurance coverage.

We should remember that the restricted market for non-group insurance is not the natural state of affairs in the non-group markets. The non-employer-group market has been squeezed both from "above" with the subsidized employer-paid market and from "below" with Medicaid and CHIP. So, what the non-group market looked like in the past may have little to do with the nature and extent of private insurance once the political uncertainty about the future of the exchanges is resolved.

One could ask the hypothetical question of what this coverage would look like in the absence of the tax-based subsidy to employer health insurance plans. In Chapter 2, we describe some general features of that world, but for here, we offer a short summary: More people are covered through employer groups in our "real" world than would occur without the subsidy, and their insurance coverage is more generous than it would otherwise be (because of the subsidy).

In parallel, absent the subsidy, non-group markets would be larger than we observe now, but the insurance coverage obtained through them would not be as generous as the employer-group coverage that we now observe. In other words, we know that there has been an expansion in coverage on net, although the exact magnitude of that expansion cannot be stated with precision. Economist Mark Pauly summarized this literature, by stating that estimates of the price elasticity of demand for health insurance typically ranged from –0.2 to numbers exceeding unity in absolute value.[20] If this summary of the price elasticity of demand for health insurance provides a reasonable guidance, we can say (within the boundaries of those summary numbers) that health insurance coverage in the United States is substantially more generous than it would be without the subsidy—certainly enough to affect the shape and size of the health care system as a whole. The next section elaborates on this issue.

How health insurance affects health care use

If the problem stopped here, it would not be that large of an issue. But health insurance has an unusual structure: unlike other types of insurance, it reduces the price of medical care when we actually consume it. So, if an insurance plan has a $25 per office visit copayment for physician visits, then consumers' cost of a visit (as they think about whether to go to the doctor) is $25, not the actual amount received by the physician.

The physician gets paid the $25 copayment fee directly, and then gets paid some other amount (usually negotiated with the insurance plan or specified by law for Medicare or Medicaid) that is usually quite a bit larger than the $25. Thus, the cost of the physician visit is subsidized by the health insurance plan. The same is true for hospital care, emergency room care, diagnostic tests, therapy, psychiatric counseling, prescription drugs, dental care, and any other type of medical treatment covered by the health insurance plan. Thus, better health insurance coverage lowers the price of health care and hence increases use of health care itself. The subsidy to health insurance gets multiplied by its effect on the use of health care. The health insurance tax subsidy's effect is leveraged into the health care market itself.

What happens to our choices about buying medical care when the price falls? That issue was the subject of a very large randomized controlled trial social experiment conducted in the 1980s by the RAND Corporation, financed by the federal government, and designed to learn how people change their medical care use with different degrees of insurance coverage. Table 1.2 summarizes the results from the study, shown here as the amount of medical care relative to a high-deductible medical insurance plan at various types of health insurance coverage such as full coverage (zero out of pocket), 25% coinsurance rate, 50% coinsurance rate, or a modest deductible ($150 per person per year, equivalent to about $450 now).[21]

The details of this large study have led to entire books being published on the results, but for our purposes here, the most salient data appear in Table 1.2. This table is scaled so that people on the "high deductible" plan are the "yardstick." Their rates of use in every category are defined as "1." The free care plan provides the greatest contrast (as one might expect). Overall expenditures on health care were about 40% more on the free care plan than on the high deductible plan. Even modest copayments (either 25%, 50%, or the moderate-sized deductible) led to utilization reductions compared with the free care plan. The biggest differences came in the things where patients have the most discretion (face-to-face visits with providers and ambulatory care costs), and the smallest differences occurred for more serious (hospitalized) events. The most important number to remember is "total cost of care: free vs. high deductible"—a 40% difference.[22]

Table 1.2 Health care spending with different insurance plans from the RAND Health Insurance Experiment. Spending is scaled so (for each category) the high-deductible plan = 1, and all other insurance plans are shown as a ratio to the high-deductible plan

		Type of medical care			
Insurance plan	Visits	Outpatient costs	Hospital admissions	Inpatient costs	Total cost
Free	1.67	1.67	1.29	1.30	1.39
25%	1.22	1.28	1.06	1.18	1.14
50%	1.11	1.10	0.93	1.43	1.06
$150 deductible	1.11	1.16	1.16	1.18	1.17
High deductible	1	1	1	1	1

Source: Revised from Phelps, 2012; original data from Manning, 1987

Now we can combine the consequences of the federal income tax subsidy to employer-paid health insurance and their downstream effects on medical care spending. Using estimates for demand for insurance (in the range described by Pauly) and those from the RAND Health Insurance Study for the demand for medical care itself,[23] it is possible to estimate the effect of the tax subsidy on the overall size of the health care economy. The results are non-trivial: overall medical spending from those covered by employer-paid health insurance (about 60% of the under-65 population) is about 10–30% larger than it would be without the tax subsidy to employer-paid health insurance, with the "best-guess" estimate centered at about 20%.[24]

We do not need to resolve this question precisely. The important point is that the tax treatment of employer-paid health insurance has unambiguously increased the amount of health insurance that people hold—quite possibly by considerable amounts—and therefore unambiguously increased our annual medical spending on medical care, which remains (on a per capita basis) by far the largest in the world.

While these results technically apply only to a proportion of the population covered by employer-paid health insurance, it is easy to see that the effects of the 1954 tax policy had more pervasive effects, particularly in the design of Medicare and Medicaid, as well as the coverage for armed forces members, their families, and retirees (TRICARE). Indeed, as we discuss more extensively in Part II of our book, Medicare was originally closely modeled after the predominant forms of health insurance coverage of the day, Blue Cross for in-hospital care (now Part A of Medicare) and "major medical insurance" with a $50 deductible and 20% copayment for physician services (now Part B of Medicare). And the ACA, for all of its complexity and detail, in many ways simply locked into place the employer-paid mechanisms (that had grown into place since World War II) and the Medicare Act of 1965.

The effect is dynamic, not static (the "gift" that keeps on "giving")

The effect does not stop just with this year's total spending, because there is also a dynamic effect that may be more important. With the insurance coverage widely in place in the United States, health care providers (hospitals, physician offices, dentist, therapists, pharmaceutical manufacturers, medical device makers, and others) understand that if they can find a new way to treat patients that has even modest chances of improving people's health, the insurance system will—in the main—pay for it. This changes the dynamics of invention of new medical procedures, new medical drugs into devices, and the way these are used in our country. Many health economists believe that significant fractions of the total increases in medical care size in our country's economy have arisen because this incentive to bring in new technologies is ultimately created by our health insurance, which is ultimately oversized because of the employer-paid health insurance tax treatment.

This concept was first introduced by Newhouse[25] to test statistically the influence of health insurance coverage on medical spending. Standard economic theory predicts that the demand for medical care should increase as the price falls (or in health care, as the patients' coinsurance rate falls). Newhouse also tested the effect of the *level* of the coinsurance rate on the rate of medical spending growth. In the classical model, we should observe no effect, but in a dynamic model taking into account introduction of new technologies, he predicted that the *level* of coinsurance should also affect the growth rate of medical spending. This is precisely what he observed. A decade later, the validity of this result was confirmed with additional data and more sophisticated estimation techniques.[26]

In a recent and comprehensive review of the literature on health care cost growth, Chernew and Newhouse state the following: "The evidence suggests that over long periods of time a primary determinant of spending growth is the development, adoption and diffusion of new medical technology..."[27] And that rate of adoption has surely been increased by the shape and structure of health insurance.

Chernew and Newhouse include in their definition not only new medical devices and new pharmaceutical products but also new practice styles or medical procedures that use existing technologies. The effect arises in numerous ways. For example, improvement in diagnostic imaging can readily lead to more surgical intervention as more operable lesions are identified, so that (in such cases) the cost of the new imaging capabilities (e.g., magnetic resonance imaging (MRI) or positron emission tomography (PET) scans) is followed by a greater use of other medical interventions.

The reverse could happen, of course, where improved imaging leads to less surgery, but that seems not to be the normal course of events. Sometimes the mere improvement in the safety of a procedure or its efficacy makes it more desirable, hence leading to more use (plus, of course, the added costs associated with the improvements in safety or efficacy). Still other interventions extend life expectancy, thereby exposing people to other treatable diseases. This is not a bad thing, of course—living longer and healthier lives is highly desirable—but it does add to health care costs.

Some innovations actually reduce costs. Pharmaceuticals that lower cholesterol can reduce later need for heart surgery. Other pharmaceuticals improve the functioning of people with mental illness, allowing them to live in mainstream society rather than in expensive institutional arrangements. Many other important examples of this phenomenon exist. But in the large sweep of things, most innovations improve health outcomes, but only with added costs. There are very few "free lunches."

Widespread and extensive health insurance affects the rate of technology introduction in a simple yet important way. In normal markets—think about personal computers, home electronics, automobiles, and the like—new technologies succeed when they pass a simple market test: do the benefits of this technology exceed the costs of producing it? But health insurance reduces the cost of health care that individuals actually see when deciding about what care to use. At the extreme, for a person with full coverage health insurance, the equivalent test essentially becomes "does this technology produce any measurable benefit," since cost is nearly irrelevant for a large fraction of the population, especially for hospital-based technologies where insurance coverage is more complete. Of course, most people pay something for their health care, but for the large majority of the US population, what they pay is far less than what it costs to create their medical care. Thus health insurance has rent asunder what the market would otherwise have put together. With cost more or less irrelevant in most medical decisions, it has hence become only moderately relevant (at best) in the introduction of new medical technologies.

Chernew and Newhouse (p. 37) summarize their work by saying:

> It is an exaggeration, but probably not a large one, to say that over the past few decades, commercially insured and most Medicare patients, who account for the bulk of health care spending in the United States, commonly received any medical advance that promised more than *de minimis* benefit for them.

The time trend of employer-paid health insurance premiums

If we wish to understand the growth rate of the sum total of employer-paid premiums, we can parse it into the following pieces:

- general inflation;
- growth of the employable-age population;
- changes in the percentage of the population who work;
- changes in the rate at which employers offer insurance;
- changes in the rate at which employees accept the offer of insurance;
- changes in the scope of benefits of the health insurance;
- changes in the actual prices paid for health care;
- changes in the per-person amount of health care consumed annually;
- introduction of new technologies into the health care system.

In general, most of these components have increased steadily over time since 1954. The only thing that has not steadily increased is the proportion of workers covered by health insurance. That climbed steadily until the early 1980s, at which time (as noted before) the Reagan tax reforms reduced the MTRs of our income tax system, and hence also reduced the gains from paying workers with health insurance instead of money. Since that time, the uninsured portion of the under-65 population climbed from 12.0% (in 1980) to a peak of 18.2% (in 2010) before the ACA began to take effect.

Combining all of these trends, we can look at the actual magnitude of employer-paid premiums over time (understanding that the "tax expenditure"—the amount of income taxes foregone by the US and State treasuries—moves

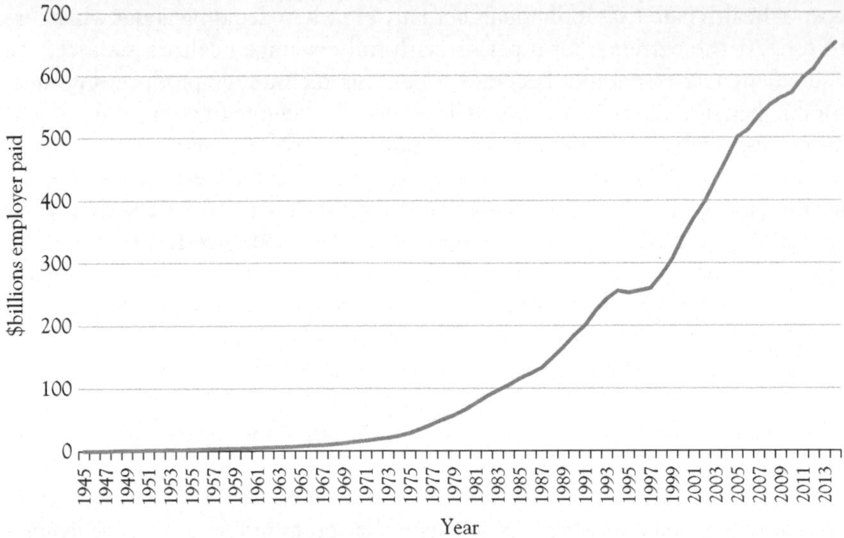

Figure 1.2

The time path of employer payments combined for health and life insurance from 1945 through 2013. Almost 100% of the payments are for health insurance in recent decades Source: Bureau of Economic Analysis

in parallel). Figure 1.2 shows the premium growth in nominal dollars. Note that this figure combines life and health insurance payments by employers, but the life insurance costs represent under 3% of the total, so this graph reflects the time path of employer-paid health insurance premiums with reasonable accuracy.

The year before the landmark Internal Revenue legislation of 1954, the magnitude of employer-paid premiums was estimated at $750 million total.[28] This is not a typographical error: The number was $750 million, not $750 billion. That represented about 7% of total private health care spending at that time. Today's total of more than $600 billion is 800 times larger than the 1953 amount. The CPI has grown by a factor of 8.85 between 1953 and now, so the inflation-adjusted ("real") growth is a factor of 90.4. The US population has almost doubled during this time, still leaving a 45-fold growth in "real" employer-paid premiums per capita in the US. That amount of increase is generated by a process with a 6.6% annual compounded growth rate: *inflation-adjusted (real), per capita* employer-paid premiums have grown at 6.6% per year for over half a century.

It is thus not surprising that in parallel, the proportion of US gross domestic product (GDP) devoted to health care also increased by a factor of 3.9, from 4.6% in 1954 to 17.8% now. The GDP share of health care has grown at a compounded annual rate of a "mere" 2.2%. The inflation-adjusted per-person premiums have grown at triple the rate of the GDP share of health care. The reason for the difference, of course, is that an increasing share of health care spending came through employer-paid health insurance over time.

The large scale of the employer payments (and the associated subsidy—about a third of the total employer premium payments) had led us to an overly generous health insurance system for those with access to this type of insurance (i.e., most workers). The recent amount shown in Figure 1.2—about $600 billion—represents the total. More than 40% of that—the most recent Congressional Budget Office (CBO) estimate—puts the tax expenditure at $248 billion—represents the loss in potential federal government income tax, Social Security, and Medicare tax revenues due to the exclusion of employer-paid premiums, and also represents the amount of money we can use to help fix the system, as our proposal detailed at the beginning of Chapter 3 outlines.

A wise policy analyst once said, "Things that can't go on forever... won't!" This is true for growth health care's GDP share, and in the growth of employer-paid premiums. But it is worth extrapolating how much growth occurs in a mere decade if the 6.6% annual growth rate continues into the future. The answer: with a 6.6% annual growth rate, things double every 11 years. Left unchecked, the $250 billion in lost tax revenue will become over $500 billion in 11 years, and only two decades from now, it will have reached well over $1 trillion.

We believe the case is clear that eliminating the subsidy to employer-paid health insurance is both a good idea and important. We are not the first health economists to propose this notion. But to date, no political mechanism has arisen that allows the shift from a subsidized to an unsubsidized market. One reason is the fear of what would happen to health insurance markets. In Chapter 2, we discuss what the health care market would look like absent the employer-paid premium subsidy. That world, we argue, is not as scary as most people might imagine. Thus we hope to dispel the frightening mythology about this market, and then (hopefully having succeeded in that task) we can move to a proposal that we believe merits serious consideration to remove this onerous distortion in the health care economy.

Notes

1 In acronym form for later use, PPACA, also known as the Affordable Care Act (ACA).
2 P.L. 83-591, August 16, 1954; Internal Revenue Code of 1954, Section 106.
3 Anderson, 1975.
4 The crowding out became more severe with the introduction of Medicaid in 1965 and the Children's Health Insurance Program (CHIP) in 1997.
5 Helms, 2008.
6 In 2012, tax expenditures for health insurance premiums paid by employers were $117 billion. The comparable exclusion for life insurance premiums was $2.8 billion—2.3% of the amount for health insurance. Source: Joint Committee on Taxation, February 1, 2013.

7 Total life and annuity premiums in the US in 2011 were $462 billion (American Council of Life Insurers, 2012, Table 4.2). The $2.8 billion in tax expenditures for group term life insurance (Joint Committee on Taxation, 2013, Table 1) is consistent with total premium payments of $12.7 billion, assuming a 22% average of the applicable marginal tax rate. Thus, the $12.7 billion represents 2.7% of the $462 billion total.

8 The issue of competitive advantage hinges on the incidence of employer-paid fringe benefits. There is widespread agreement among economists that the incidence in the short run can fall at least in part on the employer. In the long run, the incidence can still fall to a considerable extent on the employer in certain conditions (Kotlikoff and Summers, 1979). In a review of studies in US labor markets, Gruber (1997) summarizes the literature by stating "...the incidence of mandated employer benefits is fully on wages, with little to no dis-employment effect." The dis-employment issue interacts with minimum wage laws, where employers cannot offset insurance costs with lower wages (Mitchell and Phelps, 1976).

9 Congressional Budget Office, December 2, 2010.

10 Looking at the reverse side of this question, the percentage of under-65 persons without insurance hit an all-time low in 1980 of 12.0%, and then climbed within a decade to stabilize at 16–18%, increasing during recessions and declining during economic upturns. See www.cdc.gov/nchs/health_policy/trends_hc_1968_2011.htm (accessed August 7, 2017) for data. The ACA brought the percentage of uninsured down to 10.5% in 2015, the first year since 1980 where the rate dropped below 12%.

11 For an increasingly large set of taxpayers, the Alternative Minimum Tax (AMT) defines their MTR. The AMT has a nominal cap of 28% on the MTR, but which in fact imposes a 35% MTR on income for a broad band of incomes because of the systematic elimination of the ability to claim deductions. The AMT now covers about one in every eight tax filers.

12 This tax ratchets up to 1.95% for single individuals with incomes over $200,000 and jointly filing families with incomes over $250,000.

13 Keynes, 1924.

14 www.taxpolicycenter.org/taxfacts/displayafact.cfm?Docid=456, accessed August 7, 2017.

15 Pauly, 1986, Liu and Chollet, 2006.

16 http://kff.org/health-costs/report/2015-employer-health-benefits-survey/, accessed August 7, 2017.

17 On June 25, 2015, the Supreme Court of the United States upheld the mechanism for providing these subsidies in a 6–3 ruling against the plaintiffs in King v. Burwell.

18 PPOs are Preferred Provider Organizations—plans that control costs by guiding patients to panels of providers (doctors, hospitals, therapists, pharmacists, etc.) who have agreed contractually to the fees they receive for various services provided (Fee for Service, aka FFS). HMOs are Health Maintenance Organizations. Typically, they provide health care through closed panels of physicians who are paid on annual salaries rather than FFS. Point of Service (POS) plans are similar to PPOs but instead of limiting treatment to a fixed panel of providers, they pay for treatment "outside the panel" but with much higher patient copayments for "out of plan" providers.

19 By "traditional health insurance" we mean plans like 1960s era hospital and physician coverage that had little or no patient copayment and limited mechanisms to control either utilization or prices paid to providers.

20 Pauly, 1986.

21 Manning et al., 1987.

22 Using a standard economic measure, the elasticity of demand reflected in these data is about –0.1 to –0.4, depending on the type of care. The most price sensitive care was outpatient well-care, with an elasticity of –0.43. See Phelps, 2014, Table 5.3.

23 Newhouse et al., 1993.

24 Phelps, 1996, Table 5, assuming small effects on the price of medical care as demand falls. The effects are larger if permanent reductions in health care prices emerge as demand for medical care falls.
25 Newhouse, 1978.
26 Newhouse, 1988.
27 Chernew and Newhouse, 2012.
28 Mushkin, 1955.

2 An alternate universe Life without the tax subsidy

Consider an alternate universe where the employer-paid health insurance premium tax exemption had never been codified into law. While this may sound like a strange and perhaps scary universe, perhaps it is one where we can presume that the laws of economics work the same as in ours.

In this alternate universe, what, if anything, would employers offer their employees regarding health insurance? The clearest answer comes by looking at the market for life insurance, which was treated equally with health insurance in the World War II price and wage controls, but treated very differently in the 1954 revision of the tax law.

The 1954 law capped tax-protected employer contributions for life insurance at the premium to pay for term life insurance with a $50,000 death benefit. That is precisely what most employers still pay for, if anything. This is codified in the Internal Revenue Code section 79, and the exclusion applies only for insurance on the worker not for a spouse, dependent, or for any other person.

Note also that the original $50,000 life insurance limit has never been adjusted for inflation, so the $50,000 insurance policy has become less and less meaningful. The $50,000 envisioned in the 1954 tax code would require $450,000 of life insurance in 2017 to maintain the same buying power for the insurance beneficiary, and represented about 20 times the then-current per capita income. The government has let the tax benefit for life insurance wither away, and it is now worth barely one-tenth of what it was in 1954 when the tax law codified the World War II exemption from taxation—approximately the same as the 2015 annual per capita income in the US (not 20 times that amount).

We can use the behavior of employers in life insurance markets as a good template of what would happen in the absence of the exclusion of health insurance premium payments from the taxable income base. The following sections describe our best understanding of what that alternate universe would look like.

Employers would actively offer health insurance

Many employers offer term group life insurance as a benefit to employees. By recent estimates, well over 110 million people have group life insurance, with a face value of over $8 trillion.[1] Any employer premium payments for insurance in excess of $50,000 per year are reported to the Internal Revenue Service (IRS) as taxable income. A survey from Prudential Insurance in 2011 indicated that 85% of employers with a term life fringe benefit also offer at least one voluntary participation plan, almost always involving life insurance and disability insurance.[2] The compelling reason, of course, is that group administration of the plan brings with it both reduced administrative costs (and hence lower premiums) and also conveniently assembles a group of individuals for actuarial rating, thus obviating the need for personal health evaluations. Employers can provide a valuable service to their employees at low cost by having insurance companies compete not only for the sale of the $50,000 term policies but also (probably far more important to the insurance companies) access to the broad employee market to sell voluntary-participation life insurance to the employees.

The popularity of such plans is high. Among those workers offered voluntary insurance, very high fractions (up to 97% in some surveys) participate by purchasing at least some term life insurance, either by sharing in the initial $50,000 amount (if required by the employer) or purchasing additional insurance, either in fixed dollar amounts or some fixed multiple of salary (2X, 5X, 10X, etc.).

And so it would be in our alternate universe with employer-paid health insurance even without the tax subsidy. Employers would widely offer health insurance plans to their workers—they just would not pay for them in ways that we now see. Indeed, some employers might continue to buy some basic health insurance for their employees, using the logic of what is known as a "productive fringe benefit." Firms offer many such benefits to improve the health and educational skills of their work force, thereby increasing their productivity, either through improved performance or through lower sick-loss days, disability days, and their attendant absenteeism or the related "presenteeism," (i.e., workers coming to work to get paid but unable to perform well because of illness). But the form of such insurance would differ considerably from what we see now, both because of what employers would willingly pay for and what employees would desire.

Robust markets would exist beyond the employer-based health insurance market

The life insurance market operates in a commercial world with a large variety of products, features, and options, beginning with simple term insurance of various amounts, and a wide variety of insurance options that include "savings" aspects, the original product known as "whole life insurance," now with many variants. And life insurance now comes blended with combinations of life insurance, long-term care insurance, retirement annuities, and many other viable options for consumers. None of this relies upon employer-paid plans.

Similarly, in our alternate universe, we would see a thriving private health insurance market beyond what we now observe in our own universe. Private health insurance markets have essentially been crowded out, on one side by the tax subsidy to employer-provided health insurance and on the other side by widespread governmental health insurance programs (Medicaid, Children's Health Insurance Program (CHIP), the Department of Veteran's Affairs, TRICARE and other special-population programs). We would expect to see a wide variety of sponsored health insurance group offerings to compete with those offered by employers. One can envision a wide array of group health insurance sponsors, once the artificial protection of the tax-subsidy shield has been removed from employer groups. The alternate universe could include offerings from fraternal groups, labor unions, community-based organizations, perhaps even banks, credit unions, and other organizations. Non-group markets have functioned remarkably well given the crowding out; they have a bright future if put on even footing.[3]

Crowding out is a well-documented consequence of subsidized health insurance. The issue has been studied in the past on a number of occasions relating to how much public health insurance crowds out private health insurance. These studies have assessed how much total insurance coverage expands as public coverage expands. The answer is that about 60% of the expansion in public plans results from people dropping private plans, which means that crowding out is very important.[4] We think it quite likely that the tax-subsidy of employer-based plans has crowded out much of what the non-group market might have in the absence of the subsidy, but there is no way to know for sure in advance.

Even now in the US (despite the employer-plan tax subsidy), non-employer-group health plans exist through "sponsorship" of health insurance, underwritten by a private insurance company, but with enrollment sponsored by a separate "membership group." Existing membership groups offering group health insurance include the National Association for the Self-Employed, the American Association of Retired Persons, the Alliance for Affordable Services, the National Association of Female Executives, and the Small Business Service Bureau, just to name a few. The presence of these groups in the face of the tax subsidy provides evidence that they would be a more important part of the market if the subsidy did not exist.

Another window into the world of "sponsored" health insurance came with the advent of Medicare Part C (more about which is in Part II of our book). Part C created an option—now called "Medicare Advantage" (or more simply, "MA") where people can trade in their traditional Medicare coverage for a private health insurance plan. It transforms Medicare into a voluntary voucher system.

Many MA programs have emerged. In 2015 there were 1945 different MA plans offered throughout the US.[5] This over-65 market does not face the tax-subsidized competition from employer-paid insurance. It provides another example of what the under-65 market could look like if the tax subsidy did not exist. Enrollment in MA plans is climbing steadily, reaching 33% of the Medicare population in 2017 (19 million MA enrollees).

The non-employer market is important now, and would be more so without the tax subsidy (and with the health insurance exchanges created by the Affordable Care Act (ACA) and likely to continue even if the ACA is repealed). The market would be larger, richer in choice, and would cost less (for identical coverage) than we now see. The market would be richer in offerings, and hence would attract more enrollees.

In addition—a somewhat technical issue we will not venture into in detail—the adverse selection faced by the non-group market would diminish. The issue—briefly—is that the employer group mechanism tends to siphon off the most desirable insured lives—those healthy enough to work regularly—leaving those with worse health outcomes to go either in the private non-group markets or to turn to governmental programs such as Medicaid, CHIP, and VA programs. Removing the subsidy to employer group insurance would help re-balance this mix.

Non-employer markets would actively use actuarial rating

Another important difference can be observed between group-term life and privately purchased life insurance: Most life insurance (particularly whole life and its variants, but also some term insurance) is priced based on the insured-person's actuarial circumstances, including age, sex, smoking status, and for large insurance policies, sometimes a personal and family history, and even a physical examination to determine other risks of premature death. These policies also have extra premiums paid each year for people who engage in hazardous activities such as skydiving, scuba diving, and related risky endeavors, and for people engaged in risky occupations such as mining, fire protection, race car driving, and the like.

Auto insurance has the same types of pricing—riskier drivers pay more. Any person who has had a teenaged son in the family understands this well—testosterone and gasoline create an explosive mixture, made worse when alcohol is added to the mix. In fatal crashes involving teens, one-quarter have been drinking alcohol.[6] More generally, the cost of auto insurance is closely linked to many observable characteristics, including age, sex, and, most importantly, driving history. Bad drivers pay more than good drivers.

This difference in the way the insurance is priced (that is, linked to individual behavior and choices) differs remarkably from the way health insurance is priced. Indeed, the ACA allows some but precludes other lifestyle-related data in actuarial rating or determination of to whom insurance companies will sell insurance.[7] Even before the ACA, employers could not meaningfully specify price differences for health insurance due to lifestyle-related choices of employees because of restrictions in US labor laws. As a consequence of these rules, much of our health insurance system has lost the ability to charge people more when their own behavior increases their expected medical costs. And because of that limitation, some important economic incentives to avoid risky lifestyle choices—notably obesity and excessive alcohol consumption (and to a lesser extent, smoking; lesser because of the allowed use in the ACA rules)—have been blunted or entirely removed from the market for health insurance.

Even if some individual companies did not offer an array of plans that took lifestyle into account, the market would quite likely produce such a result, just as do the markets for auto insurance, life insurance, and similar financial markets such as personal lending. Economists call this concept a "separating equilibrium," a notion first analyzed by Michael Rothschild and Nobel Laureate economist Joseph Stiglitz.[8] One can readily observe either experience-rated insurance or separating equilibria in markets such as life and disability insurance, automobile insurance, and personal loan institutions.

Given this theoretical basis and the results we see in other insurance markets, we could expect to see health insurance companies specializing in non-smokers (and hence others for smokers separately), healthy-weight people (and hence for obese people separately), and so forth. Not only are such market segmentations common in other forms of insurance, they also (importantly) encourage more healthful behavior. Just as auto insurance rate-setting is believed to encourage safer driving and non-smokers life insurance leads to smoking cessation (at least to some degree), we can expect that such "experience-rated" health insurance would move people towards healthier life styles.

We must draw a distinction here between use of observable lifestyle choices such as smoking, scuba diving, skydiving, obesity, and alcohol abuse and the use of pre-existing conditions to rate health insurance premiums (a topic to which we return extensively in Chapter 6). This is not a "bright line" issue. Smoking (for example) can readily lead to numerous chronic conditions which, once they occur, are (by definition) pre-existing. These lifestyle choices affect the *probability* of an individual acquiring a chronic condition, but they are not the same thing as having a chronic condition. Further, as we discuss in Chapter 6, even some lifestyle choices (including, among others, propensity to gain weight, propensity to nicotine addiction, and propensity for alcohol abuse) are at least partly determined by genetic traits. Thus, limitations on the use of pre-existing conditions in insurance company choices (offer of coverage and price) will always blur into the potential for limitations on the use of lifestyle choices such as smoking, obesity, and alcohol abuse. We have no clear answer to the proper path here, but only note that total prohibition on the use of lifestyle choices in insurance pricing will inevitably blunt efforts to limit such health-damaging behaviors.

Ultimately there is also a fairness question—should people who live healthy lifestyles (e.g., non-smoking, non-obese people) be forced to pay for the excess health care costs of those who choose otherwise (e.g., smokers or obese people)? In other forms of insurance in our society, ranging from auto insurance to homeowners' insurance to life and disability insurance, people creating higher risks pay more for their insurance than those who create lower risks. How we proceed as a society in this realm with health insurance will in part determine the long run health burden, and hence the long run health care costs of our society. As noted previously, the ACA takes a wholly different stance on this issue, allowing up to 50% surcharges for smokers but wholly disallowing use of obesity in insurance pricing. What any Republican "replace" legislation might include remains to be seen.

We might see fewer people with health insurance ... or perhaps not

This section discusses a counter-factual situation. We ask whether voluntary coverage would increase or decrease with removal of the tax subsidy. Of course, the individual mandate of the ACA makes this question essentially moot, but with the distinct possibility that new legislation (or a different Supreme Court ruling) may overturn the individual mandate, we proceed with our analysis.

On first thought—absent the individual mandate—it would seem that abolishing the tax subsidy to employer-paid health insurance would unambiguously increase the number of persons in the United States without health insurance. This logic follows one of the primary rules of economics—when the price of something rises, people will consume less of it. This "iron law" has proven to be correct again and again, for food, clothing, housing, health care, and even addictive products such as narcotics and tobacco.[9] How could it possibly differ for health insurance?

To understand this issue more fully, we must think about how firms decide which health insurance plans to offer their employees. Some firms offer only one choice, others offer several. A few firms offer up to half a dozen or so. Rational employers (perhaps in bargaining with unions) would want to select plans that appealed most to their overall work force for any given outlay by the firm, since this would make the benefit most attractive to workers.

One analysis of the way these choices worked has concluded that one can think about the selection process as if the choice of plan were put up for vote among the employees, each worker receiving one vote.[10] In such a model, the person with "centralist" preferences (the "median voter") wins. Thus, in a firm filled with young, healthy workers, one might expect relatively lower health insurance coverage, whereas in a firm more heavily populated by older workers (or smokers, or others with known health risks), one would expect to see choices shifting towards higher coverage. In firms with unusually wide ranges of health risks (age, smoking status, etc.) the preferences of many of the workers may not jibe well with those of the "median voter" and hence the set of plans offered by the firm may not be appealing to all workers. In this case, some workers would forego the insurance coverage, all the more so to the extent that the employer's share was smaller. Or they might decide only to use coverage offered to the employee, bypassing spousal and children's coverage. Or they might seek employment in a firm with different insurance offerings. Diverse tastes in the work force also explain why some large firms offer multiple insurance options to their employees—this makes the fringe benefit more valuable to the workers.

The data are consistent with this process. Almost half of the nation's uninsured have incomes 200% or more above the poverty line, and a quarter have incomes above 300% of the poverty line.[11] Thus, significant numbers of uninsured people in the US are not those typically identified (poor, unemployed) but rather younger workers with incomes well above the poverty line. These people have either opted to work in firms without health insurance, declined to enroll, or enrolled only for themselves, leaving spouses and other family members uninsured. The latter is a common pattern, since many firms pay a greater share of the "individual" workers' insurance premium than for spouse or family coverage. These young and relatively healthy people have been identified as attractive marketing targets by the health insurance industry, but remain out of the market in large numbers.[12] The "individual mandate" of the ACA was designed to bring them into the market.

In this type of world, since employer-provided coverage has in many ways crowded out alternative markets, workers such as these might find it better to "go bare" than to accept (and pay for part of) employer-provided coverage. However, in our alternate universe, these workers could be expected to have access to a wider array of coverage choices than those currently available, and some of them would opt for insurance coverage even when they choose to forego employer-based coverage in our observed universe—the one dominated by employer-based plans.

As a consequence, one cannot predict in advance whether total insurance coverage would be greater or less in our alternative universe. The lack of the tax subsidy would push in one direction (fewer people with coverage) but the wider array of options would push in the other direction (more coverage). We would need to look into that universe to know for sure; something we cannot do at present.

To think more about this "crowding out" issue, consider an analogous world where employers paid a 30% subsidy for automobile purchases, but only if the vehicle was a high-end "luxury" vehicle, e.g., Cadillac, Chrysler, Lincoln, Lexus, Mercedes Benz, BMW, Audi, etc. The subsidy to high-end vehicles would crowd out the market for lower cost alternatives (Chevy Smart, Ford Fiesta, Smart Cars, Fiat 500s, Toyota Yaris, etc.).

What would happen if the tax subsidy for high-end autos vanished? Certainly fewer people would own high-end cars, but the expansion of the market for lower-end cars would provide more alternatives, and some people would end up owning cars who had not done so before. Thus it could also be with health insurance. We have no way to know for sure, but it remains a possible outcome that more people would end up with insurance, much of it coming in the form of low-premium High-Deductible Health Plans (HDHPs).

Job and entrepreneurship lock and insurance-related labor disputes would not exist

Without the tax subsidy and subsequent breaking of the employment-insurance link, workers in our alternate universe would not experience "job lock," the situation where people cannot change jobs because they are tied to the health insurance plan of their employer. In our actual "universe," the problem of job lock was partly eliminated by the Health Insurance Portability and Affordability Act (HIPAA) of 1996. Even with that provision in place, "job lock" has been a persistent part of workers' decision making for decades, and there may be residual effects even if the ACA rules against use of pre-existing conditions for actuarial purposes (either pricing insurance or decisions not to offer it) are retained.

The problem goes beyond job lock. Even more than a decade after HIPAA, researchers have estimated that job lock cut by a third the rate at which corporate employees chose to leave a comfortable corporate employment to start a new company (dubbed "entrepreneurship lock").[13] A market with multiple non-employer options would make it clear that the issue of job lock had become moot. The tax subsidy has locked us into an employer-based system, and hence into an increased risk of job lock and entrepreneurship lock.

The alternate-universe economy would also have fewer labor-relations problems, fewer strikes by workers, and less loss to the economy from these labor issues. Even casual observers of labor-management relations know that the key issues in bargaining and strikes over the last half century have often focused on health care benefits more than wages or other contract features. Without the tax advantage of employer-provided health insurance, these would almost never be issues for labor negotiations. Think of how seldom one hears of a labor strike over the extent of employer-paid life insurance benefits.

The income tax system would not redistribute from the poor to the rich

One of the true ironies of the current health insurance tax subsidy is that its benefits focus more on the wealthy than the poor. This comes through three common labor-market features:

- If you are not working, you cannot get employer-paid health insurance.
- If you are working but at lower wage levels, the chances that your employer offers health insurance are smaller, and when insurance is offered, it will be less generous in firms with lower average wage levels (see previous discussion above group insurance choice).
- For any given amount of health insurance premium paid by the employer, the subsidy increases with income, since workers' marginal tax rates rise with income.

Table 2.1 Share of employer premium tax benefits by income group

Income group	Share of tax benefits
Lowest 20%	8%
Next lowest 20%	14%
Middle 20%	19%
Next to highest 20%	26%
Highest 20%	34%

Source: CBO, May 2013

Combining these features, it is easy to see why the current system systematically subsidizes those with higher incomes at the expense of those with lower incomes. The employer-paid health insurance tax subsidy is not the only "tax expenditure" to do this (the homeowners' mortgage interest deduction has a similar effect), but the employer-paid health insurance subsidy is greater than any other single tax expenditure.

A recent Congressional Budget Office (CBO) study calculates the distribution of the tax subsidy for health insurance of $260 billion per year.[14] By income quintiles, the shares of benefits are as shown in Table 2.1.

The message is clear: this tax subsidy strongly and disproportionately benefits the wealthiest segments of our society. This regressive tax exclusion runs contrary to the general overall structure of our tax system. The top half of the income distribution gets 70% of the benefit (34% + 26% + half of the 19% for the middle quintile). The bottom half gets 30%.

Our "alternate universe" does not contain this regressive feature of the tax code. In addition, as we discuss in the next chapter, in our alternate universe—with a broader base of taxable income than in the "real" universe in which we live—all marginal tax rates can be set lower and still achieve the same tax revenue. And those lower marginal tax rates would produce a more robust economy than the one in which we now live.

Summary of the "alternate universe"

What would our alternate universe look like if the 1954 tax subsidy to health insurance had never happened? Employers would continue to offer health insurance policies to their employees, because the advantages of grouping together all of the workers and their families into a single group makes for a very efficient market through which insurance companies and employers can negotiate rates. However, the employers would most likely not actually pay any of the premiums. Total compensation (salary or wages plus benefits) would be the same in both settings, but their mix would differ.

Employees would see a wider array of options than they do currently, since they could shop for plans priced on an equal footing with regard to tax subsidies. Employment-related groups would continue, but alternatives would arise, including union-sponsored groups, fraternal organizations, religious organizations, college alumni organizations, and perhaps even regional governmental plans (cities or counties). Consumer choice would be greater than we now observe, a valuable outcome in any free market environment.

The most important difference, however, would be the insurance choices would be made without the tax subsidy. Without that subsidy, people would predictably select health insurance with different characteristics—higher deductibles, less generous (or no) coverage for some low-risk activities such as dental services, and more acceptance of insurance structures that control costs well. The plans most likely to thrive in such a world would include Preferred Provider Organization (PPO) plans, Health Maintenance Organization (HMO) plans with restricted provider panels, and (of more recent vintage) HDHPs with an associated Medical Savings Account—plans that offer effective cost-control while still limiting risk. We discuss these types of plans more in a later chapter.

The ACA bans the use of pre-existing conditions in the pricing of insurance, further breaking the job-insurance link, so to the extent that the law remains unchanged, the problem of job lock may decline and perhaps even wither away in our actual "universe." It never would have arisen in the alternate universe without the tax subsidy to employer-provided insurance. But even with the ACA rules about pre-existing conditions, subtle employment decisions by corporations may still lead to some job lock, since some firms may opt not to hire potential workers whom they view as potentially expensive health insurance risks.

Finally, the most important differences between our actual "universe" and the alternative universe without the tax subsidy would be the size of the health care economy and the rate of growth over time. Rather than spending 18% of gross domestic product (GDP) on health care, the alternate-universe world could be something closer to 13–14% of GDP, perhaps even lower, and it would grow less rapidly over time without the over-stimulus to the introduction of new medical technologies.

Aside from special interests (some health care providers, those with very high employer-paid insurance), this might seem like a desirable place to be. This raises the fundamental question: how might we actually get to that alternate universe? Chapter 3 provides a new pathway to get from here to there.

Notes

1 American Council of Life Insurers, 2012.
2 Prudential Insurance Company, 2011, p. 25.
3 Pauly, 2010.
4 Gruber and Simon, 2008.
5 Jacobsen et al., 2014, Exhibit 1.
6 www.cdc.gov/motorvehiclesafety/teen_drivers/teendrivers_factsheet.html, last accessed August 7, 2017.

7 The ACA allows up to a 50% surcharge for smokers, but specifically precludes obesity-related surcharges.
8 Rothschild and Stiglitz, 1976.
9 Becker et al., 1991; Grossman and Chaloupka, 1998.
10 Goldstein and Pauly, 1976.
11 Chockley et al., 2003.
12 Benko, 2003.
13 Stroupe et al., 2000.
14 CBO, May 2013.

3 How to get there from here and also grow the economy

Fix the tax law (Proposal 1)

We propose immediate and complete elimination of the favored tax treatment for employer-paid health insurance premiums, coupled with proportionate across-the-board reductions in the marginal income tax structure for personal income taxes, Social Security taxes and Medicare taxes paid by all US workers and their employers as a marginal tax on labor.

If nothing else changes, tax collections would remain unchanged—the increase in taxable income would—by design—be offset by commensurate reductions in all marginal tax rates. To be clear, we would simultaneously repeal the so-called "Cadillac tax" (due to take effect in 2020) if not already repealed.

This change in the tax law will both favorably alter the shape of the US health economy and at the same time increase economic activity because of lower marginal tax rates. It will change the way health insurance is viewed in the United States, leading people to select plans that have more cost-consciousness and are less likely to lead to regular increases in medical care spending over time.

Previous efforts and ideas

We are not the first to venture down this path. Many recent proposals for universal health insurance in the United States have included taxation of premiums to some extent, including the Affordable Care Act (ACA), which would place a 40% surcharge on "large" health insurance premiums (taxing amounts over $10,200 per year for a single individual, $27,500 for families). This so-called "Cadillac tax" would apply to a bit under 20% of large-employer health plans in the year before the ACA was implemented, fewer by 2020 as firms shift their insurance offerings to reduce the potential excise tax burden. This tax is based on the total premium cost, not the employer contribution, but for firms that pay all or most of their employees' health plan costs, these are nearly one and the same. The 40% surtax approximately offsets the consequences of the income tax-based subsidy currently embedded in the tax law, but only for the policies that rise to the taxable "Cadillac" level.[1]

In earlier years, a proposal from the Clinton administration in 1994 involved a similar sort of tax on high-cost health plans. The logic underlying this approach rests mostly on the idea that these expensive health plans are significantly more generous than other health insurance plans, and hence create more demand and more total cost in the health care system. (We later raise a parallel issue regarding "Medigap" plans that supplement standard Medicare coverage.)

Unfortunately, the "Cadillac tax" aims imprecisely. Designed to target "lavish" coverage (very low deductibles and copayments) it also affects more modest insurance plans for people who live in very high-cost areas, and has a similar effect on firms with a work force with relatively older workers (who have predictably higher health care costs). Recent research shows that "benefit design" (scope of benefits and coverage parameters) explains relatively little of the overall variation in insurance premium levels.[2] Regional differences in cost of care and other factors account for most of the variability in total premium costs.

Another common policy approach would cap the amount of employer-paid insurance that escapes income taxation. In 1983, the Reagan administration proposed limits of $175 and $70 per month for family and individual insurance, to be indexed by the Consumer Price Index (CPI). Parallel proposals appeared in legislation sponsored by Senator David Durenberger (R-MN), and Representatives Richard Gephardt (D-MO), James Jones (D-OK), David Stockman (R-MI), and Al Ulman (D-OR).[3]

The tax cap strategy has repeatedly resurfaced in policy proposals. In a 2013 essay in the *New England Journal of Medicine*, a "bipartisan gang of four" of prominent Democrat and Republican political figures (former Democrat Senator Tom Daschle, former Clinton appointee as Director of the Office of Management and Budget, Alice Rivlin, and former Republican Senate leaders Pete Dominici and Bill Frist, MD) set forth their approach to this problem: repeal the "Cadillac tax" on high-cost health plans and instead cap the level of premiums that are exempt from income taxation.[4]

Their choice to cap the tax-excluded amount rather than taxing all health insurance premiums is purely a matter of political pragmatism. The concern has been that taxing all premiums would increase the tax burden for a large fraction of the US population—about 70% of the under-65 population. That is not a typical part of any successful tax-reform legislation. The tax cap idea is designed to reduce the number of people harmed by the change in the tax law to the point where it becomes politically acceptable.

However, just as the "Cadillac tax" aims imprecisely (focusing on total premiums rather than benefit design), a capped tax-deductibility can also affect people with relatively modest insurance coverage who live in high-cost areas and similarly can sweep in employment-based groups with a relatively older work force. These defects could be reduced by having the cap linked to geographic regional costs and average age of any insured group, but these sorts of adjustments complicate the administration of the tax cap and have not been included in any tax-cap proposals of which we are aware.

Capping the tax-exempt premium level also fails to achieve the full benefits that our proposal would bring. First, it would miss a significant number of individuals, people who would continue to make decisions with the tax subsidy affecting their choices. Thus, the tax cap has less than complete effectiveness in controlling health care spending. In addition, capping the tax-exempt premium does nothing to stimulate the economy, whereas our uncapped version returns the newly-acquired tax revenue to the people through lower marginal tax rates. Capping alone can never attain this effect.

In a proposal somewhat similar to ours, Stanford health economist Alain C. Enthoven proposed to wholly eliminate the favored treatment of employer-paid health insurance premiums and to replace it with a tax credit equal to 40% of the employee's premium costs with caps similar to the Reagan administration's proposal.[5] This approach still subsidizes 40% of the insurance plan cost for those under the cap, but by using a tax credit, it removes the regressive features of the current system that systematically give larger subsidies to higher-income families. However—as with all other earlier proposals—it does not provide the assured stimulus to the economy that our across-the-board reduction in marginal tax rates creates.

Further details about our proposal

Now some details: We propose to achieve this by lowering every relevant marginal tax rate—personal income, personal FICA, personal Medicare tax, employer FICA, and employer Medicare tax—in a way that will precisely offset the increase in the tax base with proportionately lower marginal tax rates. As we detail below, we estimate that—using 2015 data—more than $600 billion in newly taxable income would be created by removing the favorable treatment of employer-paid premiums—a permanent increase in the taxable income base.

Workers have three federal taxes on their incomes—personal income taxes (with a progressive marginal tax structure), Social Security (FICA) taxes, at 6.2% of wages up to the legislatively specified ceiling ($127,200 in 2017), and Medicare taxes (1.45% on all wage income).[6] Employers pay matching FICA and Medicare taxes on employee wages (and of course self-employed people pay both the worker and employer shares). In addition, many workers face personal income taxes from state and (in some cases) local governments,[7] averaging out to 4.65% marginal rate on wage income, according to National Bureau of Economic Research (NBER) estimates using their TAXSIM model.[8]

How much money is at stake, and where does it come from? Begin with estimates of the total employer contributions towards health insurance premiums. As shown in Figure 1.2 in Chapter 1, the Department of Commerce estimated that in 2012/2013, employer-paid health contributions reached $600 billion per year—about $3000 for every individual in the United States who has any earned income. That $600 billion per year amount (approaching $700 billion in 2017) currently escapes all forms of both personal and corporate taxes. That amount has changed slightly since the 2013 data, but suffices for our discussion here and allows a useful connection to other 2013 data.[9]

If we combine the $600 billion per year estimate from the Department of Labor regarding employer contributions for health insurance with the 2013 Joint Committee on Taxation estimate of $132 billion in personal income tax expenditures,[10] a very useful number emerges—the average of the marginal personal income tax rates that would be imposed on employer-paid health insurance premiums is 22%. This counts only the personal income tax portion of the tax expenditure—not the FICA or Medicare payroll taxes. We estimate that the additional losses in revenue to the Social Security system and Medicare are (in rounded numbers) an additional $63 billion and $17 billion, respectively.[11] Thus, the total loss in federal revenue is something approximating 35% of the employer-paid premiums. So as not to overstate the precision, this estimate can be rounded to "one-third."

A Congressional Budget Office (CBO) report shows that for 2013 the total estimated personal taxable income was $10.488 trillion, representing 65.4% of total gross domestic product (GDP).[12] The $600 billion employer-paid insurance premium amount thus represents 5.7% of the taxable personal income base. Similarly, the same CBO source estimates 2013 Social Security tax base (wage income) at $7.014 trillion, so the $600 billion in employer-paid insurance represents 8.55% of the income base upon which Social Security taxes are levied. The Medicare tax is levied on all wages (about $7.46 trillion in 2013), so the $600 billion represents 8.04% of that total.

Our basic proposal would reduce all marginal tax rates in proportion to the expansion of the relevant tax base. Thus, using these 2013 estimates all federal income tax rates would fall by 5.7% of their current levels, so the overall average would fall from 22% to 20.75%. FICA taxes (both employer and employee share) would fall from 6.2% to 5.67%. Medicare taxes would fall from 1.45% to 1.33%.

To assure the neutrality of the tax system (holding labor force participation constant), it would also be necessary to widen all marginal tax brackets in the federal income tax system (and in all states with progressive income tax structures). Otherwise, the expanded income base would push some tax filers into higher marginal tax brackets than they would have been in previously. The mechanisms to accomplish this are essentially identical to the manner in which the tax brackets widen to account for annual increases in the CPI.

State income tax rates would also fall if (and only if) state governments act through legislation to follow the federal change. If they do so, the average state marginal tax rate would decline from 4.55% to 4.2%. If states left their marginal tax structures unchanged and followed the change in federal law defining the taxable income base, their tax receipts would rise, at least in the short run, but migration and industry relocation could alter that outcome in the long run. For many state income tax forms, it would take a special act by the state not to follow the federal definition of taxable income, since many state income tax forms begin with "write down your Federal adjusted gross income here" or some similar statement. Since federal income definitions would include employer-paid premiums, so would the income definition of the states unless they specifically chose otherwise.[13]

The question naturally arises as to how much income employers will give back to employees when they cease paying health insurance premiums. The answer will first hinge on how the Internal Revenue Service (IRS) rules describe the imputed income. Once again, the employer-sponsored life insurance market shows how this will work. If employers pay for life insurance premiums above the $50,000 cap for any workers, the IRS imputes income to them according to a scale related to the actuarial value of the insurance by age, as shown in Table 3.1 (rates as of 2016).

Following implementation of our proposed tax change, the IRS would necessarily create a similar table for health insurance premiums, almost certainly linked to age but probably not to other observable characteristics of their workers (including sex, smoking status, etc.). Such a table as this would be necessary for those employers who continued to pay health insurance premiums for some or all workers. Note the steep and accelerating cost of coverage as age increases in the "term life insurance" table. A similarly-shaped profile will likely emerge for health insurance premiums, since average health care costs rise at an increasing rate with age (as we discuss in a subsequent chapter on chronic diseases).

Employers will use this as the basis for converting their average monthly health insurance premiums ("per member per month") to an imputed income per worker, based upon whether they have received coverage as individuals, couples, or families. If they continue to pay the insurance premiums (unlikely, we believe, in the long run) then the premiums will be imputed as income for tax purposes. The most plausible long run outcome is that employers will shift income to workers using the IRS formulas or similar actuarial tables at least as a starting point for determining the wages shifted to workers. Market forces will

Table 3.1 IRS imputation of income for life insurance premium payments in excess of $50,000 coverage per year

Age	Cost per $1000 coverage per month
Under 25	$0.05
25–29	$0.06
30–34	$0.08
35–39	$0.09
40–44	$0.10
45–49	$0.15
50–54	$0.23
55–59	$0.43
60–64	$0.66
65–69	$1.27
70+	$2.06

Source: www.irs.gov/pub/irs-pdf/p15b.pdf, Table 2.2

lead to the proper shifting of income to workers by age category rapidly as firms, workers and (where involved) unions adjust and negotiate these transfers.

There stands our proposal in a nutshell: Add the employer-paid premiums to the taxable income base, and simultaneously reduce all relevant tax rates—income, FICA and Medicare tax rates—proportionately in such a way that if nothing else changed, tax revenues would remain unchanged. This ignores the revenue that the ACA Cadillac tax might produce, but it does not take effect until 2020, even if new legislation left it in place, and we urge immediate enactment of our proposal and simultaneous elimination of the ACA's Cadillac tax.

We also know that this is not the final resting point of the economy. Instead, with all marginal tax rates made smaller, the economy would shift to a larger equilibrium. This is not a one-time "stimulus" issue, but rather a permanent reduction in the (otherwise larger) marginal tax rate structure of the economy, and hence a permanently larger economy. We turn next to estimates of the magnitude of this effect.

The macroeconomic benefits

We have three estimates of the consequences of this change in tax law on the size of the economy. The first estimate comes from an exercise taking into account the reduction in marginal tax rates and subsequent effect on labor supply in a simple partial-equilibrium analysis.[14] The second estimate adapts the GDP effects estimated in a 2010 analysis by the CBO of the effects of a 10% across-the-board reduction in marginal tax rates (scaled to match the change in tax rates that our proposal would create).[15] The third comes from a macro-simulation model from University of Minnesota economists V.V. Chari and K. Eslami that specifically analyzes our proposal using a more complex general equilibrium model.[16]

In all three of these approaches, federal income tax revenues, Social Security, and Medicare payroll tax revenues and (as applicable) state and local income tax revenues will all increase in proportion to the increase in economic activity—payroll taxes in direct proportion to the percentage changes in employment, and income taxes in proportion to percentage changes in total GDP. In each approach, an increase is assured since the underlying changes in the tax structures (as we propose them) have wholly offsetting increases in the taxable income base and decreases in marginal tax rates. The extent of the percentage changes in tax revenues will closely follow the percentage changes in GDP or labor effort (as appropriate) estimated by each approach, the results of which we summarize next. Details appear in the Appendix for this chapter.

Summarizing the tax revenue effects

While the primary goal of our proposal is to remove the major distortion in the health economy arising from the tax subsidy to employer-paid health insurance, the mechanism we have designed also creates an assured increase in government tax receipts because of the ensured stimulus to economic activity that the reduced marginal tax rates create. Table 3.2 summarizes the results of these three approaches. The estimated changes range from a low of 0.3% (Chari and Eslami) to a high of 2.4% (partial equilibrium model with high supply elasticity). The CBO general equilibrium models (as we adjust them to fit our setting) provide estimates of 0.8 to 1.7%. Details of the calculations and uses of these three approaches appear in the Appendix to Chapter 3.

To calibrate the overall tax revenue effect, we summarize next the implications for a 1.0% increase in economic activity—an estimate approximately in the center of those available to us, and also convenient as a natural "scale" as other estimates might arise to measure the economic gains from our proposal. For example, if readers prefer the 0.3% estimate (or the 1.7% estimate), they should multiply all of the following numbers by 0.3 (or 1.7).

First, we review tax receipts in the existing world and then compare the projected gains arising from increased labor force participation and overall economic activity.

The baseline parameters in 2015 are:

- Federal personal income tax receipts: $1480 billion.
- Federal corporate tax receipts: $340 billion.
- Social Security payroll tax receipts: $1070 billion.
- Medicare payroll tax receipts: $230 billion.
- State income tax receipts (in aggregate): $360 billion.
- Total tax receipts: $3500 billion ($3.5 trillion).

Taking a summary measure of the growth in the economy of 1% and applying that in proportion to these baseline numbers, the *annual* increases (2015 dollars) in tax revenues are:

- Federal personal income tax increase: $14.8 billion.
- Federal corporate tax increase: $3.4 billion.
- Social Security increase: $10.7 billion.
- Medicare Part A increase: $2.3 billion.
- State income tax increase: $3.6 billion.
- Total increase in government tax receipts: $35 billion.

These increases occur *each year* for each 1% growth in the economy. The economics models differ in the magnitudes of change, and the actual

Table 3.2 Estimated percentage changes in labor supply, economic activity, and tax receipts

Partial Equilibrium Analysis	1.0 to 2.4
CBO General Equilibrium Model	0.8 to 1.7
Chari and Eslame Two Good Model	0.3

Source: Calculation by authors, and Chari and Eslami (2016)

results can only be known after "running the experiment." But the prospect of an increase is essentially certain because of the program design and the widespread understanding that lower tax rates on labor produce *some* increase in labor supply. The primary issue at hand is the magnitude of that increase.

These new tax receipts will not eliminate the federal deficit in a single stroke since the increased federal income tax receipt increases only represent about 3% of the projected 2015 federal deficit. But they take a step in the right direction while solving other problems in the economy. In parallel, the increases in FICA and Medicare taxes help bolster the trust funds associated with those programs, reducing the risk of having to take other programmatic steps to keep those trust funds solvent.

Concluding comments

These three approaches provide a range of estimates of the steady-state gains in economic activity in the US economy and the associated gains in federal and state income tax revenue and federal payroll tax (FICA and Medicare) revenue. They converge around an estimate suggesting approximately a 1% increase in GDP and tax revenues (in very round numbers).

We believe that choosing among these three estimates (or others that might emerge) lends little to the discussion. The economic logic involved provides strong confidence that economic growth will follow the lowering of marginal tax rates, and the structure of the proposed tax change assures (unlike discussions of the so-called Laffer Curve in the 1970s) that net tax revenues will increase. The three estimates of the magnitude of the revenue effects (and steady state GDP improvements) that we provide all support the theoretical conclusion—the economy will improve and tax receipts will rise. The only issue is by how much—an issue that we do not hold as central to the value of our proposal.

The primary goal of our proposal is to rationalize the incentives in the health economy. The tax revenue improvements—we believe—are a bonus, the existence of which we can be confident, while less so to the magnitude of the bonus. But our proposal offers something that no other previous approach has created to stem or remove the deleterious effects of the tax subsidy to employer-paid health insurance: it wholly removes the adverse incentives and at the same time grows the economy.

This combination would seem at face value to assure political support, but we would be naïve to believe so. While our proposal creates a net improvement in the economy in two ways, it clearly creates winners and losers among the population. Chapter 4 turns to a discussion of who wins and who loses upon acceptance of our proposal.

Notes

1 If the tax subsidy averages 30% (so the apparent cost of insurance is 70% of the actual cost) then the 40% excise tax approximately offsets the 30% subsidy, since 1.4 x 0.7 = 0.98 (approximately 1.0). If an individual has a marginal tax rate notably above 30%, the insurance remains subsidized even after the 40% excise tax is paid.
2 Gabel et al., 2009.
3 Enthoven, 1981.
4 Daschle et al., 2013.
5 Enthoven, 1984.
6 In recent changes, the Medicare tax grows slightly in high income brackets, a feature that we do not need to discuss extensively here.
7 These state taxes are deductible on federal tax calculations if individuals itemize, but on average, only 35% of US tax filers itemize their deductions. And the deduction of state income taxes and property taxes goes away for the nearly five million people who get hit annually by the Alternative Minimum Tax (AMT) rules.
8 http://users.nber.org/~taxsim/state-marginal/, last accessed August 7, 2017.
9 Extrapolating the most recent available data (01/01/2014) from the Bureau of Economic Analysis time series on Employer Contributions for Health and Life Insurance gives a value of $690 billion for 2016.
10 Joint Committee on Taxation, February 1, 2013.
11 We reached these estimates by comparing the FICA and Medicare taxes (and the incomes to which they apply) to the estimated 22% average marginal tax rate, and then scaling the $132 billion tax expenditure accordingly.
12 CBO, May 2013.
13 Some states do alter the federal rule. For example, California has tax filers enter their federal taxable income and then subtract off any Social Security income, which is thus taxed at the federal level but not at the state level.
14 For labor supply elasticity estimates, see Keane, 2011.
15 Congressional Budget Office, 2004.
16 Chari and Eslami, 2016.

4 Who might support or oppose our proposal?

Who will likely oppose our proposal?

Our proposal combines two ideas that each separately create two important benefits for the US economy. First, eliminating the subsidy removes an important distortion in the US health care system—the subsidy to employer-paid health insurance—which in turn distorts the size and growth rates of the US health care system. Second, taking the newly found tax revenue (achieved through the addition of $600 billion or more to the taxable income base) and converting it to lower marginal income and payroll tax rates provides a strong and permanent stimulus to the US economy—by approximately 0.3 to 1.7%, according to our best estimates. It would seem that people interested in simultaneously reducing the magnitude of our health care expenditure problem and permanently stimulating the US economy would support our proposal. Given those benefits, who would most likely oppose it? Our first answer to this question looks at the self-interest of affected individuals.

Those with high employer-paid premiums would lose ground

The first answer is quite simple—those individuals and groups who have above-average employer-paid health insurance premiums relative to their taxable income will be more likely to oppose our proposal. This group is fairly easy to describe: it consists mostly of relatively highly paid workers (but not those at the very top of the earned income distribution) and certain employment groups (commonly, but not universally, members of labor unions) that have negotiated unusually high health insurance payments as part of their total compensation package.

In addition to labor union workers in the private sector, state and local government workers will likely fall into the group that faces negative consequences from our proposal. According to Bureau of Labor Statistics data, the proportion of total compensation accounted for by health insurance for all civilian workers in late 2015 was 8.5%—but distinctly different at 7.7% for private sector workers and 11.6% for state and local government workers.[1] Thus, employees of state and local governments will, on average, have reduced after-tax incomes under our proposal. Federal workers on average have slightly higher health benefit payments than comparable private sector workers, mostly arising from more extensive post-retirement health benefits, and may be similarly affected.[2]

A further detail remains—a predictable age-related change in net tax consequences. Table 3.1 described the consequences for a worker who receives a specified dollar amount of employer-paid term life insurance premiums. We can also expect an age-gradient that will follow the inevitable Internal Revenue Service (IRS) calculations about the imputed cost of health insurance, similar to the gradient shown in Table 3.1. Thus, lower-age workers within any firm will receive less actual income transfer (or imputed income if employers continue to pay premiums), and higher-age workers will receive greater transfers. This will generally shift more after-tax income to higher-age workers within any given organization, matching the notion that the employer-paid insurance has more value to older workers (who on average have higher health care costs than younger workers). Those same older workers will face higher premium costs in the subsequent market equilibrium (just as is the case for buying life insurance) but will have more after-tax income to pay for that insurance. For example, a worker with family coverage might have $12,000 of income either imputed (if employer-paid coverage persisted) or transferred to that worker, with an increase in taxes (payroll, federal, and state income) of something in the order of $4000. A young single worker might have only $2000 in imputed income, and $600 in imputed taxes.

Therein lies the most predictable opposition to our proposal: Those who for six decades have most benefitted from the tax subsidy will likely oppose its removal most vigorously. We do not have to conjecture extensively to reach this conclusion. One must only look at the opposition to the "Cadillac tax" put in place in the Affordable Care Act (ACA).[3] By far the most vigorous opposition to that tax came from labor unions such as the United Auto Workers.[4]

To estimate the net-tax consequences for individuals and families in various situations, we developed a calculator that uses 2015 tax brackets and modified it to account for the addition of employer-paid premiums into the tax base. As noted in Chapter 3, this requires adjusting the width of all tax brackets, just as the IRS would adjust their width in the face of general inflation. Without this adjustment, adding the employer premiums to the tax base would push some people into higher marginal tax brackets, contrary to our goal of reducing marginal tax rates where possible (within the goal of revenue neutrality before labor supply response is accounted for). To do this, we widened the tax brackets by 6% (the average employer premium is 5.7% of personal income). Similarly, we expanded the FICA cutoff by 8%—approximately the proportion of FICA income represented by the added tax base. These tables assume (as would be more appropriate in the short run) that the incidence of the employer portion of FICA and Medicare taxes remains on the employer. We discuss the long-run situation (with a full shift of the employer's payroll tax costs) subsequently.

Table 4.1 shows the results for a person filing as an individual and Table 4.2 for joint filing. These two categories account for most tax filers. Results for other filing categories are similar.

For a quick summary of these tables, look at the bottom row in each one, showing the base-state employer-paid premiums that create a break-even condition in actual dollar value and as a percentage of wage income. In this break-even situation, the taxpayer has the same tax obligation either under existing tax rules or under our proposed change. The break-even amounts generally fall close to 7% of wage income both for individual and joint return filers. The small differences arise as the steps in marginal tax brackets shift and also as the FICA tax obligations end (at higher wage incomes). In round numbers, the 7% typical break-even point, "averages" the 5.8% representing the employer-paid premium share of taxable income and the 8% average of wage-tax (FICA) income.

Note that these tables represent a "worst-case" scenario for employees. In the long run, we would expect that the reductions in FICA and Medicare taxes paid by employers would also be shifted to employees as higher wages.[5] To the extent that such shifting occurred, the net changes in after-tax income for employees would be more favorable than Tables 4.1 and 4.2 show. In a natural experiment in Chile as reported by Gruber when payroll taxes were reduced across the nation, a large fraction of the employers' payroll taxes were shifted to the worker.[6]

Table 4.1 Net change in federal income tax and payroll tax, individual filing, for various combinations of adjusted gross income (AGI) and employer-paid premiums using 2015 marginal tax structure with tax brackets widened by 7% and FICA payroll tax limit increased by 7%. Final row shows the break-even point (as percent of AGI) where the net tax change is zero

Individual filer with 6% bracket expansion FICA incidence employer

Old income	20,000	40,000	60,000	80,000	100,000	150,000	200,000
Premiums							
0	−301	−826	−1242	−1675	−2236	−3207	
1000	−89	−521	−936	−1351	−1902	−2930	
2000	122	−215	−630	−1045	−1568	−2653	−3972
3000	334	91	−324	−740	−1234	−2376	−3672
4000	545	396	−19	−434	−900	−2098	−3323
5000	757	702	287	−128	−566	−1821	−2998
7500			1051	636	269	−1128	−2187
10,000			1816	1401	1104	−434	−1376
Break-even	1420	2700	4060	5420	6695	11,565	14,240
Pct of income	7.10	6.75	6.77	6.78	6.70	7.71	7.12

Source: Calculations by authors

Table 4.2 Net change in federal income tax and payroll tax, family filing, for various combinations of adjusted gross income (AGI) and employer-paid premiums using 2015 marginal tax structure with tax brackets widened by 7% and FICA payroll tax limit increased by 7%. Final row shows the break-even point (as percent of AGI) where the net tax change is zero

Old income	20,000	40,000	60,000	80,000	100,000	150,000	200,000
Premiums							
0	−300	−601	−902	−1653	−2068	−2988	
1000	−89	−390	−691	−1347	−1762	−2739	
2000	123	−178	−480	−1041	−1457	−2490	−3504
3000	334	33	−268	−735	−1151	−2241	−3227
4000	442	245	−57	−430	−845	−1992	−2950
5000	757	456	155	−124	−539	−1743	−2672
7500		985	683	640	225	−1121	−2488
10,000			1212	1404	989	−427	−1286
Breakeven	1420	2845	4270	5405	6765	11,540	14,635
Pct of income	7.10	7.11	7.12	6.76	6.77	7.69	7.32

Source: Calculations by authors

When individuals have had smaller employer-paid health insurance premiums than the break-even amount, their net tax obligation falls (shown as negative values in the tables). The smaller the previous employer-paid premiums, the better off is the individual (or family), and conversely, those with large employer-paid premiums are worse off. Those who have previously benefitted most from the tax subsidy will fare worst, and those who have received little to no previous benefit will fare best under our proposed change.

We can also consider the consequences for employers. The effects of our proposed change in tax law come in two parts—the economic equilibrium for the employer insurance payments that should follow the shift to full taxation of employer-paid premiums and the reductions in FICA and Medicare taxes paid by employers.

First, consider the employer's labor costs, which are deductible expenses before corporate profit taxes are calculated. We believe that in the steady-state (long run), employers will simply transfer the funds they have been paying as health insurance premiums into standard wage payments. In either case, their expenditures (wages or health insurance) are tax deductible expenses. Thus, their total labor costs would remain unchanged, except that any portion of the FICA and Medicare taxes not shifted to the employee would decline. Overall, if no shifting occurred, this would represent about an 8% drop in their nominal FICA and Medicare obligations, or about one-half of 1% of labor costs.[7]

To the extent that the employers' share of FICA and Medicare taxes have not been shifted to workers, these changes in the tax rates of FICA and Medicare unambiguously reduce the cost of hiring, adding further stimulus to the economy beyond that created by reductions in the taxes on work effort

(FICA, Medicare, and income taxes). As noted previously, to the extent that these reductions in FICA and Medicare taxes are shifted to employees, the net gains to employees would rise compared to those shown in Tables 4.1 and 4.2. The economic gains are relatively simple to calculate, but their distribution between firms and workers will depend upon the magnitude and rate of shifting that does or does not occur.

Given the premise—completely consistent with standard economic analysis—that employers would shift their previous health insurance payments to straight wage and salary payments, employees would then be free to use those funds to buy health insurance through arrangements made by the employer (who would most likely continue to offer health insurance as a benefit, but would not pay for any portion of the premium) or from other sources (fraternal organizations, unions, civic organizations, insurance exchanges, or individual policies). Their range of choice would expand, as we discussed in Chapter 2.

In summary, as these tables show, those with little to no insurance premiums paid by their employer have significant reductions in their net tax burdens (because of the reduced marginal tax rates on their incomes). Conversely, those with large health insurance payments (relative to their incomes) would see significant increases in their tax burdens, an effect that accelerates with income (because of the progressive tax structure in the US). However, all persons would receive reductions in their marginal tax rates—the reward for additional effort—through lower income tax rates, FICA rates, Medicare tax rates and (when implemented by states), state income tax rates.

Some health care providers could object

Health care providers with a long-run view regarding their income flows may also find our proposal disturbing. With a high degree of certainty, the large bulk of those individuals who have previously benefitted from the subsidy to employer-paid health insurance will eventually opt for different types of coverage. They will have many dimensions along which they might adjust their choices, all of which likely will affect the ways in which they use medical care. They might opt for plans with larger deductibles—shifting, for example, into the increasingly popular High-Deductible Health Plans (HDHPs) with Health Savings Accounts (HSAs). Based on the results from the RAND Health Insurance experiment and other analyses, we can expect the use of health care services by people shifting to HDHP plans to decline (see Table 1.2 in Chapter 1). This aggregate reduction in demand will generally reduce the long-term economic well-being of health care providers.

Other insured individuals may opt for other alternatives that use other mechanisms to control utilization and/or costs of care. Some of these will be shifts to Health Maintenance Organizations (HMOs) and similarly structured organizations. Others may shift to Preferred Provider Organization (PPO) types of plans that negotiate vigorously for lower prices from providers. As more and more people switch to these options, PPOs and related organizations will have more leverage to negotiate lower prices from hospitals, doctors, drug companies, device manufacturers, and others. This would accentuate any gains in bargaining power achieved by recent and ongoing mergers of private health insurers.

All of these shifts will likely have negative long-run effects on the lifetime earnings of health care providers. In the long run, the health economy will shrink in this new world—at least relative to how it would remain if the tax law remains intact with the massive subsidies to health insurance. Thus, we could expect at least some opposition to our proposal from health care providers.

The magnitude for change in physician compensation bears particular mention.[8] In a comparison of the Organisation for Economic Cooperation and Development (OECD) nations' payments to physicians relative to per capita gross domestic product (GDP), a recent analysis found the US second only to Australia in the average payment to physicians, with payments relative to per capita GDP of 5.7 for specialists and 4.1 for generalists.[9] The 4.1 ratio for generalists is the highest listed among these 16 OECD nations. Table 4.3 shows the details. These results closely mirror earlier studies using OECD data,[10] and a more detailed analysis of six industrialized nations.[11]

Does this change endanger people's health?

Some opponents to our proposal may suggest that these changes are dangerous to people's health. They may say that people will forego necessary preventive care, end up sicker, and cost more money in the long run if our proposal is enacted.

Table 4.3 Physician compensation relative to per capita GDP, top 16 OECD countries

Country	Specialists	Generalists	Average
Australia	7.60	2.80	5.20
United States	5.70	4.10	4.90
Netherlands	6.00	3.60	4.80
United Kingdom	4.90	3.90	4.40
Canada	5.10	3.40	4.25
France	5.00	3.10	4.05
Belgium	6.00	2.00	4.00
Switzerland	3.80	3.40	3.60
New Zealand	3.60	3.20	3.40
Ireland	4.00	2.80	3.40
Denmark	2.90	3.40	3.15
Greece	3.10	2.70	2.90
Germany	2.70	2.20	2.45
Norway	2.70	2.20	2.45
Finland	2.50	2.30	2.40
Sweden	2.50	2.20	2.35
Average	4.26	2.96	3.61

Source: www.insidermonkey.com/blog/16-highest-paying-countries-for-doctors-314590/?singlepage=1, last accessed August 4, 2017

To these sorts of objections, we offer two rebuttals in advance. The first rebuttal is simple: We urge that health plans create strong incentives to use preventive medical interventions in every possible way. In HDHP plans, for example, we urge a bypass around the deductible for preventive services proven to reduce health risks and/or reduce health care spending. Chapter 10 details these ideas more fully.

Second, we point to a systematic accumulation of evidence that the situation in which we now find ourselves—too much insurance and too much health care arising from that insurance—has not led to improved health outcomes. None of this evidence is perfect, but almost all of it points in the same direction—that we can introduce the proposals set forth in here in our book without meaningfully endangering people's health.

The evidence on this question comes from four types of sources: international comparisons, regional variation comparisons within the United States, randomized controlled trials of health insurance and its effects, and finally, other analyses bearing on this issue. We take up these approaches in turn.

International comparisons

International comparisons offer an important—albeit imperfect—insight into the issue. This involves two steps—an understanding about how a nation's per capita income affects its health care spending, and next, how that health care spending translates into measurable health outcomes. Both of these steps use widely available international data, adjusted (where appropriate) for purchasing power parity differences across populations.[12]

Figure 4.1 shows the first of these relationships—the strong correlation between a country's per capita income and its spending on health care. The "fit" is extremely tight: per capita income in this regression (omitting the US) explains about 90% of the variance in per capita medical spending. One almost needs to know nothing about a country except its per capita income to know how much they will spend on health care—except for the US. The relationship is essentially independent of the ways in which health care is organized in a country, ranging from purely government-provided health care (as in the British National Health Service or county-provided health care in Sweden) through mixed-economy models (such as Canada, with universal governmental insurance but private production of medical care) to Australia, Japan, Germany, and others (with a mix of private and governmental insurance and predominantly-private production of medical care).

From these data, we can also answer the question "if per capita income grows by 1%, how much will medical spending grow?" In these data, the answer is "about 1.3%" using the "best fit" line while excluding the obvious outlier of the United States. The "income elasticity" in these data is about 1.3. In economists' normal categorization, health care is a luxury good (i.e., an income elasticity greater than 1.0). The share of gross national product devoted to health care grows as income grows when the income elasticity exceeds 1.0. In the

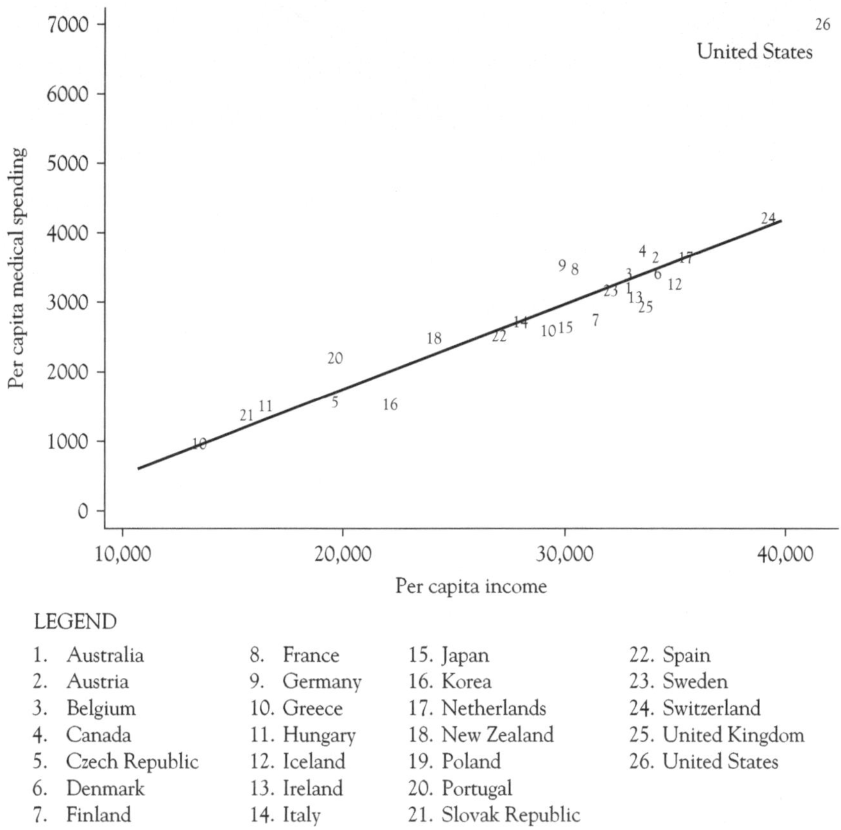

Figure 4.1

Relationship between per capita GDP and per capita medical spending, US Dollars (using purchasing power parity for currency conversion), 2010 data
Source: Data from Organisation for Economic Cooperation and Development (OECD)

US, as real per capita income has grown over the decades, the "budget share" (percent of GDP) has more than tripled, rising from about 5% in the 1950s to about 18% now.[13]

The US is an obvious outlier in these data, spending far more than the "best fit" line from the other 25 nations would suggest. This comes from a number of reasons, including notably that we pay our physicians far more compared with other workers than do other countries (see Table 4.3), we employ new technologies more aggressively, and we are worse on some important health habits (most notably obesity and smoking) than other countries. The bottom line is that we spend a lot on health care—even more than the strong income–medical-spending relationship found in other countries would suggest.

The next step looks at the health outcomes we achieve. One widely used (and important) indicator is life expectancy (see Figure 4.2). The

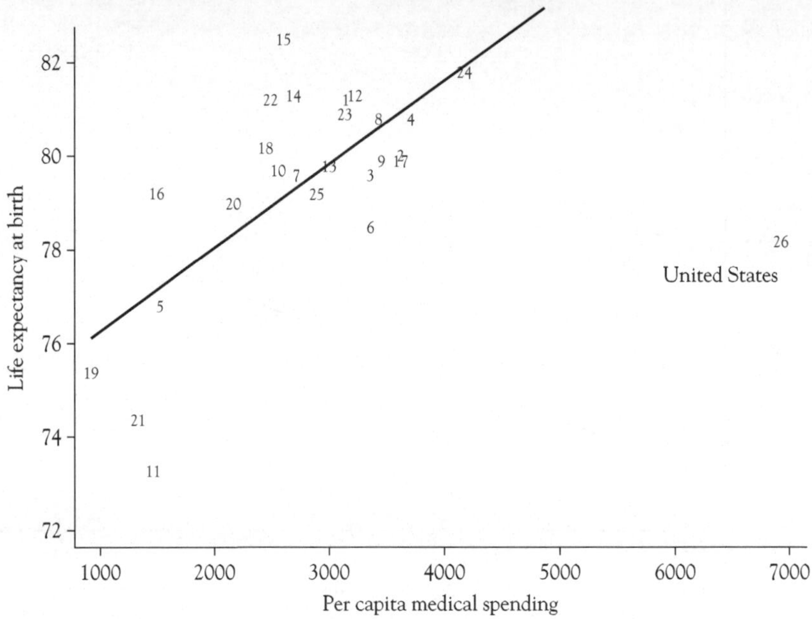

LEGEND

1. Australia
2. Austria
3. Belgium
4. Canada
5. Czech Republic
6. Denmark
7. Finland
8. France
9. Germany
10. Greece
11. Hungary
12. Iceland
13. Ireland
14. Italy
15. Japan
16. Korea
17. Netherlands
18. New Zealand
19. Poland
20. Portugal
21. Slovak Republic
22. Spain
23. Sweden
24. Switzerland
25. United Kingdom
26. United States

Figure 4.2

Relationship between per capita medical spending and life expectancy at birth, US Dollars (using purchasing power parity for currency conversion), 2010 data
Source: Data from Organisation for Economic Cooperation and Development (OECD)

relationship between medical spending and life expectancy is not as tight as the income–spending relationship shown in Figure 4.1, but the data from these OECD nations show a clear pattern of positive gains in life expectancy associated with more medical spending. But here—again—the US is a distant outlier from the "best fit" line, spending about twice as much per capita as other OECD nations on health care but having life expectancy no better than "middling." Numerous nations with far less medical spending achieve significantly better life expectancy outcomes.

Of course, many things confound this simple relationship. Higher per capita GDP creates better standards of living (e.g., clean water, safer cars…) and also comes hand in hand with higher educational attainment, which will not only improve income but also health outcomes (independently from health care).

But this does not distract from the clear fact that the US has notably worse life expectancy outcomes than the general association found in the OECD nations would predict, despite its abnormally high medical spending.

Some analysts view infant mortality as the most "medical care" sensitive indicator available in international studies such as this. Figure 4.3 shows the relationship between medical spending and infant mortality. Here the US lies a notably high distance (worse outcome) above the "best fit" line found using the other OECD nations' outcomes. Here, of course, "less" is better.

The high levels of infant mortality of course enter the calculations for overall life expectancy, leading to the question of whether our poor showing on life expectancy is driven by the poor showing on infant mortality outcomes. Figure 4.4 shows otherwise: the OECD data provide life expectancy for people who have achieved given ages, and Figure 4.4 shows the pattern for life expectancy

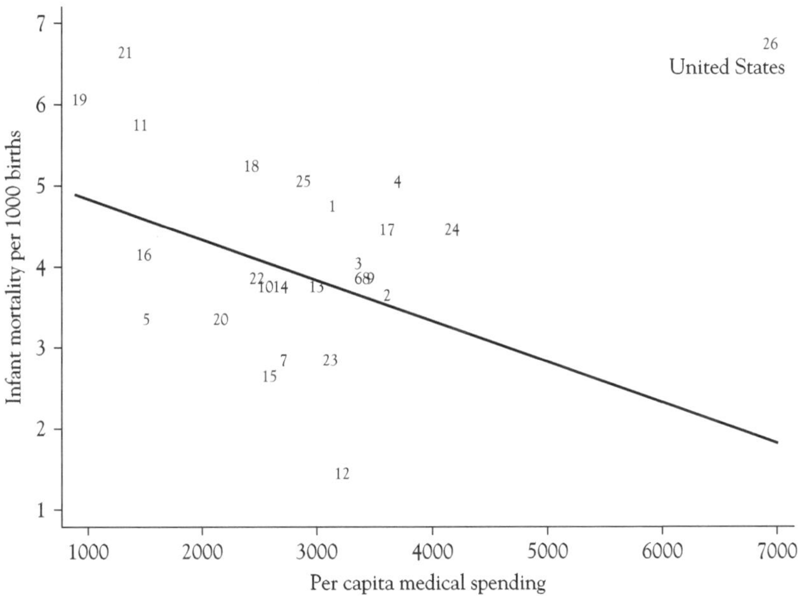

LEGEND

1. Australia
2. Austria
3. Belgium
4. Canada
5. Czech Republic
6. Denmark
7. Finland
8. France
9. Germany
10. Greece
11. Hungary
12. Iceland
13. Ireland
14. Italy
15. Japan
16. Korea
17. Netherlands
18. New Zealand
19. Poland
20. Portugal
21. Slovak Republic
22. Spain
23. Sweden
24. Switzerland
25. United Kingdom
26. United States

Figure 4.3

Relationship between per capita medical spending and infant mortality rates, US Dollars (using purchasing power parity for currency conversion), 2010 data
Source: Data from Organisation for Economic Cooperation and Development (OECD)

of those who have reached 25 years of age. The same pattern exists as for life expectancy at birth—more medical spending is associated with higher life expectancy, and (yet again) the United States sits as an unhappy outlier, far from the "best fit" line using other nations' data.

These data provide one way to think about the question of reducing our nation's medical spending. While the overall data show a weak positive relationship between medical care use and life expectancy, the US seems to have a health care system that does not fit within that model. We spend considerably more than other nations do on health care. We get considerably less for our efforts. It is clearly possible to achieve better health outcomes with less spending.

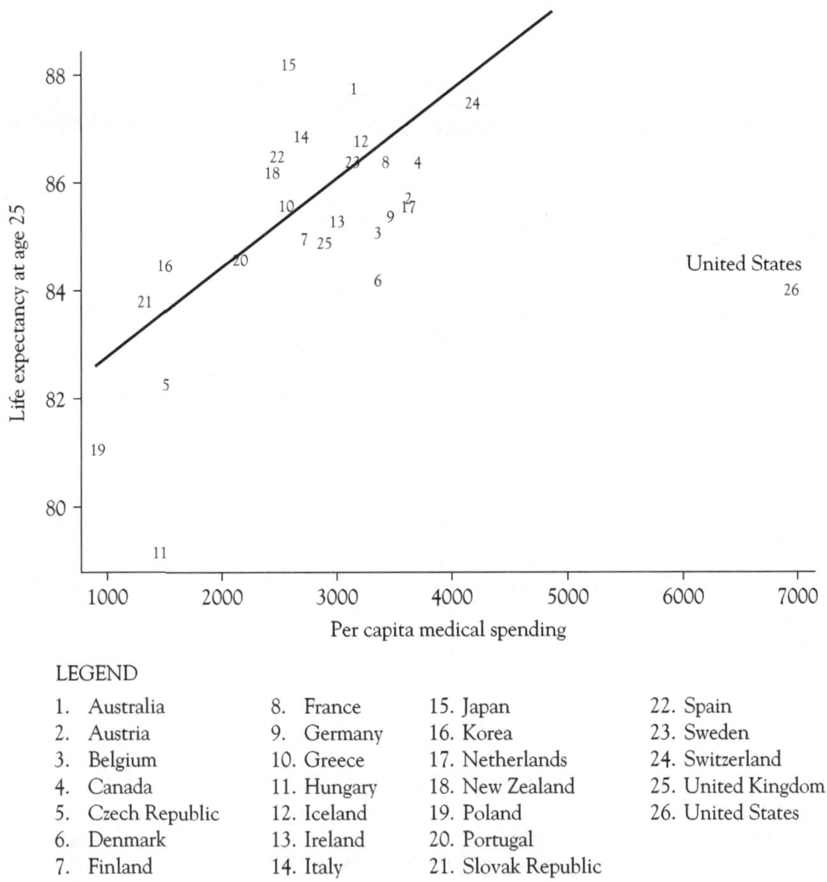

Figure 4.4

Relationship between per capita medical spending and life expectancy at age 25, US Dollars (using purchasing power parity for currency conversion), 2010 data
Source: Data from Organisation for Economic Cooperation and Development (OECD)

Regional differences in health care use and associated mortality

A second approach looks at differences in medical spending in various geographic regions across the United States, seeking to learn if more spending is associated with better health outcomes. These types of studies present numerous potential pitfalls. For example, regions with higher spending might be populated with sicker patients on average. But most studies on this issue generally conclude that only small parts of the regional variation are due to underlying differences in disease burden.[14] The differences in spending are mostly driven by differences in utilization of health care—and in particular, the rates at which variously intensive treatment settings and post-hospital services are involved. These results are not without their critics,[15] but our reading of this literature says that the primary results stated by authors of the Dartmouth Atlas (the source of the regional variations data) remain valid.

Continuing with more detail, the most expensive treatment settings are intensive care units, followed next by hospitalization in general, then (variously) skilled nursing care, outpatient treatment options, hospice care (at the end of life), and finally, down to very low-technology issues such as the use of beta blockers and anti-coagulants for patients who have suffered heart attacks. In a summary of this literature, Skinner and Fisher conclude that differences in "high technology" spending provide no measurable improvement in health outcomes in the best-controlled studies, but (encouragingly) more spending on some of the simplest low-technology interventions (e.g., maintenance medications for chronic conditions) can improve health outcomes regularly.[16]

Randomized and quasi-controlled trials

Two large randomized controlled trials and one quasi-random analysis shed light on this issue, directly addressing the specific question at hand: *does better health insurance coverage lead to better health outcomes?* Note that this shifts the discussion away from "does more *medical care* produce better health outcomes" to the exact question posed by our proposed change in tax law—do changes in the *extent and generosity of health insurance* affect health outcomes?

i. **The RAND Health Insurance Experiment.** The first of these studies was the RAND Health Insurance Experiment, discussed earlier in conjunction with the discussion of how health insurance coverage affects medical care use (discussion at Table 1.2 in Chapter 1). The RAND researchers also carefully studied a series of health outcomes—measured over three-to-five-year intervals—for people who had randomly been assigned different levels of health insurance. The insurance varied from "complete coverage for everything from the first dollar" to plans that look much like the HDHPs that are now growing in popularity in US health care markets. The health-outcomes measures included patients' self-reports, measures of ability to carry out normal activities of daily living, and other well measured health outcomes at a level far more finely tuned than "mortality."

The RAND results strongly suggest that the best health insurance coverage (full coverage for everything) had little to no measurable benefit on any of the many health outcome measures compared with the cost-sharing plans.[17] Some people have observed that the RAND results are limited because there were no over-65 individuals in their study, but for our purposes here, the RAND study covered precisely the right population—those under the age of 65 who rely on employer-sponsored health insurance as their primary source of coverage.

The primary limitation from the RAND study is its duration. Some of the study enrollees were in their randomly-chosen insurance for only three years, others for five years. Thus, the duration of experimentally-provided coverage may have been too short to allow for a full understanding of the health effects of different insurance coverage.

ii. **The Oregon Medicaid Experiment.** Another randomized controlled trial covered a similar age group—adults aged 19–64 years—carried out as part of a Medicaid expansion in the State of Oregon in 2008. The State of Oregon randomly selected among eligible citizens—all without health insurance of any sort—and offered Medicaid coverage to those who "won" the lottery. Those who "lost" the lottery became the control group in the study.

To assess the health effects of the improved insurance coverage (the lottery winners went from having no insurance to full coverage within the Medicaid system in Oregon) the study team used both personal interviews and specific measures of various health indicators, including depression, high blood pressure, long-term cardiovascular risk (using the "industry standard" Framingham risk score), elevated cholesterol, and a plasma glucose concentration test (HbA1c) that measures long-term control of diabetes-associated blood glucose. They found no significant differences between the "treatment" and "control" groups on any of these measures, but there were "statistically insignificant" improvements in each category—an 8% decrease in high blood pressure rates, a 17% decrease in high cholesterol rates, an 18% decrease in HbA1c levels, and a very modest 2.5% decrease in the Framingham cardiac risk scores.[18] They could not assess mortality differences because of the low death rates in the study population.

This study is mildly inconclusive for our purposes. They did measure some improvements in the selected health scores, but they all were small enough that they could have been due to chance. Standard medical literature statistical analysis uses a "5% rule," namely that the results in a study must occur with less than a 5% chance (if there were no true effect) in order for the result to be labeled "statistically significant." If the effects had been bigger, they could have become statistically significant under this approach, but the study had enough people in it to generally assure that if the Medicaid expansion produced significant health effects, they were likely to be relatively small.

The other issue is that the Oregon comparison here looked at people with *no insurance* vs. those with *full coverage* (Medicaid) insurance. In the world of our tax reform, we are not talking about such large differences in coverage, but typically smaller changes in coverage as the subsidy for health insurance goes away and people restructure their health insurance coverage towards less generous (and hence less expensive) plans. Thus, logically, changes in health outcomes would be smaller than those observed in the Oregon experiment, which were in turn too small to become statistically significant in that study.

iii. **A Quasi-Experiment in Massachusetts.** A more recent analysis pertinent to this issue reached a different conclusion. This 2014 "quasi-experimental" study (as self-described by the authors) analyzed the effects on population mortality of the expansion in insurance coverage arising from the Massachusetts "Health Care for All" legislation.[19] They looked at county-level death rates in Massachusetts for 2001–2005 (before the health care law came into being) and then 2007–2010. They compared the differences in mortality (county by county) with similar data from carefully matched "control" counties. They found a significant decrease in all-cause mortality associated with the Massachusetts reform, estimated at a 2.9% reduction in all-cause deaths (8.9 deaths per 100,000 adults per year), and a 4.5% reduction in health care-amenable deaths. Their approach is known in the economic literature as a "difference of differences" approach, designed to eliminate effects of other things that might have occurred in the before/after time comparison.

This analysis (like the Oregon analysis) looks at a somewhat different issue than is raised by our proposal (particularly in a world with the individual insurance mandate of the ACA). The primary effect in Massachusetts arose (as in Oregon) via a comparison of a "no insurance" status with a "high coverage" status. Our proposal would not create shifts in coverage of nearly the extent created by the Massachusetts (or Oregon) experiments. Thus, we can know with reasonable certainty that the Massachusetts study would overstate any mortality effects arising from our proposal, but by how much we cannot be certain.

In summary, none of these approaches to addressing the health-risk question are perfect, but the overall conclusion we would draw is that the sorts of changes in the generosity of health insurance coverage that would emerge from our proposed tax changes are unlikely to lead to impairments in health outcomes of the US population. The reduced mortality arising from expanded coverage in Massachusetts provides the only significant counter-example, and that experiment centered on much larger changes in insurance coverage than our plan would create. In addition, our proposal to bypass copayments and deductibles for proven preventive health care interventions further strengthens the case that our proposed tax change would—to our best understanding—cause no meaningful harm. More broadly, the expansion in after-tax per capita income associated with our plan would be expected to increase health outcomes, given the overall positive correlation between income and better health.

Other US comparisons

An extensive review assessed ten studies of the effect of health insurance coverage on the rates of chronic condition prevalence, self-reported health status, and mortality.[20] Of these all but one used comparisons of people with and without Medicaid coverage—a distinctly different issue than relates to our proposed change in tax policy for employer-provided coverage. They estimate that Medicaid expansion costs $327,000 to $867,000 per life saved, a low cost compared with many other health-affecting interventions.

Only one of the ten relevant studies assessed the health effects of private insurance coverage on mortality. That study focused precisely on the relevant population: persons with employer-sponsored insurance.[21] This study identified 672,526 individuals, determined their insurance coverage status, and then assessed whether or not they had died by 2002 using the highly reliable National Death Index. They were able to follow 643,000 persons aged 18–64 with over 5.4 million years of follow up. This study, controlling for appropriate risk factors such as smoking status and obesity, concluded that "the risk of subsequent mortality is no different for uninsured respondents than for those covered by employer sponsored group insurance at baseline." Again, we emphasize that "mortality" is not the only relevant measure of health outcomes, but it is certainly an important measure, and, for the relevant population (persons aged 18–64) for our issue, this very large sample study found no relationship between mortality rates and having (or not) employer-sponsored health insurance.

Most recently, a new analysis used a long-term study of "near-elderly" persons (aged 50–61 at enrollment), matching persons who had employer-provided health insurance with those without such insurance. Those uninsured at their initial enrollment consumed fewer health care services (as expected) but their health (while alive) did not deteriorate faster than those with insurance, and they did not die at a faster rate. The authors conclude that "... prior studies have greatly overestimated the health and mortality benefits of providing health insurance to the uninsured."[22]

Long-run effects on technology innovation and health

Neither of the experimental data sources (the RAND Health Insurance Experiment and the Oregon Medicaid study), the quasi-experiment in Massachusetts nor the longitudinal study of US adults include the potential effect of a reduced pace of technological innovation. In concept, a shift in aggregate insurance coverage for a large population (the privately insured US population in this case) that reduces demand for medical care could also reduce the rate of technological innovation, which could therefore (also in the long run) reduce health outcomes. None of these studies affected enough of the market to induce such changes.

Could the change in insurance coverage induced by our proposed change in the preferred tax status of employer-paid insurance induce such changes?

In concept, of course, the answer is "yes." But we must realistically ask how large such a change might be. The most important markets involved here include pharmaceuticals and medical devices, both of which are highly international in nature, so one must view the change in the US tax law in the context of world markets. Consider the market for pharmaceutical drugs, which has about $1 trillion annual revenue, 45% of which is in the US. But within the US, the affected market includes only the health care covered by private employer-paid health insurance, which represents 49% of persons but only one-third of all expenditures. Suppose that aggregate demand for medical care by this sub-population dropped by 10% (for simplicity of discussion) because of the tax law change. Then US demand would fall by 3.4%, and world demand would fall by 45% of that, or about 1.5%. Thus, the worldwide incentives for innovation would fall by about 1.5%. We do not believe that this represents a major threat to future health outcomes of the US population.

Even if one considered that decline to be significant, we would ask why it is desirable to subsidize this particular form of technological change vs. (say) consumer electronics, which seem to have thriving innovation worldwide without this type of demand subsidy. And even conceding that a subsidy to health-improving innovation might be desirable, we would argue that it would best be done overtly so that the magnitude could be measured and the value of the subsidy weighed against the cost—a comparison that cannot meaningfully take place with the current implicit subsidy to technological change embedded in the tax code.

Might employers drop insurance coverage to give employees access to Health Insurance Exchange subsidies?

Even without changes that may arise during Trump administration reform or repeal, employers may drop their coverage to assure that their workers would qualify for Health Insurance Exchange (HIX) subsidies. This has been a concern from the very start of the ACA. Under current law, if employers drop health insurance coverage, they will pay a per-employee penalty. Furthermore if the employee elects to receive a subsidy from the HIX, the employer will incur an additional penalty for every employee that signs up with the HIX. These rules (unless altered) will deter employers from dropping coverage.

By 2016, after three years of ACA open enrollment on the HIX and without an enforced employer mandate, the Employer Sponsored Insurance (ESI) population remained quite stable. One reason is that the rollout of the ACA health insurance marketplaces was so slow that many employers did not want to sour relations with their workers by dropping coverage. However, the marketplace in 2016 was fairly smooth in execution and the vast majority of firms still offered health insurance—even without a penalty for non-participation.

Another explanation is that the rapid rise in HIX premiums for the 2015–2017 plan years and the reduction in the number of plans being offered on the HIX may have deterred employees from wanting to switch to HIX. How this concludes will hinge greatly on how legislation deals with measures to protect insurance plans offering coverage in the HIX. Specifically—pending any changes in the way these markets work in legislation arising during the Trump administration—the re-insurance and risk corridor program will disappear for the 2017 plan year leaving only risk adjustment to modulate unexpectedly higher premiums in 2017 and beyond. This will further dampen employees' desire to switch to HIX, and if Republican changes in the law further cut into these adjustments, this effect will be even further accentuated.

Within any single firm, consider which part of the work force would be more upset by not having access to HIX subsidies. It certainly depends in part on income, because of the income-related structure of HIX subsidies. It also depends on age, since older workers are generally highly subsidized by a younger work force in the current employer-based financing system. Thus, younger workers may not prefer the HIX. This would reinforce a company staying with employer-provided health insurance to keep costs down as the population brings in younger workers to replace retiring workers.

What factors might generate support for our proposal?

We have discussed who might oppose our proposed change in the tax treatment of employer-paid health insurance. Let us turn to the parallel question—what features of our proposal might create support among some voters or politicians—independently from our key goal of removing the distortion in our health economy.

First, people who believe that the government should stay out of the lives of the citizenry could embrace this proposal. Subsidizing one type of purchase (health insurance) vs. others in fact is a major governmental intervention into private decision making. Thus, "Libertarian" minded individuals could find at least parts of our proposal appealing.

Second, individuals who wish to help the economy grow should embrace our proposal. Unlike any other proposed plan to remove or limit the favorable tax treatment of employer-paid health insurance, our plan not only provides full reversal of the distortive subsidy to health insurance, it simultaneously creates a permanent stimulus to the economy by reducing marginal tax rates on work effort—permanently. This is not a one shot "stimulus package" but rather an ongoing steady-state increase in the size of the economy. Thus, those in favor of economic prosperity should favor our proposal. This is not the arrival of economic Nirvana, but it does create a permanent (not merely a one-time stimulus) step in the right direction, although not a large step by any of our estimates.

Third, people who wish to control our health care spending in the US should see benefit in our proposal. More than any other single issue, the tax subsidy to employer-paid insurance sits at the center of health care decisions across the entire health economy. Noted health policy commentator Avik Roy has called the tax subsidy "the original sin" of our health care system.[23]

Maintaining the status quo will leave in place a distortion in our health economy that will only grow through time. Ending that distortion will permanently shift the size and growth rates of the health care sector. In addition, with the distortive tax subsidy to employer-group insurance removed, non-group insurance markets that have been squeezed out by the subsidized market should increase in scope and richness and offer consumers more choices in health coverage than they now have.

Fourth, many businessmen and others believe that the current employer-based insurance system puts the US at a competitive disadvantage in international competition. While most economists who have studied this issue believe that "in the long run" the employer-paid health insurance costs are shifted back to workers (in the form of lower wages) this issue is not fully settled, and there is agreement that at least in the short run, employers bear at least some of the burden of employer-paid premiums. Thus, there is the possibility also that our proposal will increase the strength of US firms in international competition. To the extent that this is fulfilled, the increased corporate earnings should increase corporate income tax revenue as well.

Fifth, people who believe that the income tax structure should not contain regressive elements should welcome our proposal. Our proposal eliminates a regressive component of the tax code that systematically shifts money from the poor to the rich. The upper half of the income distribution gets 70% of the tax subsidy for health insurance while the lower half gets only 30%. Our proposal removes this regressive tax structure.

Some observations about horse trading

In terms of political viability, we make the following observation: Implementing this proposal has something for almost everybody of any political persuasion both to hate and also to love. This creates natural options for political horse trading.

First, even though our proposal returns all of the tax revenue generated by the increase in the income tax base, it does so in a way (lowering marginal tax rates) that assures economic growth, and hence net increases in tax revenue. This proposal will not eliminate the federal deficit all at once, but it offers a relatively painless way to make headway against the problem. Both fiscal conservatives and liberals might welcome how this proposal reduces the stress on their finding other solutions to reduce the deficit.

Second, although we advise against it, there is room for political bargaining about how much of the increased tax revenue (from the larger taxable income base) goes towards reductions in marginal tax rates and how much goes towards direct deficit reduction. We have crafted this proposal to be revenue-neutral (before any economic growth), so both liberals and conservatives should be able to "sign on" to this model—it will not increase the tax burden in aggregate.

But the Congress might choose to opt for smaller reductions in the marginal tax rates to try to collect more revenue immediately from the expanded tax base. At a maximum, the current foregone tax revenue—called "tax expenditures" by tax and budget analysts—could be procured from the addition of the employer-paid premiums to the income tax base. Thus, the political decision will require a tradeoff between economic growth (at one end of the spectrum) and reduced federal deficit (at the other end).

Third, although our proposal clearly involves an immediate redistribution of income, it generally goes in a way that would be considered "progressive," both by eliminating the existing subsidy to the wealthy embedded in the current law and because the net change in after-tax income will be positive for many people in a vulnerable portion of the population—those currently without employer-paid health insurance.

But (to continue on a related point) the nation's highest taxable earners (those in the highest marginal tax brackets) would see the largest increases in reward for work effort, both through reductions in the FICA tax up to the legislated income limit, and through the largest reductions in the actual income tax rate (with a marginal 39.6% falling by a full 2.75% to under 37%). Pro-market conservatives should take heart in this outcome.

We know of some details that will matter significantly. The most prominent of these will be the methods used to index the income tax brackets. Just as the IRS modifies tax brackets (such as in Tables 4.1 and 4.2) to account for inflation, we believe that the tax brackets should be modified to account for the expanded taxable income base in a similar fashion. Our goal of assuring tax-neutrality would expand the brackets to account for the increased taxable income base. The data used in Tables 4.1 and 4.2 assume a 6% increase in the width of each tax bracket, but careful analysis using the actual distribution of taxable incomes will be necessary to understand the proper modifications to tax bracket width.

The Congress might also try to reshape the income tax structure by funneling more of the newly found income (from the increased tax base) into one or another segment of the income distribution. Our proposal has deliberately stayed away from that issue. The Congress always has the opportunity to redistribute income from one group to another. We see no particular reason why that issue should be appended to our proposal. Indeed, we urge against combining the two issues, unless somehow linking the two together was the only way to achieve sufficient political consensus to pass the legislation needed to achieve our goal (in which case we would favor combining the issues, so as to reach our goal). Otherwise, we treat these as wholly independent issues that should remain as such.

Notes

1 www.bls.gov/news.release/pdf/ecec.pdf, Table A, last accessed February 22, 2016.
2 Falk, 2012.
3 A Google search on the terms [unions Cadillac tax] resulted in 333,000 results in May 2015.

4 To create a specific example, in 2012, the average hourly United Auto Worker (UAW) member earned $28 per hour base pay, and a total of $33.58 per hour including fringe benefits (health and others). Although available data do not break down the $5.58 per hour in benefits, it is likely that a major proportion is for health care. As an example, suppose $4 of the $5.58 in benefits is employer-paid health care; then the UAW workers have employer-paid health benefits exceeding 14% of the average hourly wage. The national average shows employer health payments at about 6% of wages. Thus, UAW workers, as an example, are likely to have negative net change in after-tax income as a result of our proposal. This same group, of course, faced the 2018 (now 2020) implementation of the Cadillac Tax in the ACA, a tax our proposal would repeal.
5 Kotlikoff and Summers, 1979.
6 Gruber, 1997.
7 Calculation: The employers' FICA tax is 6.2% on about 95% of wage income. Medicare tax is 1.45% of all wage income. Rounding slightly, this represents a total tax obligation of just under 7% of wages paid. That would decline by about 8%, hence a decline of a bit over 0.5% of total compensation costs.
8 We might mention here that both of our wives are physicians, so this result has direct personal implications to us.
9 Congressional Research Service, 2007.
10 Zaccagnino, 1994.
11 Laugesen and Glied, 2011.
12 The graphs use the nations in the Organisation for Economic Cooperation and Development (OECD) and omits Norway, which has a highly distorted per capita income from North Sea Oil revenues.
13 The income growth over this period—per capita GDP has slightly more than tripled since 1955—would alone cause the GDP share to double from 5% to 10% based on the best fit of the non-US OECD nations. The extra growth is "something special" about the US. For the most recent GDP share estimate, see www.cms.gov/research-statistics-data-and-systems/statistics-trends-and-reports/nationalhealthexpenddata/nationalhealthaccountshistorical.html, last accessed August 7, 2017.
14 Skinner, 2012, Skinner and Fisher, 2010.
15 *The New York Times* in 2010 published an essay critical of the Dartmouth Atlas results by Abelson and Harris (see www.nytimes.com/2010/06/03/business/03dartmouth.html, last accessed August 2, 2017), leading to an extensive exchange and series of rebuttals and counter-rebuttals by the participants. A more recent challenge to the Dartmouth Atlas methodology appears in Hadley et al. (2011). They analyze individual-level data and find that increased medical spending for the past three years for these individuals resulted in higher health outcomes, other things held equal, in conflict with the general Dartmouth Atlas findings that regions with higher spending have no meaningful health outcome improvements associated with that higher spending.
16 Skinner and Fisher, 2010.
17 Newhouse et al., 1993.
18 Baicker et al., May 2013; Baiker and Finkelstein, August 2013.
19 Sommers et al., 2014.
20 Sommers et al., 2017.
21 Kronich, 2009.
22 Black et al., 2017.
23 www.forbes.com/sites/theapothecary/2012/05/12/how-employer-sponsored-insurance-drives-up-health-costs/, last accessed August 7, 2017.

5 What else needs fixing?

While the tax-law change is the most important part of our proposals to get incentives properly aligned in the non-Medicare health economy, several other issues also loom large, issues to which we turn next.

Eliminate the employer mandate (Proposal 2)

It almost goes without saying, but it is important to be clear that the employer mandate in the Affordable Care Act (ACA) should be repealed in parallel with the adoption of our proposed change in the tax law. While—as we discussed in Chapter 2—most (if not all) employers who offered health insurance to their employees before the ACA will continue to do so, it will no longer make great sense for them to continue to pay for part or all of it. Over time—perhaps quite rapidly—employers will shift to paying straight salary rather than health insurance premiums, thereby allowing employees to choose among a much wider range of options (employer offerings plus the rest of the market for health insurance) on even terms. But the ACA mandate forces many employers (particularly small employers) to get into the business of health insurance in an unhealthy way (or to pay a large per-worker tax that goes to subsidizing insurance purchased through the health insurance exchanges (HIXs)). And it is not just the ACA that embeds this approach: almost all previous attempts to achieve universal health insurance coverage in the US, ranging from Presidents Nixon, Carter, and Clinton to Senator Kennedy and others, relied on an employer mandate as an essential feature of their proposals. We urge against such tendencies in the future, *so long as the tax subsidy has been eliminated.*

If employers (as we would anticipate) pass the same dollar amount to all employees and at the same time eliminate any payments for health insurance, the shift will add relatively more cash to the compensation of lower-paid workers. For example, if the employer were paying $6000 per year for individual coverage (the approximate current average) and shifted that amount to all workers who had single-worker coverage, then a worker with $30,000 cash income before would now have $36,000—a 20% increase—with half of the relative effect (only a 10% increase) on a worker who previously was paid $60,000, etc.

Employers who did not previously offer health insurance were a fairly predictable group—primarily small firms with a relatively large proportion of part-time workers. There is a good reason for this—they pay more to buy the same insurance coverage than larger employers do.

The "price of insurance" is the "load" charged by insurance companies (usually expressed as a percent of the average benefits paid) to cover the costs of administration and the risk-bearing assumed by the insurer. For a variety of reasons, the loading fee charged by insurance companies for employer-based group insurance systematically declines as the number of "covered lives" increases. The effect is quite large. Two separate estimates using different data lead to similar results. In one analysis, small groups (under 100 people) face (on average) a loading fee of 34%. Groups over 100 in size (on average) face an average loading fee of only 15%, but the effect continues as firms get larger and larger. Firms with more than 10,000 employees face (on average) loading fees of only 4%.[1] A second analysis estimated the loading fee for individual policies (40 to 100% loading), groups of size 1–20 employees (34% loading fee), groups of 100–500 covered lives (16%) and separately, over 10,000 covered lives (4–6%).[2] These two estimates from very different data sources converge to very similar estimates of the group-size gradient for loading fees: Small groups face a 34% load, medium-size groups face a 16% load, and very large groups face a 4–6% load.

As a consequence, requiring all firms to provide health insurance for their employees systematically taxes smaller firms more than larger firms. The costs of providing (say) a Bronze plan (the minimum coverage allowed to meet the ACA employer mandate) will be about one-third more per worker for small firms (under 100 workers) than for the largest firms (over 10,000 workers). This extra cost strains a set of firms that in many ways are the source of growth in the economy—startups that nurture creative economic endeavors.

The ACA recognized this burden (incompletely) by offering tax credits to assist in the provision of health insurance for firms with 25 or fewer full-time employees, and a separate assistance (Small Business Health Options Program, aka SHOP) for firms with 100 or fewer full-time employees (as of 2016). However, the cutoff of 100 employees (the definition of "small" firms) still misses the reality of how loading fees work in the real world. The loading fee remains very high for firms well above the 100-worker cutoff.

The employer mandate has a separate negative consequence that affects low-wage workers, particularly those in small firms and those near or at the minimum wage: It can cost them their jobs. If a firm is mandated to provide health insurance (as the current ACA does), they normally have the option of shifting the costs of that health insurance back to the worker in the form of lower wages, at least in the long run (e.g., by giving out small or no raises, or simply by reducing wage income immediately). But if the worker is at or near the prevailing minimum wage law, that option no longer exists, and to the extent that minimum wage laws increase over time (relative to median wages), they capture more and more workers in this net. Providing transitional subsidies to small firms does not help—the combination of mandatory employer-paid health insurance coverage and minimum wage laws necessarily decrease employment (at least in the legal employment sector) when they are jointly applied.[3]

Eliminate the "precious metals" ranking system (Proposal 3)

One important negative feature of the ACA is the ranking system for health insurance plans, which both led to the withdrawal of some desirable plans from the market in late 2013 and sets the wrong standard for the future. This ranking system uses a "precious metals" standard evoking the Olympics, with a super-powered extra (better than Gold!) ranking included:

Platinum—at least 90% of enrollees' costs covered.
Gold—at least 80%.
Silver—at least 70%.
Bronze—at least 60%.

President Obama famously promised in 2009 "if you like your plan, you can keep it." He actually said this or some variant of it 37 times.[4] The "precious metals" ranking system throws out some plans that many people liked enough to have chosen for themselves. With these rating systems in place, he probably should have said "if you like your plan *and* I like your plan, you can keep it."

The problem is that the "precious metal" metrics focus on the wrong thing. The fraction of all expenses covered is the wrong target. Indeed, a plan covering 100% of all costs is a waste-inducing plan, leading people with such coverage to be very profligate in their use of medical care. The RAND Health Insurance Experiment (see Table 1.2 in Chapter 1) showed this clearly: people with 100% coverage used about 40% more medical care than those with some copayments (either a deductible or a 25% coinsurance), but with no meaningful improvements in their health.[5]

There is a good reason for this—when something is free, you use more of it that if you pay for it, even if it provides only the smallest possible addition to overall health or happiness. Full coverage health plans are wasteful and expensive, and few rational people would buy them without the tax subsidy we have had for nearly three-quarters of a century in the US. Plans that cover 90% or more are almost as bad, for similar reasons. The "platinum" rating suggests that these are the most-desirable plans—if you can afford them.

Now look at the other end of the spectrum—the Bronze plans. They must cover at least 60% of expected costs to qualify, and the ACA rules do not count as legitimate any plans that have lower average coverage. But many rational people might well like such plans, especially if they do not have the benefit of the tax subsidy to help support the purchase.

We need instead an alternative ranking system that focuses on risk protection, access to providers of choice, and proper balancing of risk protection vs. incentives to over-use health care, access to care, and quality of care.

As Nobel Laureate Kenneth J. Arrow proved, optimal insurance in its simplest form contains a deductible and then full coverage for losses above the deductible.[6] He also showed situations where a coinsurance for expenses above the deductible makes sense. Later work shows that the optimal coinsurance closely relates to the degree to which health insurance increases the demand for medical care by reducing the price faced by consumers.[7] The greater the price sensitivity of demand (larger demand elasticity), the greater the optimal coinsurance. And conversely, the greater the financial risk (as from extended hospitalizations), the lower the optimal coinsurance. The true "best" balances the reduction of financial risk (desirable) with the effects of overly increasing medical care use (undesirable).

With this notion in mind, it seems clear that insurance rating systems should provide information on maximum losses facing the insured person or family, not just the percent of medical costs covered. The rankings should illuminate how well the plan controls financial risk. The maximum loss is probably best expressed as a percent of family income rather than an absolute amount, since a loss of $5000 means something entirely different to a person with $40,000 annual income and one with $400,000 annual income.

A good ranking system would also include information on the plan's effect on access to care. Some plans achieve cost savings by creating narrow "panels" of providers (doctors and hospitals). Some of these (called "point of service plans") have substantially higher copayments for use of providers not in the main "panel," giving strong incentives to stay with approved providers. But these approaches have intrinsic drawbacks, particularly in employer-based insurance arrangements. Employers commonly let out their employee plans for bids, and select (at least in part) on the proposed insurance premium. If the plans under review have different panels, then if the employer changes insurance carrier, many of their employees (and their families) will have to change their usual sources of care (primary care provider and others)—known to have adverse health effects.

A variant of this issue is the breadth of choice of providers that consumers have within various plans. Narrow panel Preferred Provider Organizations (PPOs) and Health Maintenance Organizations (HMOs) by definition have limited choice, but help control health care costs by other methods. Other plans (most notably High-Deductible Health Plans (HDHPs) with Health Savings Accounts (HSAs)) control cost (and limit financial risk) using different approaches, but (by not relying on narrow provider panels) offer wide choice of provider. As we discuss in Part II, this issue has a special importance for Medicaid enrollees, who face a very narrow market of physicians open to new Medicaid patient enrollment.

Plan rankings could also provide information on the quality of care provided within the plan. The Centers for Medicare and Medicaid Services (CMS) already now do this for Medicare Advantage plans, using information from three separate sources to describe quality of care with their "Star" rating system, with separate criteria for plans with and without prescription drug coverage.[8] As the breadth of data about quality of care increases (as will assuredly occur with plans to expand these ratings in CMS), the ability to inform consumers about quality of care within all health plans should similarly expand.

Rankings of plans could also illuminate the "loading fee" associated with the plan. Under our proposal, people will likely have many more options for health coverage than they have now, and differences in premiums will arise both from differences in operating efficiency and/or profits of the insurers (as reflected in the loading fee) and the exact benefits offered. Providing information on loading fees will help consumers make good choices, just as providing information about cost-per-pound in food of different packaging sizes helps consumers select what to buy in the grocery store.

Our proposal to replace the "precious metals" ratings would instead provide data on these key quality issues to all consumers for all health plans, and hence would allow individuals and families to incorporate relevant data in ways that matched their own tastes and preferences. Some might place highest value on risk coverage; some might prefer to focus more on quality of care or provider access issues. Others might wish to focus on the loading fee or the total premium cost, or some combination thereof. A single-metric approach to ranking multi-faceted health plans cannot be optimal. A multi-attribute approach will serve all consumers better, allowing them to incorporate their own preferences with relevant data about potential health plans.

Fix the Health Insurance Exchanges (Proposal 4)

Expansion of private insurance coverage was one of the primary goals of the ACA. Insurance coverage is projected by the CMS Office of the Actuary to be expanded by 34 million citizens by 2019.[9] This expansion is planned to use competitive bidding of private insurers to offer a set options that will be available on an HIX and rebranded by CMS as Health Insurance Marketplaces. In 2013, the Obama administration followed the example of Massachusetts in setting up a network of federal and state exchanges for insurance contracts as part of comprehensive health reform strategy.

At this writing, the Trump administration and Republicans controlling in both the House of Representatives and the US Senate have promised (in their 2016 political campaigns) to repeal and replace the ACA. In mid-2017, as we write, the House, after one failure, passed one version of the American Health Care Act (AHCA), and the Senate never actually voted on their alternative plan, and then failed to pass a "skinny" repeal of the ACA's individual and employer mandates and some of the ACA taxes. Whatever transpires in the future, we are confident that the basic idea of HIXs will persist in many states, even if abandoned at the federal level. The idea arose, of course, in two states with Republican control of the political process (Massachusetts and Minnesota), and has seen not only widespread appeal in the population generally but has led to major increases in health insurance coverage (in combination with expansions of state Medicaid programs with federal support). We believe that these exchanges will remain a prominent feature of the US landscape, and thus offer ways to improve their functioning.

The federal HIX offered to the public on October 1, 2013 may have constituted the worst-ever national information technology (IT) roll-out of a consumer product, with only handfuls of individuals able to sign up for 2014 private insurance.[10] Public policy reporters at the time described it as one of the low points of the Obama administration when its signature public policy program failed to launch comprehensively.[11] However, significant improvements were made in the HIX after initial public embarrassment and the subsequent year's HIX was far better and garnered millions of sign-ups within its first month of operation in late 2014.[12] In 2015 through 2017, the HIX continued to improve and get more enrollees. However, work remains to improve the HIX as suggested by the fraud claims from a recent Government Accountability Office (GAO) report.[13]

In late 2013, President Obama described concerns with HIX website healthcare.gov as something to be expected in a new startup.[14] This would have been a stronger statement had HIX technology not already been over a decade old. In their most basic form, the HIX would serve as vehicles to post prices for health insurance similar to what ehealthinsurance.com began in 2000.

One of the complicating components of the ACA version of exchanges assigned them the role of subsidy dispenser at the state or federal level (following relevant Internal Revenue Service (IRS) rules) to expand health insurance to those at 100–400% of the federal poverty line (FPL). As proposed by the ACA, competition can only increase if insurers start offering new products or state insurance commissioners allow out of state offers of health insurance. Without these exceptions to the current individual insurance status quo, it is unlikely that true premium competition will emerge to lower premium prices sufficient to keep health care price inflation close to the general inflation insurance rate.

These subsidies dispensed through the HIX formed the basis for a major legal challenge to the ACA (King v Burwell). At stake was the issue of whether the *federal* exchange could dispense subsidies, since the language of the act referred to "exchanges administered by the states." Since many states had not created exchanges, the federal exchange (healthcare.gov) provided the subsidies to a large proportion of those receiving subsidies through exchanges. In June 2015, the Supreme Court ruled 6–3 in favor of the Obama administration, ending what could have been a major blow to the legislation. How these subsidies persist or change in subsequent "replace" legislation from the Republican Congress and the Trump administration is unknown at this writing.

While HIX startup was more complicated and less smooth than expected as part of the ACA, and while improvements have occurred in subsequent years, we propose five enhancements that could further improve their capability. These ideas build on existing technology platforms and experiments. They are evolutionary rather than revolutionary provisions. In operation, they would align incentives better and create better long-term viability for insurance exchanges.

Proposal 4a: franchise HIX to allow private operation of federal and state sites

The first improvement would have the federal and/or state governments create franchise contracts with private corporations to operate exchanges. Prior to their embarrassing roll-out in 2013, the Obama administration characterized the exchanges as equivalent to shopping at Expedia for travel. They could have just as easily described it as shopping at ehealthinsurance.com (EHealth), where two million individuals were buying their coverage prior to 2013. In fairness, tens of millions of people knew about Expedia more than EHealth. Still, once the federal and state HIX were in full operation, they bore a remarkable resemblance to EHealth. Furthermore, when the federal and state HIX were littered with glitches, the "fixes" came from private health IT vendors who were not allowed previously to bid on the work—but who were waived through to create fixes, software patches, and innovations to make the HIX viable by the end of the open enrollment period in 2014.

Creating a franchise mechanism would encourage innovation among IT vendors as well. EHealth would be invited to apply, but it would not be the only vendor available to consumers. Just as consumers benefit from four competing credit bureaus in the US, so too could consumers benefit from multiple HIXs, all operating within rules prescribed by the government. Thus, the Expedia illustration would be complete; multiple websites would be available to sell health insurance and they would compete on how engaging consumers found each of the available sites.

To be clear, it is wholly commonplace for the federal government to turn over major software and operations activities in health insurance to private contractors. CMS, in fact, bids out the entire operation of administering Medicare to regional contractors. If CMS allows private contractors to bid on and administer Medicare, we believe that they also operate healthcare.gov and state plans.

Proposal 4b: make health plan bidding dynamic

The second improvement in the HIX would have health plans make dynamic bids for premiums and have them be available to other plans bidding before the plans are sold annually. This would require a reverse auction mechanism to be created for the HIX. Fortunately, there was a 2000–2002 experiment that did this on a national scale for multiple large employer contracts being bid upon by large insurers across the United States, managed by the Hewitt Associates, LLC. An Appendix to this chapter describes those experience in more detail. We can learn from it how to make auctions better.

Many pieces of the ACA would make a Hewitt-style auction a greater success today. With the "precious metal" plan designs—or with any successor ranking system that might replace it—health insurance is much more like a commodity product than before. Nobel Laureate economist Alvin Roth has emphasized how standardization of product descriptions improves market functions, providing numerous examples of how markets moved from complex and expensive processes to simple and highly automated transactions, e.g., with markets for wheat (where wheat is graded on a number of categories important to flour millers and their customers) and coffee (where blinded tasters classify coffee before it goes to market).[15]

This standardization of the elements of insurance benefits design (e.g., a deductible not greater than $5000 for a family contract) would greatly reduce the transaction cost experienced by Hewitt and hence enable a more sustainable model. The advances in IT since the Hewitt auctions were last conducted allows for such automation, as has been demonstrated in the high profile Federal Communications Commission (FCC) spectrum auctions. The standard plan descriptions for "Medigap plans" (see later discussion in Chapters 7 and 8) assisted that market for Medicare supplemental insurance in a similar way.

One of the main benefits of online procurement auctions is reduced transaction costs. To achieve that, however, the entire process needs be allowed to proceed electronically. Although the employers and insurers of 2000 and 2001 were not ready for a completely electronic market, today companies have moved to a much more electronic transaction environment.

Insurers offering additional benefits such as disease management for chronic conditions or personal health records should provide separate *a la carte* prices for easily identifiable standard products that are complementary to basic medical and pharmacy insurance coverage. This would allow greater transparency of pricing differences and most likely invite greater competition because insurers with comparative advantage in niche health insurance markets could compete over small points of distinction.

Insurers should be asked to submit their plan's quality assurances prior to the auctions—not during. This would enable buyers to evaluate the guarantees provided by the plans. Further, the guarantees submitted prior to the auctions could be included in the qualifying criteria (along with the past performance scores) for auction participation.

In summary, from 2014 on, health insurance reform as prescribed by ACA legislation created federal and state exchanges. Franchised HIXs could use a competitive bidding process for the provision of private and public insurance contracts. Further, we see no reason why these results could not be used for public insurance bidding as well as for Medicaid contracts. As health insurance premiums continue to rise, online auctions may be useful in achieving the overarching goal of providing high quality affordable health care.

Proposal 4c: allow and encourage national bidding and competition

A third improvement for the HIX would allow health insurers to bid nationally rather than through state insurance agencies. This improvement is perhaps already completed but not recognized by the policy community. The federal HIX must take bids from insurers to sell insurance in multiple state markets. Many of these insurers are large national firms, the large insurers generally known as BUCA (**B**lue Cross Blue Shield, **U**nited Health Group, **C**igna and **A**etna). The BUCA firms generally sell products where they do not also own delivery systems (unlike complete HMOs such as Kaiser Permanente or Humana). One exception in the BUCA environment is Blue Cross Blue Shield, where roughly half of its members are part of for-profit WellPoint and the other half are part of non-profit state-based or regional plans. For our discussion of national bidding, the "Blue" part of BUCA is their WellPoint multi-state for-profit firm.

The rationale for permitting national bids is to reduce transaction costs to the HIX franchises as well as generate as much choice as possible for consumers. It also recognizes how most consumers see national health insurance brands already in the marketplace. And it allows new-entrant insurers perhaps to compete on a national basis if their platform is sufficiently competitive in terms of premium and economies of scale to operate across state lines.

Proposal 4d: allow insurance sales across state lines

This leads to our fourth proposed HIX improvement—the sale of insurance across state lines. This improvement may be less important than when it was proposed by 2008 presidential candidate John McCain prior to the passage of ACA in 2010, since the ACA has created a federal health benefits commodity structure that did not exist previously. As a result, far more uniform health insurance designs exist now after ACA implementation as well as mandatory modified community rating and guaranteed issue. These common features may have raised premiums for some, but coupled with ACA subsidies the actual price paid by consumers has been reduced on average.

What would be the post-ACA passage value of selling insurance across state lines? It will provide more robust competition in regions where a handful of local insurers dominate a market and could be offering insurance at a far more competitive premium price.[16] In addition, national insurers are more comfortable managing narrow networks of providers or offering an HDHP than current local market insurers. Cross-state competitors would be able to inject design as well as premium competition into various markets.

Proposal 4e: passive, not active, management of the HIX market

The fifth and final improvement we propose is passive—as opposed to active—HIX market management. To get the maximum value out of the aforementioned changes of: a) franchise, b) auctions, c) national market, and d) interstate sale, the sale of insurance must be not actively managed by the federal or state governments. The distinction between active and passive management is how heavily governments want to manage entry and exit of insurers in the HIX. Passive management means just posting premium prices (following auction completion) and letting the consumers find their products of choice. Active management means a government restricts an insurer from even entering the market or has its premiums revised based on the government's assessment of the viability of insurers' bid premium. Our perspective is that if an insurers' bid is too low they will go out of business and burn out their reserves. If their bid is too high they will be priced out of the market. So the only required regulation is assurance of sufficient reserves at the initial qualification of insurers.

With all of these changes, there would be potential concern regarding ongoing oversight. Here we are agnostic in that we acknowledge that state insurance agencies play vital roles in consumer protection and should continue to do so if there is a breach of insurance contract. However, beyond that, the changes we advocate would make the health insurance market substantially more modern, flexible, and competitive.

Proposal 4f: rationalize and solidify reinsurance mechanisms

Health insurance markets in the HIX remain in flux in 2017 for several reasons. Most important is the political uncertainty about the Trump administration's intention regarding reinsurance and other protections for health insurers. But a second issue looms large as well—enforcement of the individual mandate. Health insurers must estimate (some would say "guess") about the mix of people who will enroll in the plans they offer on the HIX. Will they get a standard mix of healthy and sick people, or will only those with the greatest risk enroll? This in part depends on the magnitude of the penalty for failing to obtain coverage and the effort spent to enforce the law and the penalty for non-compliance. With elimination of the mandate (one potential political outcome) or with reduced enforcement, the incentives for the healthiest of the non-enrolled persons to enroll shrink, and the average cost of those who actually enroll rises.

One of the potential counter-measures to rising premiums following elimination of the individual mandate is a robust reinsurance mechanism. The ACA's reinsurance mechanism stopped at the start of the 2017 plan year. The GOP House of Representatives passed legislation in the form of the 2017 AHCA to create a premium stabilization fund that would reinstate some form of reinsurance to absorb the financial hit on insurers if a less healthy population enrolls after the 2017 plan year. The funds, totaling over $130 billion over ten years, would have supported states' generating high-risk pools modelled on Maine's successful implementation of an "invisible high risk" pool. In that model, the state would intervene to cover high-cost cases if they exceed expected premiums after ACA risk adjustment. Under the GOP legislation, the federal government would have the option of providing a federal reinsurance program and also incentives for individuals in various health situations to enroll. We see this approach as a valuable template for future legislation, even though the AHCA was not enacted.

This approach could include a more traditional stop-loss program for high-cost patients where expenses *above* $300,000 (for example) would be covered by the reinsurance mechanism. This would contrast with the ACA reinsurance program that ran in 2014–2016 plan years where *only expenses between $45,000 and $250,000 were covered* by the reinsurance program in 2014 and 2015. In 2016, the last year of the program, these "attachment points" changed to $90,000 for the start of reinsurance and $250,000 for the threshold where the insurer would pay medical expenses from premium and tax credit contributions.[17] A stop-loss reinsurance mechanism with only one high attachment point ($300,000) would likely entice health insurance issuers who left the ACA HIX with a more attractive alternative than offering ACA vintage 2014 to 2016 policies. Having this type of a stop-loss provision (above which all expenses would be paid by the federal government's reinsurance program) would protect insurers against the costs of the most-expensive patients. This should increase their incentives to bid in the HIX markets even if the individual mandate was removed.

Summary

Our proposed changes would reduce transaction costs and create better incentives for consumers to price-shop and thus for insurers to restrict their monopolistic urges. Better information about plans rather than the overly simplistic and misguided "precious metals" standard will simplify comparison shopping on dimensions that matter to people. Our set of proposals to improve the operation of the HIX will create further gains for shoppers. This will have desirable spillover effects—those who engage in comparison price shopping "police the market" for non-shoppers. Good public policy can help increase the number of shoppers by reducing transactions cost.[18]

Notes

1 Karaca-Mandic et al., 2011.
2 Pauly, 2010, Table 3.
3 Mitchell and Phelps, 1976.
4 Politifact.com, www.politifact.com/obama-like-health-care-keep/, last accessed August 7, 2017.
5 Newhouse et al., 1993.
6 Arrow, 1963.
7 Phelps, 1973, 1976, 2012.
8 www.medicare.gov/find-a-plan/staticpages/rating/planrating-help.aspx, last accessed February 27, 2016.
9 www.cms.gov/ActuarialStudies/downloads/PPACA_2010-04-22.pdf, last accessed January 15, 2012.
10 www.nytimes.com/2013/10/13/us/politics/from-the-start-signs-of-trouble-at-health-portal.html?_r=1&, last accessed January 10, 2015.
11 www.washingtonpost.com/blogs/the-switch/wp/2013/10/09/heres-everything-you-need-to-know-about-obamacares-error-plagued-web-sites/, last accessed January 10, 2015.
12 www.nydailynews.com/news/politics/obamacare-enrollment-deadline-set-monday-night-article-1.2045076, last accessed January 10, 2015.
13 www.gao.gov/products/GAO-16-29, last accessed August 7, 2017.
14 www.cnet.com/news/obama-on-healthcare-gov-bugs-patience-even-apple-has-issues/, last accessed January 10, 2015.
15 Roth, 2015.
16 This idea formed an essential centerpiece of the early discussions by then-GOP presidential candidate Donald Trump of his health policy plan to replace the ACA, as described by him in the GOP debate on February 25, 2016 that CNN hosted.
17 Explaining Health Care Reform: Risk Adjustment, Reinsurance, and Risk Corridors. Kaiser Family Foundation, www.kff.org/health-reform/issue-brief/explaining-health-care-reform-risk-adjustment-reinsurance-and-risk-corridors/, last accessed June 13, 2017.
18 Schwartz and Wilde, 1979, 1982a, 1982b, Sadanand and Wilde, 1982.

6 Pre-existing conditions and the individual mandate[1]

This chapter considers what may seem to some as unrelated topics, but in our analysis, they are highly intertwined. Thus, we begin with the question of whether we should allow or forbid health insurance companies' use of pre-existing conditions as part of their underwriting practices—deciding to whom they will offer insurance, and, if so, at what price. The Affordable Care Act (ACA) generally forbids such practices, but debate remains about the economic desirability and consequences of such rules, and their status in subsequent GOP-led alternatives remains uncertain. This then leads to a discussion about the importance of the individual mandate in the ACA (and any subsequent revisions or replacement) and its own desirability.

Some observations about "experience rating" in insurance markets

"Experience rating" in insurance means that insurers account for known factors about the insured person (or car or home) that are statistically correlated with the costs the insurer might expect. In auto insurance, such factors can include the city where the car is used, miles driven, the driver's age and sex (teenage males are notoriously dangerous drivers, for example), and of course the value and age of the vehicle. In homeowners' insurance, factors can include the geographic region (and region-related risks such as crime, fires, floods, etc.), size, quality, and age of the home (and hence its value), and sometimes such conditions as whether the owners smoke or not (smoking at home increases the risk of household fires).

In "individual" disability and life insurance markets, quotes depend on the person's age and sex (females on average live about five years longer than males in the US and hence commonly receive lower rates than same-aged males), and often a history of illnesses either of the person or in the family, in addition to listing of dangerous occupations or hobbies the person might undertake (police or fire fighter, private aircraft flying, scuba diving, parachute jumping, etc.). And they often include information such as weight and height (to estimate obesity levels) as well and whether or not a person smokes. Sometimes (for larger valued life insurance policies) they may also include a physical examination that may include urine and blood samples for laboratory testing for such things as pre-diabetes risk, smoking status, liver disease, cholesterol levels, etc.

We can make several observations about these practices. As noted previously, if Companies A, B, and C use experience rating tools, and if Companies D, E, and F choose not to do so—instead offering a flat rate to all customers—then the "good" risks will migrate to A, B, and C, and the "bad" risks will migrate to D, E, and F. Eventually, the market will segment itself (economists call this a "separating equilibrium"[2]) and D, E, and F will have to charge an insurance premium commensurate with the higher risks that they collectively insure. So the market will evolve towards full "experience rating" even if some individual companies choose not to.

Next, this "experience rating" system fulfills some important social goals. Consider the example of automobile insurance: First, it means that good drivers are not subsidizing bad drivers. Second, it gives bad drivers an incentive either to improve their skills or reduce their driving in risky situations (e.g., after consuming alcohol). So at least in concept, experience rating can lead to safer highways overall (although the magnitude of any such effect is difficult to determine). Similarly, experience rating can lead to increases in fire protection or prevention in homes, reduced burglaries, and safer environments (e.g., safer stairwells or porches). Thus, experience rating can lead to improvements in health and safety.

We next observe that collecting and using some of this information may be socially undesirable. Regional pricing of home insurance may lead to implicit (if not explicit) "redlining" that adversely affects some identifiable groups (e.g., minority communities) even if "race" is not officially considered in insurance underwriting.

In an era where no data bank can be considered 100% safe from intrusion (not even those of the National Security Agency!), personal health records create a special concern. A whole array of US laws (most importantly, the 1996 Health Insurance Portability and Accountability Act—HIPAA) detail the methods by which health care providers must protect health data, and these have generally been effective. As with most security breaches, most HIPAA violations occur when somebody doesn't follow the rules (e.g., a health care provider puts HIPAA information onto a laptop, leaves it in a car, and the car is stolen). However, having experience-rating data in health insurers' data banks creates an added risk from security breaches.

With those general issues in mind, let us now turn to two specific issues in health insurance relating most strongly to a single part of the ACA legislation—the prohibition against insurers' using information about pre-existing conditions as part of their underwriting. These two issues lead in conflicting directions. One looks at genetic risks, over which humans have no meaningful control, and the other looks at pre-existing conditions arising from behavioral choices such as cigarette smoking, obesity, and excessive alcohol consumption. Both of these relate to the *risk* of some health condition emerging that then becomes "pre-existing," not the actual presence of the condition itself.

Different risk factors leading to pre-existing conditions

Genetic risk

Most of us carry around one or more genetic time bombs that may eventually erupt into an active (commonly, chronic) disease. The more we learn about the human genome, the more we understand how many of our proclivities towards various diseases are predetermined by our genetic heritage. These genetic time bombs increase the risk of numerous illnesses, and hence create downstream financial risks from medical treatment for these diseases.

We know about many of these genetically-linked diseases, which span every major health risk category. But many remain unknown. Even seemingly behaviorally-related issues have known genetic links, including propensity towards obesity[3] and the propensity to become addicted to nicotine.[4]

When genetically-related diseases actually emerge, pre-existing condition exclusions may make many of them uninsurable. Some of these are known because of strong familial links. One form of such genetic diseases can be passed from either parent that carries the gene—an autosomal dominant disorder. Humans receive two copies of each gene—one from the mother and one from the father. With autosomal dominant diseases, if either parent carries the genetic code for the disease, each child has a 50% chance of becoming afflicted with the disorder. (The odds go up to three out of four if both parents carry the disorder.) These diseases include a variety of neurologic disorders, some cancers (breast and colon most notably), some cardiac diseases and some skeletal disorders. Geneticists estimate that seven persons per 1000 are affected by an autosomal dominant disorder. Some common autosomal dominant disorders (and their risks of occurrence) include:

- Familial combined hyperlipidemia (1:200).
- Familial hypercholesterolemia (1:500).
- Huntington's disease (1:2000).
- Neurofibromatosis (1:2500).

A second type of genetic disorder is called autosomal recessive disease. The parents can be "carriers" without having the disease, since to actually exhibit the disease, a person must have the "tagged" gene from both the father and mother. Carrier parents have one chance in two of passing along the defective gene to a child, so if both of a child's parents "carry" the unfavorable gene, that child has one chance in four of acquiring the gene-linked disease.

Geneticists estimate that the probability of a person being a carrier of at least one autosomal recessive genetic disorder ranges from 1:10 to 1:200, depending on the person's genetic heritage. Some populations (e.g., Ashkenazi Jews) have a notably high risk of autosomal recessive genetic risk. To date, scientists know of some 4000 autosomal recessive diseases.

The incidence of autosomal recessive disease is about one in every 400 babies (consistent with an overall population risk of a person being a carrier of about 1:100, since only one-quarter of all children of two carriers is affected by the disease. Some of the prominent and common autosomal recessive diseases include (in an incomplete list):

- Cystic fibrosis (incidence 1:2500).
- Hemochromatosis (incidence 1:400).
- Phenylketonuria—PKU (incidence 1:5000).
- Spinal muscular atrophy (incidence 1:10,000).

Another series of genetic risks are carried only on the X-chromosome. These include:

- Hemophilia A and B (1:10,000 to 25,000).
- Color blindness (1:500 to 2000).
- Muscular dystrophy Duchenne or Becker (1:3000).

Summarizing all of these risks, the Royal College of Physicians in Great Britain has estimated that 2–3% of all births in the UK results in babies with either a congenital anomaly or (much more common) a genetic abnormality.[5] More important, they have estimated that 5.5% of the population will have developed a genetic disorder by the age of 25, and the risk of having some genetically-linked disease rises to 60% over a person's lifetime. This is why some of the best advice about staying healthy can be summarized in four words: "Choose your parents carefully."

Most rational people would like to be able to insure against such a serious risk.[6] But particularly for those diseases that have hidden inheritance patterns (most of them), people cannot know that they are at risk until the disease strikes, and then they have the dreaded "pre-existing condition." If insurance markets eliminate coverage for such diseases, they have become uninsurable through no action of their own taking. They have no way to control this risk, and if pre-existing conditions are allowed in health insurance underwriting, only limited ways exist (at best) to insure against these types of risks.

Banning the use of pre-existing conditions offers the only known complete remedy, and creates *de facto* insurance against such risks. We view this as a strong reason for public policy to intervene in health insurance markets and to ban all underwriting practices that would rely on pre-existing conditions.

No individual insurance company can do this alone, since any company that unilaterally covered pre-existing conditions (when other companies did not) would face significant adverse selection costs. For example, people could easily wait until they were sick and then buy or upgrade their insurance, and firms not using pre-existing condition clauses would attract all of the business of such persons.

Thus, all insurers must act together, therefore requiring regulatory intervention. Otherwise, each insurer's "best choice"—limiting coverage of pre-existing conditions—leads to the wrong market outcome—a classic "prisoners' dilemma" problem that emerges in many areas of the economy, ranging from health care to bankruptcy law.[7]

Under US anti-trust law, insurers could not safely proceed to agree together to ban the use of pre-existing conditions, since that would include activities specifically banned by the Sherman Act (and later US legislation) that specifically precludes companies from cooperatively setting prices or terms of sale. Discussing such activities is a *per se* violation of the Sherman Act, and carries with it the risk of extensive terms in federal prison for executives of companies that violate the terms of the Act. These are not conditions conducive to encouraging insurance companies to negotiate a ban on the use of pre-existing conditions among themselves. This reinforces our belief that the proper remedy is to regulate the insurance market to preclude such behavior.

Note also that if the use of genetic information (a specialized form of pre-existing conditions) were allowed, insurance companies would be forced by market pressure to accumulate such information, thereby raising the previously discussed risks of deliberate or inadvertent disclosure of an individual's genetic makeup—a major reduction in the protection of privacy.

Behavioral choices

We discuss these issues in depth in Chapter 10, so we provide a short preview here. Just as genetic conditions lie beyond the control of individuals—and hence conditions that eventually manifest themselves as pre-existing conditions—some pre-existing conditions predictably arise because of the behavioral choices of individuals. As Chapter 10 provides in detail, the most important of these are tobacco use (cigarettes primarily), obesity and lack of exercise, and excessive consumption of alcohol. These three behaviors alone lead to *increases in risk* of death from various diseases with these *increased risks* accounting for over three-eighths of all deaths in the United States annually.[8] The costs of treating these diseases run in close parallel to their contributions to deaths. Most of these increased risks manifest themselves at some point as chronic conditions—heart disease, stroke, diabetes, liver disease, chronic obstructive lung disease, and many others. When these conditions emerge because of lifestyle choices—smoking, obesity, and alcohol abuse, among others—then health care costs for the affected individuals rise because of their choices.

In many ways, pricing health insurance to account for extra costs imposed by behavioral choices would seem rational and equitable. Why make other people pay for the higher health care costs incurred (predictably) by smokers? A wide array of research (detailed in Chapter 10) shows how financial incentives alter the rates at which this sort of risk-taking occurs, so aligning health insurance prices with these behaviors might seem desirable.

One obvious problem is that many of the relevant diseases—heart disease, cancer, stroke, diabetes, and many others—also have powerful genetic risk components, and, at least at present, we have no way to determine whether a particular illness event manifested itself because of the genetic component, the behavioral component, or some combination. This is further complicated by the growing body of knowledge that at least some of these behaviors (e.g., risk of nicotine addiction or risk of abuse of alcohol) have genetic links as well.

We conclude that the ban on using pre-existing condition information for insurance underwriting (access and pricing) is the proper outcome, and that it must be done through regulation, since normal market forces would lead to its use. We specifically include genetic information itself in this ban. This does not say, however, that public policy should ban the use of information about *behaviors* that increase the risk of future disease—smoking, obesity, and alcohol abuse being three examples. Chapter 10 discusses these issues in more detail.

The individual mandate

This now takes us to the final step in the process: If the government bans the use of pre-existing conditions in insurance underwriting, then it must also require the purchase of insurance to allow the market to function well—the "individual mandate." To see this, note that if we merely had a ban on the use of pre-existing conditions in health-insurance underwriting, no rational person would buy health insurance (perhaps beyond minimalist coverage for major accidents) until they actually became sick, at which point they would buy very high-coverage insurance. The Appendix to Chapter 6 discusses this issue further in the context of the constitutionality of the individual mandate.

To draw an analogy, imagine the market for auto insurance where the government had banned the use of "pre-existing conditions" in pricing auto insurance (e.g., the fact that you had just had an at-fault accident). No rational person would buy more than minimal insurance (if any) until they had a crash, and then they would buy full coverage insurance. The major difference, of course, is that "pre-existing" auto crashes are well within the control of the insured individual, while many health-related pre-existing conditions (most importantly, those arising from genetic heritage) lie beyond individuals' control.

Job lock and entrepreneurship lock

Separate from the issue of genetic risk, other important reasons exist to ban the use of pre-existing conditions in health insurance. In a world where health insurance is linked to employment status, changing employers becomes potentially risky for anybody with any ongoing treatment, since, even after the HIPAA legislation, insurers could preclude coverage of pre-existing conditions for anything diagnosed or treated within six months previous to the issuance of new coverage. Thus coverage can be denied on almost any chronic condition. Even if a new insurer might cover pre-existing conditions, it forms an important risk—perceived or actual—and creates a significant drag on the efficiency of labor markets.

Pre-HIPAA research estimated that job lock reduced voluntary turnover rates from 16% per year possibly down to 12%.[9] Recent research shows that the problem focuses particularly heavily on those with chronic conditions; research in 2000 estimated that employer-insured persons with chronic illnesses had 40% less job mobility than otherwise-similar individuals without chronic illnesses.[10] In addition, chronic conditions are quite common: 45% of working-age (18–65) people have at least one chronic condition, and 20% have two or more, and this holds across all income strata. People with chronic conditions consume 85% of all health care spending in the United States.[11]

Recent data also show that employees leave their jobs to form new companies one-third less often when they have access only to their own employer-based insurance—a phenomenon called "entrepreneurship lock." The link to employer-based insurance is estimated to reduce the formation of new startup firms by one-third.[12] Thus a key engine of economic growth is crippled.

The ACA banned all uses of pre-existing conditions for insurance underwriting—both in terms of offers of coverage and rates charged. We support this ban, and hence the requirement of the individual mandate, because of the perverse effects on the US economy that persist even after HIPAA rules restricted such underwriting practices. But this—as noted—requires an individual mandate. This may create a dilemma for Republican "replace" legislation, where preliminary discussions have supported both continuing the ban on the use of pre-existing conditions and also elimination of the individual mandate. In our view, the market cannot function well without the individual mandate, so long as regulation bans the use of pre-existing information. Alternatives such as the Republican proposal of guaranteed renewability attempt to achieve similar aims as individual mandate, but the comparative efficiency of this mechanism in a national application to achieve a stable risk pool compared to an individual mandate is not clear; further, this approach discourages people from shopping for better coverage with different carriers.

Thus, the ban on using pre-existing conditions has two strong economic pillars upon which to stand: the ban eliminates job lock and entrepreneurship lock (and hence removes a significant drag on our economy) and it opens up an effective insurance market against genetically-related risks that cannot otherwise be insured against. We believe it is a good idea.

It's not about broccoli—it's about free-riders

The political discussion about the individual mandate in the ACA centered around the notion that this mandate was forcing people to buy something they didn't want—health insurance—with the analogy made that it would be like forcing people to eat broccoli (apparently former President George H.W. Bush's least-favorite food).[13] But this misses a key point. A good case can be made that we should require people to buy insurance, not because it is "good for them," but because it protects us. The same sort of logic leads to compulsory auto insurance for drivers to cover damages people cause when they cause an accident.

Some people who have no health insurance currently differ in many ways from the usual stereotype. People envision low-income, poverty-ridden families as the only people who "can't afford" insurance, but another significant group exists who can most likely afford it and choose not to: 17% of the uninsured (non-elderly) population have incomes 400% or more above the federal poverty level and nearly half (45%) have incomes above 200% of the federal poverty level, but choose not to buy health insurance.[14]

What do these uninsured people do when they get quite sick or badly injured? They go to the emergency rooms and hospitals in our communities, which are required by law to treat them,[15] at least until they are medically stabilized, and then transferred to a local county-run hospital (if such is available). Most large counties in the US have such hospitals, and they end up being the health care provider of last resort for those without insurance. Next on the list, if such other providers are not available, are large teaching hospitals affiliated with medical schools throughout the country.

Most hospitals in the US operate as not-for-profit organizations under Internal Revenue Service (IRS) Section 501(c)(3), which grants tax-exempt status automatically to churches and educational institutions (colleges and universities) but not automatically to hospitals. Hospitals must earn their tax-exempt status by providing charity care—often implicitly set at a level of about 5% of their operating revenue. Our point here is that those people without insurance often end up receiving care that the rest of us pay for, either explicitly (through county-supported hospitals) or implicitly (through higher prices charged by health care providers to cover the costs of uncompensated care).

Here we wish to concentrate on the issue of the individual mandate. Even with the high level of ambiguity about the boundary between bad debt and charity care (and the inflated prices used to calculate these amounts—an issue discussed in Chapter 14), hospitals, emergency rooms, urgent care facilities, and even some doctors' offices serve as the health care provider of last resort on many occasions, and they sometimes end up with truly uncompensated care—either bad debt or charity care. Recent estimates place this amount at $85 billion (in 2013), 60% provided by hospitals, but 14% (over $10 billion) by office-based physicians.[16]

In the end, all consumers pay for this, either through our own bills being inflated to cover the bad debt and charity work, or through Medicaid and Medicare rules that give extra payments to hospitals that provide unusually high levels of such care, through a mechanism known as Disproportionate Share (DSH) payments. The ACA included plans to reduce these payments over time on the premise that they will no longer be necessary once everybody has the mandated coverage embedded in the ACA rules. To give some understanding of the magnitude, the ACA plan would reduce DSH Medicare payments by 75% in anticipation of reduced charity-care losses by hospitals.

So this becomes Case 3 for mandatory individual coverage—without it, people would continue to free-ride off of others, knowing that hospitals are obligated to treat them, either because of state law or the IRS implicit requirement for providing significant amounts of charity care to receive their IRS Section 501(c)(3) charitable institution designation.

Although the outcome is not certain (see discussion in Chapter 2), the loss of the income tax-based subsidy for employer-paid insurance might exacerbate this problem without the individual mandate, thus making the individual mandate potentially more important to help avoid free-riders in the market for health care itself.

Notes

1 We express appreciation to Thomas H. Jackson for helping us think through many of the ideas in this chapter relating to the individual mandate. See the Appendix to this chapter for a specific analysis of the constitutionality of the individual mandate that he helped to originate.
2 Rothschild and Stiglitz, 1976.
3 Frayling et al., 2007.
4 Saccone et al., 2007.
5 Royal College of Physicians of London, 1991.
6 Arrow, 1963, Zeckhauser, 1970, Phelps, 2012, 2014.
7 Jackson, 1986.
8 Mokdad et al., 2004.
9 Madrian, 1994.
10 Stroupe et al., 2000.
11 Anderson, 2010.
12 Fairlie et al., 2011.
13 Dowd, 1990.
14 http://kff.org/uninsured/state-indicator/distribution-by-fpl-2/, last accessed February 22, 2016.
15 The law is the Emergency Medical Treatment and Active Labor Act (EMTALA), passed in 1986 as part of the Consolidated Omnibus Budget Reconciliation Act of 1985 (COBRA) legislation.
16 Coughlin et al., May 2014.

Part II

Medicare and Medicaid

7 Understanding Medicare and Medicaid

Medicare and Medicaid have their own problems, and are partway to being fixed compared with their inception-state in 1965, but cannot become completely healed without further help. With Medicare, the problems relate to almost every facet of its formulation, including the way enrollees pay premiums, the copayments they face at the point of service, and the way coverage determinations are made as to what Medicare does and does not cover. To understand these issues fully, let us begin with a brief review of the history of Medicare.

As with our analysis of the private health insurance market for those not enrolled in Medicare or eligible for Medicaid, we focus our attention on the incentives created by laws and regulations, seeking to learn how these legal structures create distorted incentives that lead people into behavioral paths that are not desirable from a societal point of view. We find such problems widespread throughout the structures of Medicare and Medicaid, but in almost all cases, these problems can be repaired while leaving the basic structure of Medicare and Medicaid intact.

A full understanding of the problems now prevalent in Medicare and Medicaid begins with an understanding of the history of these landmark public health insurance programs, now having passed their 50th anniversary.[1]

History and roots

Medicare

Medicare became law of the land in 1965, with coverage essentially mimicking the types of coverage prevalent in privately purchased health insurance at the time—nearly full coverage for hospitalization and in-hospital doctor fees, and other medical expenses covered by a "major medical" plan paying 80% of costs above a deductible (commonly $50 or $100 at the time, equivalent to about $250 to $500 in 2017).

The within-hospital coverage almost all came from Blue Cross (hospital care) and Blue Shield (physicians and surgeons) plans, all originally organized as not-for-profit corporations under special enabling legislation established by the various states, which have dominion over insurance regulation. And since they were organized within-state, with a few exceptions, they never competed against each other. And they seldom covered costs outside of the hospital setting.[2]

Then came new competition from commercial (for profit) insurers with a wholly new type of coverage known as "major medical" insurance. The common structure of major medical insurance closely matched the form of insurance shown by Nobel Laureate Kenneth Arrow[3] as ideal—full coverage above a deductible, or a variant of combining a deductible with a copayment percentage. Plans offered widely in the 1950s and early 1960s had annual deductibles of $50 to $100 per person per year, and commonly offered plans paying 75 or 80% of eligible health care costs above the deductible. These plans were in widespread use at the time Medicare was adopted.[4]

Thus, we can see the market origins of Medicare's original structure, closely following the types of coverage that retirees (at mandatory retirement age of 65) had acquired through employer-paid insurance. Part A essentially replicated Blue Cross coverage, with the addition of a deductible per hospitalization that was set to equal the average cost of a hospital day within the United States—$40 per day at the time.

It is worth noting that the structure of private insurance that Medicare closely mimicked in 1965 had developed beginning with the World War II wage–price-control-spawned insurance, formalized and uncapped with the 1954 legislation that created the tax-based subsidy to employer-provided health insurance. Thus, the insurance that Medicare mimicked—if anything—was likely to have been overly generous relative to an unsubsidized insurance structure.

Part A of Medicare was mandatory for all persons over the age of 65, with costs paid for through an addition to standard "social security" payroll taxes—both by employers and employees up to the FICA wage limit. The rate was 0.45% in the first year. A later uncapped Medicare payroll tax (now at 1.45% each for employer and employee with surcharges in high income brackets) finances the program's costs. The current rate is more than triple the original rate, and applies to all wage income, not just FICA-capped wages.

Part B covered physician services, but rather than limiting these to within-hospital care (as many Blue Shield plans did at the time), Part B essentially adopted the widely prevalent "major medical" coverage for out of hospital care, with an initial annual deductible of $50 per person per year and a 20% copayment (unending) for all services above the initial deductible.

Part B was established as "voluntary" and enrollees paid a fraction of the actuarial cost every year. Medicare's planners had little idea at the time how much it would actually cost, but set the annual premium charged to enrollees at $3 per month, intended to cover half of the program's costs. The Part B premiums increased less rapidly than the costs of the program over time, and

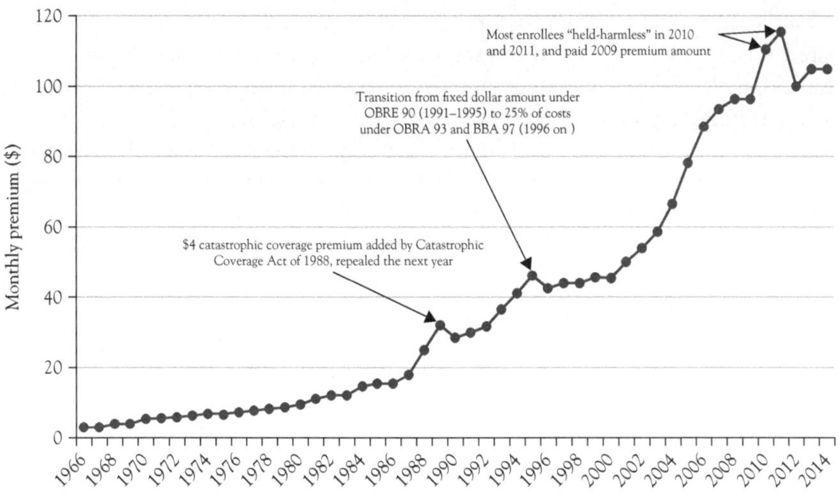

Figure 7.1

Time path of Part B premiums over time from 1966 to 2014
Source: Center for Medicare and Medicaid Services

within several decades, the premiums had eroded to cover less than a quarter of the program costs. After a series of stop-gap measures, the Balanced Budget Act (BBA) of 1997 established in law that Part B premiums should cover 25% of the program's actuarial cost.[5] As Figure 7.1 shows, the premiums steadily rose from an initial level of $3 per month to $45 per month in 1995, and now triple that currently ($134 per month in 2017[6]) for the "standard premium," higher for those in upper income brackets (up to a maximum of $428.60 in 2017—3.2 times the basic rate). Smoothing across the "stairsteps," these premiums constitute about 2% of a household's gross income—more at the lowest levels of income and less at very high incomes.

Medicaid

Medicaid took a wholly different path. First, it is not a uniform federal program, but rather a system of federal support for state-by-state programs to provide health care for low-income individuals and families. In its initial years, the federal rules required that all state programs have full coverage for all medical services for all enrollees. State eligibility levels varied greatly (and still do), with eligibility generally covering a greater set of people in higher-income states than in lower income states. In the initial federal support structure, states were forbidden from using any copayments for any covered services, so for those who gained coverage, all health care was free.

Medicaid programs have historically paid very low rates to providers compared either with private insurance or Medicare itself. A recent analysis by the Urban Institute estimated that the various state Medicaid programs (on average) in 2012 paid only 66% of the fees paid by Medicare.[7] This ratio ranged from 37% (Rhode Island) to 134% (North Dakota), with several large states also having lower-than-average payment rates. For example, California registered a 51% ratio, New York registered 55%, and Florida registered 57%.

Low provider payment rates bring with them a lower provider willingness to participate in the program. A CMS study of physician participation (using 2009 data) estimated that about two-thirds of all physicians see at least some Medicaid enrollees, but this participation clusters into two types of providers: the large bulk of physicians see only a small number of Medicaid enrollees, and a small percentage concentrate their practices in service of Medicaid enrollees.[8] They concluded that "more than 50% of all physicians either did not participate or participated nominally." A more recent study in 2013 showed that about a third of all physicians would not accept new Medicaid patients.[9] Access to health care providers has been an ongoing issue for Medicaid programs, a topic to which we return subsequently.

Some key changes in Medicare provider payment methods

Medicare's original payment structure was almost an open checkbook to health care providers. For every patient treated, hospitals could bill Medicare for everything done on behalf of the patients, and would get paid in direct proportion to that bill (but not necessarily all of it.)[10] Thus, although they did not get their full billed charges, hospitals gained more revenue by doing more billable things to and/or on behalf of the patient. So hospitals billed for each fractional hour of operating room time, each IV bottle, each injection given, each x-ray, each lab test, and even each bedpan used, and most importantly, each day the patient stayed in the hospital. Since "later" hospital days (during a patient's recovery period) are usually lower-cost than "earlier" hospital days, hospitals could make money simply by having the doctor extend the patient's length of stay by a day or two.

The folly of that system soon became apparent, and Medicare's first major structural change began in 1983 when Medicare adopted a model of paying for patients on the basis of their discharge diagnosis, with a lump sum payment calculated to match the typical costs of treating patients with that diagnosis. This "Prospective Payment System" (PPS) was based originally on over 450 (now about 750) "Diagnosis-Related Groups" (DRGs).

The key feature of the PPS was that the incentives facing hospitals dramatically shifted (incentives being a common theme in our book). Rather than having incentives for longer hospital stays, hospitals now had incentives to shorten the length of stay, with some concerns that it would lead patients to be discharged overly early ("sicker and quicker" was the catchphrase of the day). After some modest tuning, this DRG-based PPS system has not only persisted in Medicare but has been widely adopted by private insurance carriers around the country. We can readily say that the PPS payment scheme was a solid economic winner in terms of enhancing hospital operational efficiency and provides a key example of Medicare's potential leadership role in introducing efficiency-enhancing changes in health care payment.

The original Part B payment to physicians also closely matched what private insurance (e.g., Blue Shield) did at the time. It paid doctors whatever they billed, subject to several "screens" to exclude excessive fees. The system was called "Usual, Customary, and Reasonable" (UCR). The "usual" fee screen related to the average within the geographic region for all doctors providing a particular service (e.g., a routine office visit or a particular surgical procedure). The "customary" referred to the doctor's own practice—what was the most common charge to the doctor's patients? The "reasonable" screen typically involved looking at the distribution of prices charged within a region, and stating that anything above (say) the 80th percentile of the distribution of charges was not reasonable. Medicare referred to the common Blue Shield payment methods (UCR) without ever giving precise definitions. So at least initially in Medicare, physicians had even more of an open checkbook than did hospitals.

As with hospital care, Medicare eventually reformed its payment model for physicians, shifting to an administratively-determined price schedule for various procedures performed by physicians based on a combination of physician time (and other resources) and procedural complexity. This system—called the Resource-Based Relative Value System (RBRVS)—began in 1992 in Medicare, and (again) has been widely adopted or mimicked in the private sector, but not without controversy. Nevertheless, its widespread use in the private sector suggests that it was a beneficial change from the previous UCR system.

Changes in Medicare coverage options

Two other major changes came to Medicare that we discuss further below. The first was the creation (as part of the BBA of 1997) a new form of insurance within Medicare, denoted originally as Part C, now called "Medicare Advantage" (MA). Medicare enrollees who choose MA do so by enrolling in a private health insurance plan—typically a Preferred Provider Organization (PPO) or Health Maintenance Organization (HMO)—using their Medicare dollars as a voucher to buy private insurance. Enrollees must continue to pay the Part B premium (part of the resources Medicare uses to pay the private insurance companies who offer MA plans). Since being initially offered in 1997, MA plans have steadily gained market share, and now constitute the insurance plan of choice for 19 million enrollees—over one-third of Medicare's 55 million enrollees. For these people, Medicare has become a voluntary voucher system.

We anticipate that a growing proportion of Medicare enrollees will use MA for their coverage. Using the 5% sample of Medicare enrollees, researchers have shown that a steadily growing percentage of first-time Medicare enrollees opt for MA.[11] Thus, the market share of MA within Medicare enrollees overall should continue to grow over time as new enrollees enter the system and older enrollees (who entered without the MA option and had become accustomed to "original Medicare") die and hence leave the system.

Then in 2003 in the Medicare Modernization Act (MMA) came the final large structural change in Medicare—the creation of Part D Prescription Drug Insurance. These plans—sold by private insurance companies with federal subsidies for low-income persons—provided for the first time (but in flawed ways) coverage for out of hospital prescription drug expenses.

The major problem with Part D as originally created was the "donut hole" in drug coverage, whereby consumers: (a) faced a separate Part D deductible; then (b) had high quality drug coverage for a modest range of drug expenditures; then (c) had in effect another deductible to meet—far larger than the initial deductible—and finally; (d) catastrophic risk protection with only very small copayments for costs beyond the "donut hole" in coverage. The original program design was difficult for enrollees to manage or even understand, and did a very poor job of balancing risk protection against the creation of adverse incentives for over-use.

The Affordable Care Act (ACA) built into it a phased elimination of the donut hole feature with and end-point where consumers will pay 25% of prescription drug costs once the initial deductible has been met. The phase-in period runs from 2011–2019, with full effect reached in 2020. With these changes in the Part D structure, we see no major remaining changes as necessary, although some fine-tuning may be desirable in the future. How any Republican "replace" legislation alters this time path remains to be seen, but we believe that the end "target" for Part D under the ACA is much more rational than the initial structure.

What may be more important in the future is a way to integrate Part D formularies and pricing structure to account for various drugs' effect on the total cost of care. In particular, some drugs are expensive (by themselves) but lower total cost of care for patients using them. Such drugs are treated wrongly in Part D, because those designing the formulary and drug pricing rules are rewarded by keeping total prescription cost low, not by worrying about total cost of care. We discuss ways to solve this problem in a later section.

How Medicare decides what to pay for

The original Medicare enabling legislation contained precious few words about how Medicare would decide what to pay for. At the time of Medicare's introduction in 1965, only a small fraction of all possible medical care was "proven" by modern methods of randomized controlled trials. The Food and Drug

Administration (FDA) regulated prescription drugs to assure safety (since 1938) and efficacy (since 1962), and Medicare's founders added nothing to the regulatory structure to determine what particular diagnostic and treatment interventions would be covered. The legislation contained only the following vague guidance: Medicare was to pay for diagnosis and treatment that was "necessary and reasonable." These vague words guide all Medicare coverage decisions, which consider whether the item or service is safe, effective, and appropriate (which generally relates to the severity of the illness at hand) and whether it leads to improved health outcomes. There is no formal consideration of cost.

The original FDA mandate considered only drug safety, but expanded to require proof of effectiveness in 1962 (the Kefauver–Harris amendments to the FDA legislation). But not until 1976 did FDA rules cover medical devices. The 1976 law confronted an almost insurmountable problem: what to do about devices that existed at the time of the law. They chose to allow those devices to continue to be sold, and in fact used them as a basis for allowing new devices into use. The FDA so-called 510(k) process allows a device to be sold once it is proven as "substantially equivalent" to a device already in use in 1976 or one subsequently approved. Thus, all of the pre-1976 technologies (and those "substantially equivalent" new technologies) get a free pass. The FDA uses post-marketing surveillance and event-reporting to catch devices that create health risks, and have on occasion withdrawn approval of devices using data gathered through this system.

The FDA mission to determine safety and efficacy of drugs and medical devices is clear, and we do not suggest that their general role should change. However, just because something is safe and effective does not mean that it is a good idea to use it regularly. The Concorde Supersonic Transport was generally safe,[12] and very effective in moving passengers across the ocean at very high speeds. But it was not a good economic idea, particularly as fuel costs rose, and it was retired far sooner than most commercial airliners.[13] The same is true of some medical interventions—they might well be safe and effective (the FDA's determination) but not worth using.

Determining when it is a good idea to use various health care interventions is the role of health care payment agencies (such as CMS or private insurance companies) and, of course, ultimately, health care providers—doctors, nurses, pharmacists, and others—and the organizations in which they work, including hospitals, HMOs, medical practice groups, clinics, and the like. CMS has "led the way" in the most diffuse possible way, relying only on the vague "necessary and reasonable" language of the 1965 legislation. Our later recommendations suggest ways to improve upon this ambiguity.

Medigap plans

Medicare's structure was so inherently flawed, even at the beginning, that a large private insurance sector arose to provide "fixes" to the problems left unsolved in the original Medicare structure. Because of the considerable financial risk associated with both Part A and Part B, plus the original omission of prescription drugs from coverage, the private sector rapidly responded with a set of plans known as "Medigap" coverage—filling in the gaps left by Medicare. The immediate proliferation of such plans provides crucial evidence that the original Medicare's structure was badly flawed from the consumer perspective. Employers rapidly offered post-retirement Medigap coverage to employees (using the tax subsidy discussed in Part I of our work to reduce the costs to employees), and active individual and "affinity group" markets (such as the American Association of Retired Persons (AARP)) thrived. In addition, low-income Medicare enrollees are "dually eligible for both Medicare and Medicaid" and in those cases, state Medicaid programs cover the Medicare program gaps, thus providing free health care to Medicaid-eligible Medicare enrollees.

The proliferation of Medigap plans left consumers facing a dizzying array of difference coverage options, so much so that Medicare adopted rules that standardized plans' coverage while still allowing use of the term "Medigap." The set of such plans has expanded, now with Plans A, B, C,... now through M and N. Each has different coverage packages. Since 2006, new Medigap plans cannot cover prescription drugs, which are now separately covered by Plan D coverage. These "standard plans" helped to promote competition by allowing consumers to compare prices of competing plans without worrying about coverage differences, a process well understood to help markets function.[14]

The most popular Medigap plans (particularly those provided as tax-subsidized post-retirement benefits) have very extensive coverage, often wholly eliminating the deductibles and copayments built into Medicare as cost-containment devices (in the same way that almost all private insurance uses deductibles and copayments to control costs). This creates a perverse outcome—utilization expands by as much as 30–50% when deductibles and copayments are eliminated[15] or even more,[16] so Medicare's cost-control efforts are thrown out the door when people enroll in full-coverage Medigap plans. But the premium the Medigap enrollees pay covers only the Medigap plan's share (e.g., 20% of physician care under Medicare Part B coverage), and Medicare (i.e., the tax paying public) picks up the remaining tab as part of the general program cost. We return to this issue in Chapter 8.

Some key changes in Medicaid structure

All states' Medicaid programs initially were required to have zero copayments for covered services, and Medicaid programs responded widely by using lower provider payments to control costs. States began to use managed care networks for Medicaid enrollment in the 1980s, and currently all but three states offer the option of Medicaid Managed Care to enrollees, either a Primary Care Case Management Program or a Managed Care Organization (MCO). State

Medicaid programs pay these programs on a capitation basis, and enrollment is commonly (but not uniformly) voluntary on the part of enrollees. In almost all cases, when MCO enrollment is mandatory, at least two options are available to enrollees. As of 2015, 72% of all Medicaid enrollees receive most or all of their care through a managed care arrangement.[17]

Conclusion

The complicated legislative history of Medicare has left us with a flawed system, but one which we believe is fixable with some important and necessary changes. The essential problem is that throughout the system, people face incentives that lead them in the wrong direction. Some of the original flaws have been fixed, at least to some extent, primarily through the way Medicare now pays hospitals (the DRG-based PPS) and physicians (the RBRVS rather than the old and outdated UCR system). But distorted incentives still abound: The Part A deductible is too high, the Part B deductible is too low, the Part D structure is an irrational mess (with the donut hole the most obvious problem), Part C (Medicare Advantage) plans are crippled in numerous ways, and Medigap plans impose costs on the Medicare system that the enrollees' premium payments do not account for. We now turn to our prescriptions to fix these problems—all though rationalizing the incentives facing patients and providers within the Medicare system.

Medicaid has its own set of issues, dominated by low provider payments (relative to Medicare) that lead in turn to low provider participation, and hence limited access for enrollees. The shift towards Medicaid Managed Care has provided another option for many enrollees (and is mandatory in Tennessee), but the tensions created by cost control (especially for low-income states) will likely continue to produce a system with limited choice of providers, either by limited direct participation or mandatory enrollment in an MCO, or both.

Notes

1 Medicare and Medicaid were originally created as Titles XVIII and XIX of the Social Security Act, with the legislation signed into law by President Lyndon B. Johnson on July 30, 1965.
2 Anderson, 1975.
3 Arrow, 1963.
4 Phelps, 1973.
5 www.ssa.gov/policy/docs/statcomps/supplement/2011/2b-2c.html#table2.c1, last accessed August 3, 2017.
6 While the nominal premium is $121.80, the "hold harmless" 2015 level applies to about 70% of Medicare Part B enrollees since the Social Security System had no cost of living adjustment (COLA) in 2016.
7 http://kff.org/medicaid/state-indicator/medicaid-to-medicare-fee-index/, last accessed May 18, 2015.

8 www.cms.gov/Research-Statistics-Data-and-Systems/Computer-Data-and-Systems/MedicaidDataSourcesGenInfo/Downloads/MAX_IB11_PhysicianParticipation.pdf, last accessed August 7, 2017.

9 http://content.healthaffairs.org/content/32/7/1183.abstract, last accessed August 7, 2017.

10 Medicare would calculate the total costs for every hospital, and then the total charges it had levied, and then create the ratio of costs to charges, typically a number smaller than 1.0, for example, 0.9. Then it would apply that ratio to every bill submitted by the hospital for Medicare patients, thus the label "Ratio of Costs to Charges Applied to Charges" aka RCCAC.

11 Jacobson et al., 2015.

12 The only fatalities involved with Concorde flights occurred in a crash after takeoff from Paris in July 2000 when the aircraft struck a piece of debris that had fallen from a different aircraft onto the runway moments before the Concorde takeoff.

13 The Concorde was introduced in 1976 and retired from service in 2003. Only 20 were built. By contrast, the Boeing 737 (as one example) entered service in 1968, with new models projected for use for decades to come, with over 9300 aircraft produced to date.

14 Roth, 2015.

15 Keeler et al., 1988.

16 Government Accountability Office, 2013.

17 http://kff.org/medicaid/state-indicator/total-medicaid-mc-enrollment/, last accessed 7 August, 2017. Only Alaska, Connecticut, New Hampshire and Wyoming have no regular managed care enrollment.

8 Rationalizing Medicare and Medicaid

As outlined in the preceding chapter, given Medicare and Medicaid's many flaws, one might be tempted to simply scrap it and start over. Its flaws match the magnitude and severity of those in the Affordable Care Act, perhaps worse. However, given that Medicare and Medicaid have passed their 50th anniversary, wholesale destruction and rebirth seems unlikely at best, and probably not desirable. Rather than starting *de novo*, we envision a simple pathway from where we are to a better Medicare and Medicaid, achievable by simply altering some of the incentives and rules embedded in the current mix of legislation that we now have in hand.

Ten specific proposals

In keeping with our general premise, we seek to remove adverse incentives that lead people to making choices that are bad both for them and for our society. While some of these may seem trivial, they interact in important ways. Specifically, we offer ten specific proposals (each with a brief statement of the underlying logic supporting our proposal, and with subsequent expanded discussion). Chapter 9 provides more extended discussions of the logic behind these proposals, which we summarize next.

Proposal 1: *Reset the annual Part B deductible to something between $350 and $400, and then annually adjust it using the Consumer Price Index (CPI).*

Logic: The Part B deductible per year was originally set at a reasonable level, but over time, increases have not kept pace with inflation. A full CPI adjustment would bring the annual deductible to approximately $390, not the actual $183 value for 2017. This step will help control Medicare costs for all years into the future, thus extending the time frame where the Medicare Trust Fund can assuredly fulfill its promises to the citizens of the nation.

Proposal 2: *Using similar logic, reset the Part A deductible to something near $700—a bit over half of the current $1316 per hospital admission deductible* *(in 2017), and remove the higher cost-sharing parts of Medicare Part A (for hospitalizations exceeding 60 days in length). Index the Part A deducible annually using annual changes in the CPI to adjust for inflation.*

Logic: The current Part A structure imposes great financial risk on enrollees without achieving meaningful reduction in hospitalization. The incentives facing providers (the prospective payment system using Diagnosis-Related Groups (DRGs)) assure that they carefully monitor hospital lengths of stay, obviating the need for consumer-based incentives. The original copayments for hospitalizations lasting days 60 and longer have become much less relevant with the prospective payment system used for paying hospitals.

Combined Effect: Increasing the Part B deductible will likely reduce hospitalization rates such that the combined effect of these two changes will likely lead to a lower total Part A program cost, even with major reduction in enrollees' cost sharing in Part A. On net, enrollees' financial risk will fall, and the incentives for over-utilization will have been curbed. But one cannot safely undertake Proposal 2 without also achieving Proposal 1.

Proposal 3: *Using a phased-in approach, alter Part B premiums and the Medicare payroll taxes levied on both employers and employees to adjust for regional costs of treating Medicare patients.*

Logic: The current system does not recognize the well-documented differences in the cost of providing health care for enrollees, differences that have nothing to do with the age or health status of the enrollees[1] and which have no measurable effect on the health outcomes of the enrollees.[2] As a consequence, the current payment structure creates a steady flow of income from cost-conscious areas to high-spending areas, a subsidy paid by the thrifty to the profligate, and (with less specificity) from low-income people to higher-income people. The pricing of Part D, Medigap, and Medicare Advantage (MA) plans already follows this path, so this change merely brings Original Medicare A+B into line with these more modern programs.

The logic for regionally pricing Medicare taxes for employers and employees may seem disconnected, but we have a specific purpose in mind: employers and employees use the same health care system as Medicare enrollees, and making these tax payments sensitive to the regional cost-of-care differences serves is the only available mechanism we can imagine that will bring community voices together in high-cost communities to find ways to reduce unwarranted variations in medical spending.

The phase-in would allow time for communities (through discussions involving employers, employees, Medicare enrollees and B most importantly, health care providers) to adjust treatment styles and modes of care. Those communities wishing to maintain lavish treatment styles could do so, but would do so without the cross-subsidy currently embedded in the current law.

Proposal 4: *Remove the shackles from MA (Part C) High-Deductible Health Plans (HDHPs) so they become as attractive as possible, including: (a) allowing coverage of prescription drugs within HDHPs; and (b) allowing Medicare enrollees to personally add funds into a Medical Savings Account (MSA). In addition, to encourage low-income Medicare enrollees to opt for HDHP coverage, establish a system where Medical Savings Accounts (MSAs) are appropriately seeded with public funds in a way tied to family income.*

Logic: Two barriers exist for enrollees considering otherwise-desirable HDHPs within the MA structure. First, they must purchase separate Part D coverage, whereas other MA plans can and almost always do incorporate prescription drug coverage comparable to Part D coverage. Second, under current law, individuals cannot add funds to MSA plans associated with HDHP MA plans. Removing this unwarranted restriction will put Medicare enrollees into HDHP plans on even par with under-65 people using HDHP plans with an associated MSA.

With MSAs seeded appropriately for lower-income enrollees, they could meaningfully consider HDHPs along with other MA coverage or standard Medicare A+B coverage. This has the same effect as creating income-related HDHPs, but will be easier to administer in multiple ways than creating income-related HDHP structures, and also assures the privacy of individuals when they seek care, since their income status would remain unknown to providers. Medicare Part B premiums are already linked to income, so linking HDHP MSA plans to income would be administratively simple.

With the current limitations on HDHP options within MA, the HDHP option is simply not available except in very small geographic areas, with only six plans offered nationally. Removing these arbitrary restrictions is an essential step to rationalizing Medicare.

Proposal 5: *Require (as a condition of federal support) states to offer HDHP plans to Medicaid enrollees with appropriately seeded MSA accounts matching the HDHP plans, the amount of "seeding" taking enrollee income into account.*

Logic: Standard Medicaid plans, while differing greatly from state to state, have a common feature: only a limited subset of providers accept Medicaid payment as payment in full, since it typically covers only a fraction of providers' actual costs. As a consequence, Medicaid enrollees often have difficulty finding physicians and other providers who will treat them. Offering an HDHP plan with an associated MSA account provides Medicaid enrollees a pathway to attaining care in a reasonable and humane way, while appropriately sharing in the costs of such treatment through their own contributions to their MSAs and payments for treatments until they meet their HDHP deductible. Experiments in Indiana and elsewhere demonstrate the potential value of an HDHP option for Medicaid enrollees.

Proposal 6: *In Medicare Part B, Part D, and all MA programs (Part C), create mechanisms to bypass deductibles and coinsurance for prescription drugs and treatments that are reasonably demonstrated to lower overall cost of care and/or create health improvements at relatively low cost.*

Logic: Particularly for people with chronic conditions, daily use of prescription drugs and regular monitoring of health status by physicians or other appropriate providers can actually reduce the total cost of care or create health improvements at relatively low cost. When such circumstances are reasonably demonstrated, such treatments should be exempted from Part B and Part D deductibles and copayments. The same should hold for that set of MA plans that mimic traditional A+B coverage, although intelligent insurers offering alternative MA plans would logically incorporate these ideas into all plans. These "bypass" rules would be particularly important in HDHP plans.

Proposal 7: *Alter the legislative mandate controlling Centers for Medicare and Medicaid Services (CMS) National Coverage Determinations (NCDs). The original Medicare legislation required that Medicare cover services be "necessary and reasonable" without providing guidance on the meaning of this important pair of words. We would instead propose that CMS coverage determinations be made on the basis of safety, efficacy, cost-effectiveness, and other relevant attributes.*[3]

Logic: Modern approaches to evaluating medical interventions use cost-effectiveness analysis to guide coverage decisions. It is well understood that in a world of constrained resources, population health improves when resources are deployed in a cost-effective manner.[4] Other relevant attributes might include such parameters as effect on equitable access of health care, geographic availability, availability of alternatives to treat or prevent the disease or condition, and others.

Proposal 8: *Tax Medigap plans sufficiently so that the tax receipts recoup the extra costs paid by Medicare when these Medigap plans remove deductible and copayments, which serve important purposes in controlling utilization.*

Logic: The original program structure of Medicare left important financial risk facing enrollees, the result of which was a blossoming of various "Medigap" plans, designed to reduce or remove that risk. But in so doing, particularly in those plans removing Part B deductible and copayments, the Medigap plans increased utilization of the basic Medicare A+B programs excessively, thereby adding to Medicare's program costs. In effect, they allow people to buy full coverage insurance without having to pay the full added costs that such coverage creates, thereby shifting those costs to the primary sources of Medicare financing—other people.

Two more proposals call for new experimentation within the structure of the Center for Medicare and Medicaid Innovation—CMMI—that the Congress enabled to carry out experiments in ways to improve the way Medicare and Medicaid function. We believe that these two areas represent ways to improve the incentives confronting enrollees, insurance plans, and providers, but we do not know the best ways to move in these areas. Thus, we seek experimentation using the CMMI as the source of needed experimentation.

> **Proposal 9:** *Within the structure of the CMMI, allow Medicare MA plans to offer insurance with a set of covered services that is not required to match those covered by standard Medicare. Part D prescription drug coverage allows plan-specific coverages of drugs. This proposal would extend this option to MA plans for all medical services.*

Logic: Medicare's processes for determining what new technologies and services are covered are badly flawed (see Proposal 7), so that it provides coverage for some services that are very costly with little meaningful benefit and at the same time prohibits coverage for some highly desirable services. This proposal would seek ways to introduce competition into insurers' decisions about scope of benefits and covered treatments and diagnostic tests, while at the same time, assuring that people could continue their current coverage if they wish.

Part D prescription drug plans already allow plans to specify different ways to cover drug expenditures. This proposal would extend that freedom to all of Medicare.

> **Proposal 10:** *Within the structure of the CMMI, accelerate research and innovation in physician payment reform, moving away from fee for service (FFS) towards value-based payment methods, and increase research on the consequences and effectiveness of various payment methods, including understanding of how physician ownership of ancillary resources affects health care pricing and utilization.*

Logic: One can envision a continuum of payment between pure FFS at one end and capitation at the other. Currently these "boundaries" are the only mechanisms employed within Medicare. Small experiments are underway to assess alternative payment mechanisms for physician services, but in every case, these experiments focus on physician services either before or immediately after a hospitalization. One can envision (in concept) in-between physician payment plans that "carve out" other parts of ambulatory care for non-FFS payment. For example, one could carve out primary care as the focus of capitation, or one could carve out treatment for chronic conditions, leaving other care paid by FFS. Medicare's CMMI is the best available mechanism to experiment with such options.

In addition to these ten specific proposals, we also offer proposals to modernize the Information Technology (IT) infrastructure of CMS relating to fraud detection and electronic health records.

Since these should be done in concert with private sector insurers for the under-65 population, we defer discussion of these issues to Part III of our book—"Things that affect everybody."

The combined effect

These proposals, taken together, will ensure that Medicare enrollees have access to a wider variety of health insurance coverage than they now see. Perhaps most importantly, by removing the fetters from HDHP plans (allowing prescription drug coverage, allowing MSAs, and providing for governmental "seeding" of MSAs for low-income enrollees), these proposals will provide enrollees with something unimaginable within the current Medicare structure (except for buying the excessive coverage in Medigap Plan F supplements)—a guarantee that limits their maximum out of pocket expenditure in any single year. We believe that when such plans emerge in the marketplace, they will prove quite popular. HDHP plans for the under-65 population are by far the fastest growing type of health insurance coverage of any offered in the United States, but participation in similar plans in Medicare is limited by the exclusion of prescription drug coverage and by prohibition of establishing and using MSA accounts to help smooth medical expenditures. We wish to again emphasize that we do not intend to make HDHP enrollment mandatory, but merely to increase the value of these coverage packages to consumers.

With this set of proposals enacted, Medicare beneficiaries will face a better future than they now have. Individually, they will have a greater set of options available to them than they now have, including fully functional HDPHs with attached MSA accounts. Their plans will provide outstanding coverage for medical interventions that have the greatest potential for reducing health burdens and (thereby) medical costs. They will maintain the option of staying in Original Medicare, but they would also be able to switch into plans that serve them better.

In aggregate, the nation will also be better off. These proposals will help to bend the cost curve by introducing higher sensitivity to costs among participants (particularly as more people shift to HDHPs and other MA plans with the changes we propose). Introducing consideration of cost into Medicare NCDs will further add in this direction. And for the first time, all Medicare and Medicaid participants will have the option of using a single source of coverage that provides true catastrophic medical expense protection now.

Our proposals also remove some important inequities in the system. Most particularly, we propose to end the large-scale cross subsidies flowing from regions with lower-cost health systems to those with profligate health care systems. Those who live in high-cost regions will find this change uncomfortable, but it will also encourage badly-needed community-wide discussions about regional costs of care.

We also would end the cross subsidy from general Medicare financing to those who acquire high-coverage Medigap plans that remove cost sharing from Original Medicare. Those who have enjoyed this hidden subsidy will object, but we see no reason to continue it. And of course, with improved HDHP plans, most of the inherent logic for people to buy full-coverage Medigap plans will evaporate, since true catastrophic protection plans would be available to all through our improved MA-HDHP offerings.

With this summary in mind, we now proceed to a more extended discussion of the logic behind our proposals.

Notes

1 Fisher et al., 2003a.
2 Fisher et al., 2003b.
3 Safety and efficacy would be determined in a manner consistent with current Food and Drug Administration (FDA) practice.
4 Gold et al., 1996, Garber and Phelps, 1997, Neumann et al., 2017.

9 Further discussion of our Medicare and Medicaid proposals

Proposals 1 and 2: reset Parts A and B deductibles

The original Medicare legislation treated the Part A and Part B programs very differently. The enabling legislation (Title XVIII of the Social Security Act) initially specified that the Part A deductible would be set annually to equal the average cost of a hospital day in the United States—$40 per day at the time, and the Part B deductible was set at $50 per year.[1] Since then, the Part A deductible has been decoupled from the average cost per day, but the deductible has still increased dramatically more than inflation over time, as Figure 9.1a shows. Had the Part A deductible followed a straightforward Consumer Price Index (CPI) adjustment path, it would be about $330, a quarter of the actual $1316 amount set for 2017 by the Centers for Medicare and Medicaid Services (CMS).

Part B's deductible seems to have lived in a wholly separate universe. The original legislation specified the Part B deductible at $50, but said nothing about altering it through time with inflation—regular CPI or some component part related to the costs of providing medical care. It was clear that the original legislative intent was to have the Part B deductible be a significant amount—$50 per year in 1965, which closely matched the typical deductible for the semi-comparable "major medical insurance" plans of that era. As Figure 9.1b shows, the initial step in 1972 from $50 to $60 brought the Part B deductible into line with what a CPI adjustment would show, but only briefly. After that, the Part B deductible rapidly lagged behind the CPI-adjusted equivalent, beginning with the period of high inflation in the 1970s, and then more slowly in subsequent years, but nevertheless regularly declining in real value. The purchasing-power equivalent in 2017 of the original $50 Part B deductible would be $390—over double the actual $183 per year amount specified by CMS for 2017.

However, *both* mechanisms of adjustment fail a test of rationality. Suppose for a moment that the original deductibles of $40 per hospitalization and $50 per year for Part B were approximately correct.[2] Now proceed over half a century

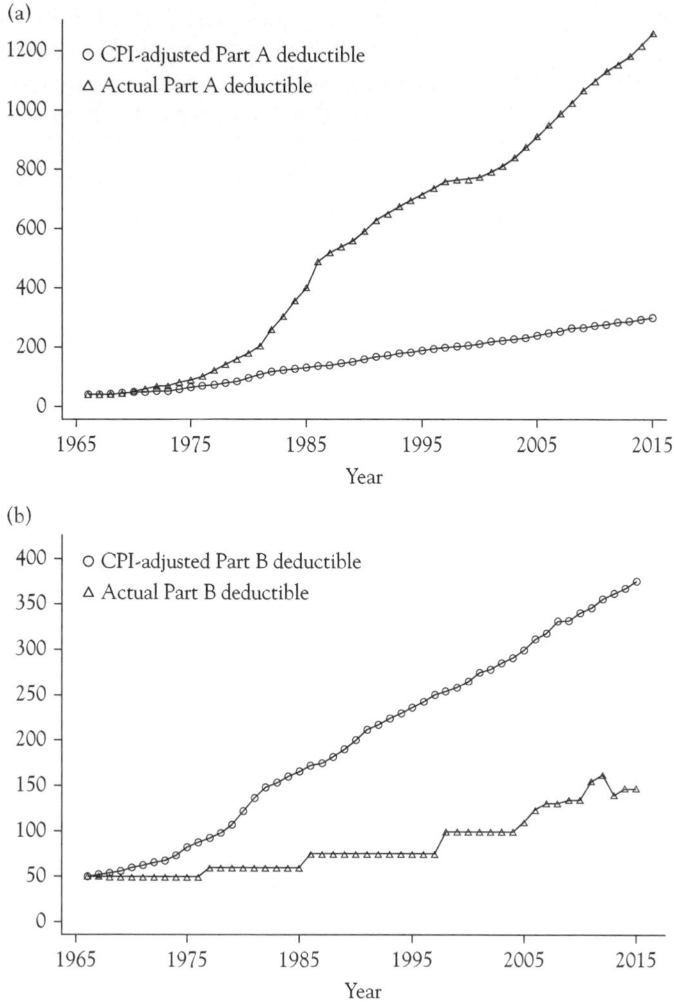

Figure 9.1

Actual and CPI-adjusted Medicare deductibles for Part A (panel a) and Part B (panel b)
Source: Calculations by authors; data for deductibles from Center for Medicare and Medicaid Services; data for CPI adjustment from Bureau of Labor Statistics, http://data.bls.gov/cgi-bin/cpicalc.pl

with background inflation *and* differentially high inflation in the medical care sector. Economic theory would say that the proper adjustment of the Part A and Part B deductible would adjust by the CPI index—not the Medical CPI factor, and certainly not the average cost of hospitalization (the Part A adjustment originally mandated by law) or the low rates of adjustment seen in Part B. With this approach, the "real buying power" of the deductibles should move with inflation, so that an individual would have to forego in 2017 the same buying power as what a similar person would have foregone in 1965 (Part A = $40, Part B = $50). The CPI adjustment provides a standard way to do that. Under that premise, the Part B deductible would be $390, not $183. But similarly, the Part A deductible would be $312, not $1316.

A separate approach to assessing the proper hospital deductible starts with the basic tradeoff between risk-spreading and the "moral hazard" effect on utilization. This approach bypasses the necessity of assuming that the original 1965 levels were set properly and, instead, estimates the optimal deductible levels using economic models and data about best estimates of risk aversion.[3] That approach suggests (for 2017) that the Part A deductible should be near $700, about double the simple "inflation-adjusted" estimate but about half of the current level.[4] The Part A deductible is two to four times too large, and the Part B deductible is about half of what it should be. The proper levels would be somewhere between $350 and $700 for Part A and $375 for Part B. For reasons we discuss below (related to the overall effect on Medicare's budget), we prefer the larger of these two estimates for the proper Part A deductible. *We propose to shift the Part A and Part B deductibles to these new levels immediately, and then to have them automatically indexed by the CPI in years thereafter.*[5]

These shifts would have several important consequences. Shifting the Part B deductible upwards would lead Medicare enrollees to be more cost-conscious, reducing utilization, and also adding incentives for Medicare enrollees to consider Medicare Advantage (MA) plans (which we would endorse as generally desirable). Research from the RAND Health Insurance Experiment suggests that this shift in the Part B deductible would reduce overall medical care utilization by approximately 10%, although to be clear, the RAND study did not include persons over the age of 65, so this is an extrapolation of those data from the under-65 population.[6]

Reducing the Part A deductible by a factor of two would have the reverse effect on hospital use, but the effect would be quite small. Hospital care is much less sensitive to price than are other types of medical care. The same RAND studies (with the same *caveat*) would predict negligible increases in hospital use, particularly when coupled with the increase in the Part B deductible, which would be expected to create a small reduction in hospital use.

Perhaps of more importance, it would reduce a significant financial risk looming over Medicare enrollees—larger than the original Medicare legislation imagined, and larger than makes economic sense 50 years later. This is particularly true for people who face repeated hospitalizations each year—an event not uncommon within the higher-aged Medicare population.

The reduction in the Part A deductible (and elimination of the long-stay copayments) would have the additional benefit of reducing the apparent need for enrollees to purchase Medigap insurance, which creates its own problems for Medicare (and which we discuss momentarily).

We also considered the effect of our proposed changes in Part A and Part B deductibles (taken as a pair, not separately) on the aggregate financial burden faced by enrollees. To a first-order estimate, the net burden remains essentially unchanged (depending slightly on where the Part A deductible is set), but, more importantly, that burden is redistributed away from the most vulnerable part of the Medicare population—those sick enough to be hospitalized—and spread out among almost the entire Medicare enrolled population.

To see this, note first that the Part B deductible is met by almost all Medicare enrollees each year, so for our purposes, we can assume that essentially 100% meet the current $183 annual Part B deductible. Raising that to $375 will reduce Medicare's payments (shifting them to enrollees) by approximately $192 per person.

The Part A deductible is paid for every hospitalization. CMS data show that there are approximately 300 discharges per 1000 enrollees per year, so (on average) each Medicare beneficiary currently pays the $1316 Part A deductible with 30% probability, or $395 per person on average. If that deductible were cut to $700 per hospitalization, the average savings would be $616 per hospitalization, or (since paid with 30% probability) $185 per year lower average hospital deductible payments. Thus, on average, enrollees' total payments of deductibles—Parts A and B combined—would increase by about $7 per year.[7]

On net, Medicare's "balance of payments" would change very little per enrollee but, as noted earlier, the distribution of these coinsurance payments would spread across almost the entire Medicare population (those using Part B) rather than those most financially vulnerable and those in the worst health status—those requiring hospitalizations—and this improved risk-spreading is a second bonus from our proposed plans for altering the Part A and Part B deductibles. We prefer the shift to $700 for the Part A deductible primarily because it maintains an even-level budget for CMS, rather than increasing it with a further reduction in the Part A deductible, a shift that could in turn trigger complicated budget negotiations to achieve.

Proposal 3: set Medicare premiums to match regional cost differences

Medicare's financing system creates a huge shuffling of money from region to region, all quite predictable, and none of it matching sound public policy. The flow of money unambiguously runs from areas with low-cost medical styles to regions with high-cost medical styles. Figure 9.2 shows the overall pattern of the average cost of treating Medicare patients by region. The differences are remarkable. The highest-cost regions have double the average cost of treating Medicare patients nationally, even after adjusting for differences in the age and sex composition of the populations. The lowest cost regions have about

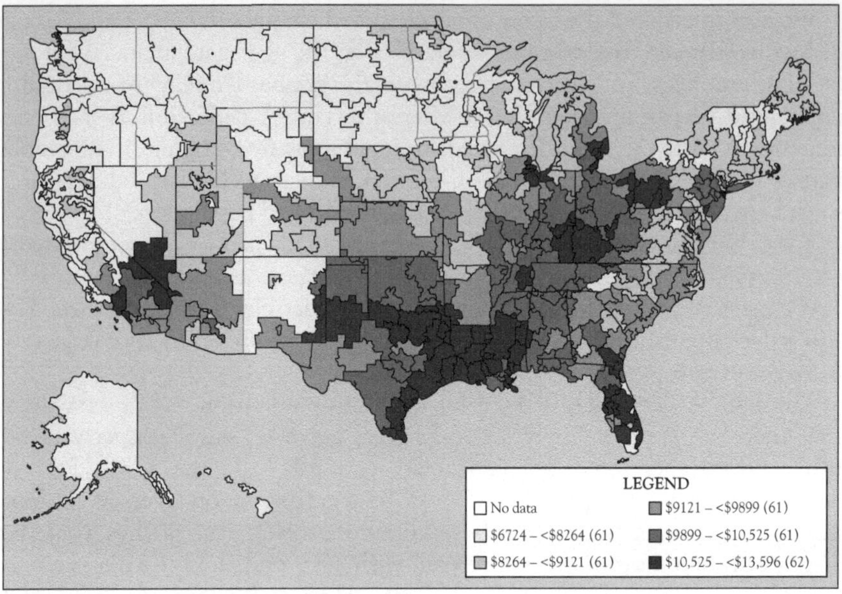

Figure 9.2

Total Medicare spending per enrollee, 2012 data, adjusted for age, sex, race, and price
Source: www.dartmouthatlas.org/data/topic/topic.aspx?cat=21

half the national average. These differences remain steady over time—they do not occur simply because of random fluctuations of illness levels within community populations. They come from the treatment style that providers have adopted.

Whether these treatment styles are led by providers or responses to the preferences of consumers does not matter here—the differences create systematic and large-scale transfers of wealth to high-cost regions from regions that use health care more conservatively. Sound public policy would align the program's costs to users with the system's behavior.

The primary source of these differences is the amount of health care used in each region. Differences in prices of services, poverty levels, and adjustments for illness differences have generally been found to have only a modest effect on the overall message that utilization drives these differences. In a frequently asked questions (FAQ)-style commentary, the Dartmouth Atlas builders have the following observations about their work:[8]

- "Adjusting for price differences leads to only a modest decline in overall variations. It is utilization—the amount of care delivered to patients—that explains most of the regional variation in Medicare spending."
- "...[the rates of] poverty explained little of the variation in health care spending across regions—at most 4%."

- "The most reliable approach to addressing the problem of illness-adjustment ... continues to show more than twofold variation in utilization across the U.S."

As we noted in Chapter 4, these results do not stand undisputed, but our reading of this literature says that the basic issue is valid, namely that at least a significant proportion of inter-regional variation in health care costs arises from differences in utilization. In an extensive literature review and original research, the Institute of Medicine's 2013 report on this matter (led by prominent health economists Joseph P. Newhouse and Alan Garber) concluded (among other things) the following:[9]

- "Geographic variation in spending and utilization is real, and not an artifact reflecting random noise; it persists across geographic units and health care services and over time."
- "... after accounting for differences in age, sex, and health status, geographic variation is not further explained by other beneficiary demographic factors, insurance plan factors, or market-level characteristics. In fact, after controlling for all factors measurable within the data used for this analysis, a large amount of variation remains unexplained."
- "Variation in total Medicare spending across geographic areas is driven largely by variation in the utilization of post-acute care services, and to a lesser extent by variation in the utilization of acute care services."

The second of these three quotes reminds us that some of the variation can be explained by factors such as health status differences, and age and sex mix of various regions' population. The proper adjustment to premiums paid by Part A enrollees and (if any) in Medicare payroll tax rates should, of course, be limited to the variation that cannot be attributed to other factors beyond utilization and systemic differences is prices attributable to general economic conditions in the various regions.

Part A is funded entirely by a special tax on all wage income—1.45% each for the employer and employee, for a total of 2.9%. These funds flow into a special Medicare Hospital Trust fund, which is then used to pay for hospital care (or part of the MA premiums to private insurers) of Medicare enrollees.

Part B is funded through two separate mechanisms. Enrollees—by statute—pay a premium that covers 25% of the Part B program costs. The remainder comes from US general revenues, the sources of which are personal income tax (70%), corporate income tax (17%), and other miscellaneous taxes (13%). For wage income (such as in Part A funding), the location where people work closely links to where they receive care, and the complexity (and hence the costs) of health care are linked to income levels in the community. The current uniform tax of 2.9% of wages for Part A and the uniform Part B premium charges thus both create a systematic flow of money from low-cost to high-cost regions.

Think of the following analogy: Suppose everybody in the United States was taxed to create a national pool of money that would then finance the purchase of automobiles by citizens on some orderly basis (e.g., a new car every five years), and this program paid for 75% of the costs of new cars. Individuals would pay the remaining 25%. (These numbers mimic the proportion of Part B costs paid by enrollees and the general public, of course.)

Two things would obviously happen. The first is that people would—on average—purchase more expensive and luxurious cars, since they would directly pay for only 25% of the costs of their decisions along the dimension of luxury. But we would also see regional differences in the costs of cars purchased. New York City (in this program) would have relatively low cost, because the cost of maintaining a car is very high (parking costs, for example), and many people would choose not to buy a car at all, despite the 75% subsidy. People living in wealthier suburbs would purchase more vehicles per household, and they would choose more luxurious cars. People who lived in mountainous or rural areas would more likely purchase pickup trucks, sport utility vehicles (SUVs), or some similar vehicle appropriate to their needs, e.g., to better assist in the operation of ranches and farms or to navigate safely on less-predictable roads and highways.

On net, we would see considerable differences in the average spending on motor vehicles in such a program. And there would be predictable flows of money across regions associated with such a program. In general, we would expect that poorer regions would have fewer and less expensive vehicles, and thus would end up shipping money to wealthier suburbanites.

Of course, such a program does not exist in the US, and if it somehow came into existence, the cross-regional and cross-income subsidies would create a political firestorm, and soon the program would be dissolved or changed to repair these defects. Yet this is precisely the sort of cross-regional and cross-income transfers that the current Medicare financing program creates.

The two newest parts of Medicare—Parts C (MA) and D (Prescription Drugs)—do not contain this defect. Since the insurance coverage from Parts C and D are sold by private insurance companies, regional difference in the cost of operating these programs naturally appears in the premiums charged by the insurers.

In MA programs, this appears as supplemental costs of the MA coverage beyond the amount provided by Medicare. The most basic part of an insurance company's bid to provide MA coverage begins with a cost bid that is compared *at the very beginning* against *county level* costs of providing Medicare coverage to enrollees. Other adjustments follow (relating to the age mix of the enrollees in the plan, for example), but the payment made by Medicare to the MA carrier always has this up-front regional adjustment. The current pricing of Original Medicare (ignoring regional differences in costs) is wholly at odds with the more modern (and economically appropriate) way in which MA plans are priced.

Economists call these types of problems a "tragedy of the commons," a situation where incentives to conserve a resource (such as forests or groundwater) diminish when ownership rights are blurred or other situations exist that blur or blunt the proper economic incentives. The current Medicare payment system creates a large tragedy of the commons. We propose to fix it by adjusting Part B premium costs and employer and employee payroll taxes for the Medicare trust fund to match regional costs of care, just as Medicare Part C and D premiums naturally do, and just as CMS does when considering an insurer's bid to become an MA provider.

One might ask why employers and workers living in a high-cost region should bear the burden of treating the Medicare enrollees in their region. Our answer to this question is that they share the same health care services as used by the Medicare population, and the only way we can envision to get them involved in rationalizing the health care delivery in their region is to have them confront the actual costs of care in the Medicare payroll tax rates. Providers alone (even if they wished to do so) cannot coordinate an effort to alter patterns of medical care utilization safely. They run the risk of violating the anti-trust laws of the United States (the Sherman Act) by merely discussing ways to alter prices or utilization patterns. But if citizens and businesses organize a cost-control effort in their community, it will withstand anti-trust concerns. So our logic for regionally adjusting the Medicare payroll tax burden rests on the desire to precipitate community discussion about regional treatment styles. If those discussions are not to happen, then our proposal to regionally adjust Medicare payroll taxes can be set aside.

Proposal 4: unshackle HDHP Medicare Advantage plans

While the current law allows MA programs to offer High-Deductible Health Plan (HDHP) choices, they in fact almost do not exist. Only six such plans were offered in 2016, four of them by a single carrier (MVP in New York), and the only other two in Wisconsin. A bit under 2900 people were enrolled (mostly in Wisconsin)—a trivial proportion of the overall MA enrollment.

There is also a variant on HDHP plans embedded in one type of Medigap plan. Plan F—widely described as the most generous of all Medigap plans—essentially eliminates all Medicare copayments and deductibles. However, Plan F offerings also contain an odd anomaly, wherein individuals have total elimination of their Medicare copayments and deductibles, *but only after an out of pocket expenditure has reached a pre-set level* that is generally comparable to HDHP plan deductibles. There is an important difference: standard HDHP plans provide full coverage after the deductible is met using *total medical spending amounts* as the trigger. The high-deductible Plan F coverage only provides full coverage once *Medicare copayments and deductibles* reach the trigger level. Both provide the assurance of "stop-loss" catastrophic risk protection, but the high-deductible Plan F does so only for much higher total annual expenditures. Thus, it is an imperfect substitute for a true HDHP plan.

One might ask why HDHP plans have such limited appeal among the Medicare population when they are by far the fastest growing segment of the under-65 health insurance market. We believe that the reason is simple: current Medicare legislation puts two important shackles on HDHP plans within the overall MA program: (a) Individuals cannot put their own money into the associated Medical Savings Account (MSA—like the Health Savings Account (HSA) in under-65 HDHP plans); and (b) MA-HDHP plans cannot—by law—cover prescription drugs. Enrollees who might want the HDHP option must purchase a separate Part D plan. This restriction does not exist for any other MA plan, so this restriction obviously drives people away from thinking about an HDHP plan, even if one might exist in their region. And the lack of potential demand accounts for the lack of apparent supply. Realistically, very few Medicare enrollees have a viable HDHP option.

Let us return to the MSA issue. Only the MA-HDHP plan can place money into the MSA account. Individuals are forbidden to add to these accounts. The amount the health plan might actually place into the MSA is not specified in the law. Presumably, if meaningful competition existed among such plans, that competition would lead to appropriate "seeding" of the MSA accounts, passing back to enrollees the medical cost savings arising from the incentives created by the HDHP plans. But as we noted before, no meaningful competition exists. Four of the six HDHP-MA plans offered in 2016 come from the same organization (MVP in New York), and any HDHP option at all is only available in small parts of the country.

HSA accounts are important for the under-65 HDHP plans. They allow people to smooth out the cash flows associated with random "hits" to their bank accounts associated with unpredictable changes in medical care use. Their importance is well understood in allowing HDHP plans to thrive, and their tax-preferred status speaks to the recognition of their importance. The tax-deferred status in some sense places HSA monies on even footing with tax-preferred employer-paid insurance premiums, but they serve a loftier purpose—they help people move into plans that help control national medical spending patterns, rather than (as the tax preferred status of employer-paid premiums does) encourage people to over-insure, thereby contributing to (rather than reducing) the overall national problem of growing medical spending.

The second important shackle on HDHP plans is the rule prohibiting them from including prescription drugs coverage. In many parts of the country, other MA plans are offered that include prescription drug coverage, *often with little or no monthly premium payment by the enrollee beyond the standard requirement of paying the Part B premium*.

For 2017, the average Part D premium bid was $61 per month, about $732 per year. Given the ability to choose many more traditional MA plans that covered prescription drugs, why would any rational person think about taking on the added risk from an HDHP plan *and* paying an extra $700 to $750 or more per year for Part D coverage? It would be irrational, of course, and knowing that, almost no carriers offer such coverage, and very few people opt for the few plans that do exist.

HDHPs are the fastest growing segment of the private health insurance market, and for good reason. These plans provide the clearest and lowest cost way to protect against catastrophic medical expense, and when coupled with an HSA, do so in a way that can maintain smooth control of expenditures. However, within the MA program, enrollees are forbidden from using MSA accounts to smooth income flows, and HDHP plans within MA are forbidden from covering prescription drugs. Reversing both of these needless rules would put HDHPs on an even footing with other forms of MA plans. We see no reason to continue crippling HDHP plans in these ways. They may thrive, or they may remain rare, but they should be allowed to compete on even terms.

We have reason to believe that HDHP plans can compete and thrive. Consider the costs of a person who wishes to wholly limit their out of pocket expenditures in a predictable way. The most common way to do this would be to enroll in Original Medicare A+B, then purchase a Part D plan, and then supplement that with a Medigap Plan C or Plan F. The Medicare Part B premium is the same in all of these options, so consider two options: a person enrolling in A+B plus Part D plus a Plan F vs. a person enrolling in an HDHP option in Medicare (if it were sensibly structured). The "standard approach" would incur costs for Part B, plus an average of $732 per year for Part D, plus an average of about $2400 per year for the Medigap Plan C or F. Thus, to obtain assured risk protection against catastrophic loss, a person must spend *with certainty* more than $3000 per year on top of their Part B premium.

We cannot know for sure what competitive HDHP plans would look like, but let us assume that plans would emerge that cover prescription drugs and (in a sort of "worst case" analysis) add *nothing* into the MSA account. In that case, the enrollee would be responsible for the HDHP deductible *as a worst-case outcome* but would end up spending less if they had a relative low-cost year of medical expenses.

What would those limits look like? Only a true market competition would tell, but under Internal Revenue Service (IRS) rules for under-65 HSA-eligible HDHP plans, the annual deductible must be at least $1300 per person (twice that for a family) and *no more than* $6450 per person (twice that for a family).

We also know—based on the annual employee benefit survey of the Kaiser Family Foundation—that the average deductible for individual HDHP plans with an associated HSA in 2014 was $2098, and about twice that for family coverage. As with any other MA plan, enrollees would pay their normal Part B premium, and then the underwriting insurance companies would receive a flat amount from CMS to pay for the HDHP plan. Adding prescription drug coverage, we know that many Health Maintenance Organization (HMO) and Preferred Provider Organization (PPO) MA plans charge either nothing or small monthly additional premiums. We also know that HDHP plans are typically less expensive than PPO or HMO plans. Thus, we would expect that competition would lead to some significant seeding of the Medicare HDHP plans, reducing the net out of pocket risk of enrollees dollar for dollar.

Where would the market end up? We cannot know for sure without actually allowing such plans unfettered access to the market. We think it plausible that the net out of pocket risk to Medicare enrollees could be lower than the current *certain* expenditures necessary to achieve guaranteed risk protection. Buying an average Part D plan and an average Medigap Plan C or F *assures* that a single person must spend well over $3000 annually on insurance premiums. It is not a far stretch to see how completion could bring the maximum risk in an HDHP Medicare plan to the range of $3000 per year, perhaps lower. Recall that the average HDHP deductible in the under-65 market is only about $2100. If these plans can reach a deductible of $3000 or lower without adding premiums beyond the Medicare Part B premium requirement, they will logically dominate a combination of Medicare A+B+D plus a generous Medigap plan.

To find out what would actually happen in Medicare, we must unshackle these plans. There is no rational reason to continue to limit the market for Medicare HDHP plans. Once put on even footing, they may succeed, or they may prove unpopular. Our point is not to force such plans on everybody, but rather to make them accessible on an even footing to everybody. Then the market will tell us what is best. Nothing less than this will serve the Medicare enrollee community well.

We anticipate concerns that the elderly are not capable of dealing with the complexity of these plans. We are not convinced: If passing the age of 65 disqualifies people from making serious decisions, then (using age profiles from early 2017) 45 of the current 100 members of the US Senate should be removed from office (a majority by the end of 2018) and five members of the Supreme Court of the United States should retire, as well as should any President or Vice President over the age of 65. We do not endorse this belief about automatic age-related competency inferences in any way.

Proposal 5: require HDHP options with seeded MSA accounts for Medicaid enrollees

Most policy makers have avoided any thought of HDHP plans for Medicaid enrollees on the grounds that they are too poor to have HDHP plans make any sense. We disagree. If combined with an MSA, seeded annually with appropriate funds (which could be closely tailored to enrollee's income status), HDHP plans can become a powerful tool in the hands of Medicaid enrollees and for public policy.

A fundamental problem with Medicaid centers on the original requirement that enrollees pay no cost when they seek care. This leads to much wasteful care-seeking, such as using emergency rooms as a primary care source, and (because the costs are covered by Medicaid) using ambulance services instead of buses, taxis, or rides from friends or relatives to go to the emergency room (ER) or clinic.

In parallel, to control such costs, state Medicaid officials almost uniformly set provider compensation rates *far* below other rates, including Medicare and private negotiated rates. This in turn leads to many providers refusing to treat Medicaid patients, which leaves Medicaid patients unable to find local care-givers, which in turn leads them to using ER providers as primary care givers—a classic vicious cycle. Providing Medicaid HDHPs can break it.

One additional important change—beyond providing the new coverage option to Medicaid enrollees—would require that these HDHP plans pay health care providers at acceptable rates rather than the minimal rates adopted by most Medicaid plans. An obvious choice would have these plans reimburse providers at Medicare rates, which are accepted by almost all health care providers. With that assurance, almost all health providers would readily accept Medicaid patients, in contrast to the current estimates that over half of all physicians either do not accept Medicaid patients or do so only nominally with but a small handful of patients in their practices.[10]

On first thought, it might seem that giving Medicaid recipients below the poverty line an MSA would be an undesirable and/or inefficient way to offer health insurance. However, experiments in Michigan and Indiana have shown promise and a new experiment in Arkansas may go even farther to show Medicaid MSAs as a viable national option to give poor populations access to medical care.

The obvious concerns from patient advocates are that MSAs would discourage low-income people from getting care that they need. Supporters of Medicaid MSA believe they will help beneficiaries toward becoming more cost-conscious health care consumers. Several recent experiments with Medicaid MSAs can help sort out the consequences.

Four years after the start of MSAs nationally, Indiana was granted a waiver in 2007 to modify its Medicaid program. The state sought to expand Medicaid to a group of people who were not then eligible for the program, and the state's effort required no additional outlays from the federal government. The proposed expansion was paid for with a 44-cent increase in the state's cigarette tax.

The Indiana plan design was quite similar to commercially-available HDHP plans combined with MSAs, called POWER accounts. Individuals needed to make mandatory contributions into the POWER account between to 2 to 5% of their income up to $92 a month. Participants would lose their coverage if they did not make their payments within 60 days of their due date. Once beneficiaries made their contribution, they had no other cost-sharing requirements (copays, deductibles, etc.) except for non-urgent use of emergency rooms. The state added funds to the POWER account, bringing it to $1100, which corresponded to the size of the plan's deductible.

At the end of the year, the beneficiary could apply the balance remaining in the POWER account to next year's contributions as long as they obtained a specified amount of preventive care: annual physical exams, pap smears and mammograms for women, cholesterol tests, flu shots, blood glucose screens, and tetanus-diphtheria screens. This was deliberately designed to encourage preventive care and counter critics' concerns that Medicaid MSA beneficiaries would under-use preventive care.

The program was quite successful with a large waiting list—tens of thousands—to enroll in Healthy Indiana. Ninety percent of enrollees made their required monthly contributions and it had a level of satisfaction of 98%. A 2010 study by Mathematica Policy Research found that the program dramatically increased the percentage of beneficiaries who obtained preventive care, from 39% in the first six months of enrollment to 59% after one year.[11] Of the members who had money left in the POWER accounts at the end of the year, 71% met the preventive care requirement and were able to carry the balances over to the following year. The remaining 29% could carry over their personal contributions, but not the state contributions to their POWER accounts.

In 2011, Indiana applied to renew and extend their waiver past the 2012 deadline. The Obama administration refused to extend the waiver and demanded that the plan be discontinued into order to conform to the Medicaid expansion planned in the Affordable Care Act (ACA).

The Health Indiana POWER account program effectively dealt with one of the largest concerns about the existing Medicaid program—lack of physician access. The lack of physician access is an important factor in understanding why health outcomes for Medicaid patients lag behind those of individuals with private insurance, and even behind those with no insurance at all. Healthy Indiana completely reversed this trend, achieving preventive care participation rates that are higher than the privately-insured population.

In 2014, the Obama administration reversed course and permitted the state of Arkansas to implement its own version of MSAs. Beginning in 2015, enrolled Arkansas Medicaid beneficiaries have been required to make monthly contributions to so-called Health Independence Accounts. This plan will provide further evidence on the desirability of HDHP arrangements for the Medicaid population. For 2015, Arkansas also wanted to expand its experiment by introducing the Health Independence Accounts. Nearly all beneficiaries earning between 50 and 138% of the poverty level ($5835 to $16,105 for an individual) would participate through monthly contributions of between $5 and $25, depending on their income, or face cost-sharing requirements capped at 5% of income by Medicaid rules.[12] Iowa and Pennsylvania are also experimenting with using Medicaid funds to enroll new Medicaid-eligible beneficiaries in private health insurance through the ACA marketplace.

The foundation for Medicaid MSAs is quite strong since the implementation of the ACA has become permissive after the previous Indiana shutdown. At least 40 states charge premiums or cost sharing for at least some Medicaid beneficiaries. Given the positive Indiana experience, it seems plausible that beneficiaries may be willing to pay more for better provider access—through HDHP/MSA plans—access that they cannot receive under traditional Medicaid plans.

Making the plans available in the health insurance exchanges makes them less stigmatizing and provides for easier workplace transitions as people move from Medicaid status to financial independence.

Proposal 6: eliminate copayments for selected highly effective drugs and treatments

Some health care analysts envision a major problem with HDHP plans—the concern that people will avoid using "necessary" medical care and end up with greater illness burdens that not only harm their health but add total costs to the Medicare budget as their more expensive illnesses are dealt with.

Notwithstanding those concerns, it is clear that some interventions (diagnostic tests, preventive interventions such as vaccines, and use of prescription drugs in chronic illness conditions) either save money on a total cost-of-care basis or at least create health improvements at low cost relative to the health gains. Medicare already exempts some screening activities from copayments, such as regular cervical cancer screening, mammography, prostate-specific antigen (PSA) tests for prostate cancer, diabetes screening for at-risk patients, and many others (some only when known risk factors are present).[13]

CMS has the right idea, but it needs to expand the scope, particularly in the domain of prescription drugs for chronic care. The key areas of chronic illness that account for the largest health (and medical spending) burdens are hypertension, hyperlipedemia (high cholesterol), ischemic heart disease (IHD), diabetes, and rheumatoid and osteoarthritis. We will focus on these, but the concepts generalize to all forms of chronic illness and conditions.

Two observations drive our thinking: First, for treatment of virtually all of these conditions, generic drugs are available that are quite effective, and available at much lower cost than non-generic alternatives (many of which are only minimally more effective than the generics for many people). Thus, CMS policy should focus on directing people to generic drugs as one important approach to increase adherence to prescription protocols. Second, the frequency with which these conditions occur is strongly exacerbated by common human behaviors, most notably tobacco use, obesity and lack of exercise, and excessive alcohol consumption. We turn to these issues next.

Prescription drug coverage cost, adherence, and total cost of care

Cost and adherence

In treating chronic conditions, adherence to medication has a dramatic effect on use of health care and total costs of care. A recent study combined data from medical care use and prescription drug use for a three-and-one-half-year period, and selected people with diagnoses (based on insurance claims information) with four important chronic conditions—congestive heart failure (CHF), hypertension, diabetes and dyslipidemia (abnormal cholesterol). The study included 135,000 individuals, each with three consecutive years of insurance claims.[14] They measured adherence through prescription refill rates from which they estimated the percentage of days when each subject would have had drugs on hand to take (a standard measure in such studies), and classified patients as adherent if their "possession ratio" reached at least 0.8 (again, a common metric in such studies).

They measured the difference in health care costs for adherent vs. non-adherent patients in each of the four chronic condition classes, looking at the number of hospital days used, the annual number of outpatient MD visits and similarly for Emergency Department (ED) visits. They also summarized these in the total cost of care. The dramatic difference in utilization came with reduced hospitalization—strongly significant in both those under and above the age of 65, with the greatest hospitalization reductions coming in the patients with CHF. Table 9.1 shows their results for the total cost of care for those persons aged 65 and older. (Results for the total population including under-65 were quite similar, but we focus here on those in Medicare-age groups.) Drugs spending went up (as expected) by different amounts in the four disease groups, but in the general range of $400 to $1000 per year (see Table 9.1). But in response to the increased adherence, total cost of care fell dramatically—mostly due to reduced hospitalizations. The total savings—including the increased drug costs—were $7823 per year for CHF patients, $3908 for hypertension patients, $3756 for diabetics, and $1258 for those with dyslipidemia. The returns on investment (savings vs. spending on drugs) ranged from about 2:1 to 9:1 for these four conditions.

Other individual drugs—even some that are expensive and non-generic—have shown the same effect. For example, an expensive but highly effective drug to treat angina pectoris was shown to add significantly to prescription drug costs but reduced overall cost of care for patients with refractory angina pectoris.[15] Our goal is not to specify the exact drugs that would be exempted from

Table 9.1 Differences in total medical spending by chronic disease class for patients adherent (or not) to chronic drug prescription protocols. Prescription drug costs are higher for adherent patients, but total costs of all other medical care is lower, leading to net savings per patient per year as shown in row 3

	Congestive heart failure	Dyslipidemia	Diabetes	Hypertension
Prescription drugs	1058	601	656	429
Total cost of care	8881	1860	4413	4337
Net savings for adherent vs non-adherent	7823	1258	3756	3908
Return on drug spending (ROI)	7.4	2.1	5.7	9.1

Source: Data from Roebuck et al., 2011

copayments, but rather to set in place mechanisms within CMS that would regularly review available prescription drugs to see if they fit these criteria, and to add them to the "exempt" list as appropriate (or remove them if other alternatives changed the picture). Here, as it has done elsewhere, CMS could provide important leadership for the private health insurance sector.

The bifurcated decision problem

These results bring into sharp focus a structural problem in Medicare (and indeed, in the private insurance sector as well). Decisions about what drugs are included in Part D plans and the copayment (which "Tier" of pricing) faced by enrollees are all decisions made independently by people paid to keep prescription drug insurance premiums low, wholly ignoring the consequences of their decisions on the total cost of care for their enrollees. Part D decisions affect all other health care costs in Parts A, B, and MA plans (Part C), but these consequences never enter the decisions of Part D formulary design and tier (pricing) assignment.

Even in organizations that have the opportunity for a complete overview of the total cost of care, the prescription drug coverage choices (formulary and pricing) are commonly segmented into separate organizational silos, with managers rewarded in the same way as in free-standing drug plans—"keep the drug costs down."[16] We conjecture that these structural arrangements arose because prescription drug coverage was an "add on" to existing plans (as consumers increasingly sought such coverage through their employer group plans and elsewhere), but whatever the origins, the bifurcation of prescription drug coverage and pricing choices seems almost universal in our experience.

The same problem appears in reverse in the newly-emerging field of "companion diagnostics" in cancer therapy and other highly expensive drugs. Many of these drugs work only on a subset—sometimes a small subset—of people diagnosed with a particular disease. As scientists learn more about the underlying biology, it has become clear that in many cases, highly specialized diagnostic tests can determine in advance with patients will be responders (R) and non-responders (NR). The problem is that with the bifurcation of Part D and Part B in Medicare (and equivalently in most private insurance plans), nobody has any incentive to pay for these companion diagnostic tests, and hence the market for their development remains weak.

To see how this works, consider the key insurance decision makers. Part B (which pays for diagnostic testing) does not share in any of the rewards from saving unnecessary and futile drug costs (not to mention the major side effects of some of these drugs on the patients themselves. So the Part B decision makers have no incentive to pay for them. On the flip side, Part D plans by law only pay for prescription drugs. Thus, they cannot pay for companion diagnostic tests even if they wanted to. And finally, it is not in the interests of pharmaceutical companies themselves, since the current payment structure rewards them for volume of sales. Inherently, companion diagnostic testing *reduces* sales volumes of drugs. So they have no interest in seeing these tests developed either, given the current method of paying for drugs in the US.

In the world with separate Part D prescription drug coverage, the natural equilibrium will continue to have drug coverage decisions made independently from their effect on total cost of care.[17] This problem occurs both in preventive drugs for chronic conditions *and* in the development and use of companion diagnostic tests for expensive chemotherapy (and similar) drugs. This brings us to our next specific proposal for Medicare reform.

The necessary action

Achieving our goal of zero cost sharing for appropriate drugs cannot happen without direct CMS action. To get to this point, CMS must require that all Part D plans (including MA with Prescription Drug coverage) include a defined set of chronic care maintenance drugs at no cost to enrollees (using generic drugs when possible, but not necessarily limited to such). If CMS does not mandate this change, the bifurcated structure of Medicare coverage—wherein Part D programs stand alone and hence do not take into account drugs' effects on total cost of care—then competition will necessarily lead individual Part D plans to avoid taking the necessary step. This is a natural outcome of a non-cooperative game such as would play out if the Part D plans were left to their own decision making.

More generally, this same shift in thinking should extend to all secondary prevention activities that have demonstrable cost-savings and/or produce health gains at very low cost (mostly affecting Medicare Part B and MA plans).

The US Preventive Services Task Force (USPSTF) does not routinely consider drugs such as this (so-called "secondary prevention") or (more generally) the broad range of secondary prevention activities, so CMS will need a separate process to define and regularly update the minimum set of drugs to be included in the "free to patients" category or the USPSTF must receive a modified charter to take on this work.

Two further comments are in order. First, in order to assess whether secondary prevention interventions (drugs and others) actually save costs, *somebody* will have to undertake what constitutes simple analysis—find interventions that actually save money overall. The most logical locus of such work now is the Patient-Centered Outcomes Research Institute (PCORI), but the legislative mandate for it precludes the use of cost information *when calculating cost-effectiveness ratios to rank desirability of medical interventions*. Nothing in this mandate precludes PCORI from actually collecting and analyzing cost information—it just precludes the use of incremental cost-effectiveness ratios in recommendations about use of various medical interventions.[18] Nevertheless, the ACA language regarding cost-effectiveness analysis has dampened even the measurement of cost in health services research.

The second observation is that a "must-save-money" test has never been applied to other medical interventions, but only to preventive endeavors.

This is, of course, illogical, but nevertheless has been a widely shared viewpoint about insurance coverage of prevention. Purely rational thinking on this matter would say that preventive interventions (either primary or secondary) should face the same tests as any other medical intervention. In a world that allows use of cost-effectiveness analysis for making resource allocation decisions in health care (which excludes PCORI at this point in time), the same criteria would apply to prevention as to other medical interventions, namely that the incremental cost-effectiveness ratio falls beneath some socially determined cut-off (e.g., $50,000 to $100,000 per Quality-Adjusted Life Year (QALY) or some such number). Thus, in combination with our Proposal 7 (regarding use of cost in Medicare's National Coverage Determinations), we also recommend that prevention fall under the same umbrella. But of course, this also means that things that are "dominant strategies" in the nomenclature of cost-effectiveness analysis (those that improve health outcomes *and* lower total cost of care) get special treatment—they should be available for free to enrollees without any deductibles or copayments, no matter what form of insurance they hold (Medicare Parts A and B, MA, or even HDHP plans within MA).

A parallel change must occur with respect to companion diagnostics—requiring their coverage in the "medical" side of health insurance even when the primary consequence is reduction of prescription drug costs in Part D plans.

Links to lifestyle choices

As a second central issue, almost all of these key chronic illness conditions have strong links to health-related behaviors, most notably use of tobacco, excessive use of alcohol, and obesity and lack of exercise. Again, CMS has moved in the right direction, but much more can be done. Medicare regularly pays for counseling (at least for those "at risk") for smoking cessation, alcohol abuse, and obesity. But the extent of coverage is limited, in many cases without strong evidence (one way or the other) about how much intervention would have good payoff.

For example, Medicare pays for one physician visit per year for counseling to reduce cardiovascular risk with zero out of pocket cost for enrollees. Why "one visit per year?" We cannot ascertain why. There is very little good evidence (one way or the other) about the efficacy of such counseling. The same is true for depression screening in a primary care setting, alcohol misuse screening, HIV testing and some others—once per year.

Other behavioral interventions are available on a more specifically tailored basis. There are no limits for obesity counseling and intervention (without copayments) for people with a Body Mass Index (BMI) over 30 (i.e., those at high risk). Counseling about sexually transmitted infections (STIs) is available for free to enrollees twice per year. Tobacco cessation counseling is available up to eight times per year with an odd twist—these sessions are free to the enrollee (no copayments) if no tobacco-related disease conditions are present, but at the usual 20% Medicare copayment cost if one or more tobacco-related diseases are present. Up to ten hours of diabetes self-management training is available for diabetics, but only at the 20% Medicare copayment rate in Part B. Why charge the 20%? We cannot know. Perhaps diabetes self-management training is so effective that it actually reduces health burden and total cost of care. If so, the services should at least be available for free, and perhaps people should be "bribed" to use them.

These issues are ripe for further evidence-based thinking. It almost surely cannot be true that once per year is the optimal intervention rate for cardiovascular risk behavioral therapy, depression screening, alcohol abuse, and HIV screening. The choices of when to apply and when to exempt screening and counseling from the 20% copayments seem almost random.

We urge that the Center for Medicare and Medicaid Innovation (CMMI) systematically evaluate these chronic-disease and similar interventions and create evidence-based protocols to determine how often these are eligible for payment and at what out of pocket cost to enrollees.

Proposal 7: introduce and encourage consideration of costs in National Coverage Determinations (NCDs)

The original Medicare legislation required that Parts A and B cover services that are "necessary and reasonable," a vague pair of words that lends little guidance to CMS administrators. While nothing in that language officially precludes consideration of cost, there has been a long-standing *de facto* prohibition on using cost as part of Medicare determinations of what procedures and technologies are covered. And by law, the choices made by CMS in Part A and B spill over to MA (Part C) plans, which must cover everything covered in Original Medicare, and may add other medical interventions as they wish.

Leading observers of Medicare and the world of cost-effectiveness analysis have reached the following conclusion: "The use of cost-effectiveness analysis can help Medicare to target its health care resources more efficiently. The obstacles to wider use of such analysis are not primarily methodologic but, instead, matters of politics, process, and leadership."[19]

The problem was exacerbated in the ACA's creation of the PCORI, which is charged with studying the comparative effectiveness of various medical interventions that treat the same condition. As we have noted, the ACA specifically precludes PCORI from using the incremental cost-effectiveness (ICER) measure for recommending or precluding use of medical interventions. That metric is widely used in medical and health economics literature and which is embedded formally into the decisions of organizations such as the United Kingdom's National Institute for Clinical Effectiveness (NICE) and similar organizations in the US and around the world. The Advisory Committee on Immunization Practices (ACIP) of the Centers for Disease Control and Prevention (CDC) formally takes ICERs into account in their recommendations for vaccination protocols, but with no precise methods for introducing economic considerations into their recommendations. That committee says that "Currently, although cost-effectiveness and similar analyses are presented and discussed for the introduction of every new vaccine, there is no clear consensus on the weight that should be given to economic data."[20]

The original Medicare language about using cost to help determine coverage choices (and the newer ACA language regarding PCORI) is counterproductive in meeting the goals of controlling health care cost growth and Medicare expenditure growth. Any person who derides the use of cost in Medicare coverage determinations and at the same time decries cost growth in Medicare is behaving inconsistently. One cannot ask for cost control and at the same time deny the most powerful tools available to achieve that goal. Yet that is where we are in current legislation. The time has come to remove the inconsistency and not only allow but specifically endorse the use of cost considerations in Medicare coverage determinations.

Proposal 8: tax Medigap plans to account for extra cost burden imposed on Medicare

Medigap policies were a consequence of the failures of the original Medicare. Part A imposed significant financial risk for long hospitalizations, which were far more common before the prospective payment system introduced payment per hospitalization rather than payment for each item used. Once patients exceeded 60 days during a hospital stay, financial risk rose rapidly with 25% copays for days 61–90, 50% copays for days 91–120, and the possibility of no insurance coverage at all for very long stays. While insurance conceptually should provide protection against catastrophic risks, Medicare Part A did just the opposite—it left enrollees facing large risks for the costs of extended hospitalizations.[21]

Medigap insurance plans sought to solve that problem. They covered the hospital costs left uninsured by Part A. At the same time, they also began to cover the Medicare Part B deductible ($50 originally) and the 20% coinsurance payments as well. And since Medicare did not cover prescription drugs, many of the Medigap plans also offered coverage for at least some of those costs.

The variety of options for these "wraparound" policies became staggering, and of course the premiums charged for them varied not only by the nuances of coverage provided but also by geographic region of the country. To help consumers sort out the options, the Health Care Finance Administration (HCFA), the predecessor of the current CMS, published a list of "standard" coverage packages (designated as A, B, ... J, and newer plans K, L, M, and N) that contained different mixes of coverage options. They enforced the use of this by ruling that the term "Medigap" could not be used by commercial insurers unless their plans conformed to the pre-specified packages designed by HCFA. Thus the market quickly evolved to all private Medigap policies offered following the HCFA designations, and consumers could easily price the options they wanted from different insurance carriers. As noted elsewhere, this sort of "product standardization" reduces the cost of price comparisons and helps markets to function better as more shoppers "police the market."[22]

With the exception of the low-end Plan A, the average monthly premiums for Medigap plans recently ranged from about $170 to $195, or about $2000 to $2400 per year (rounding slightly).[23]

At the peak year (1987), three-quarters of Medicare beneficiaries either had employer-sponsored supplemental coverage (35%) or had purchased a separate Medigap plan (40%). These numbers have fallen steadily through the years as MA programs have increased in enrollment. MA coverage essentially eliminates the need for Medigap plans and, by law, people who enroll in an MA plan cannot purchase a Medigap plan. In 2015, insurance industry sources reported about 12 million covered lives in Medigap plans, representing about one in five Medicare enrollees.[24]

Medigap plans have an unfortunate side effect: By eliminating the Part B deductible and coinsurance, Medigap plans increased utilization under the standard Part B and Part A plans. While we have no perfect measure of the consequences of this, the RAND Health Insurance Study (HIS) provides a close proxy, using data for persons under 65. One of the RAND experimental plans had $50 deductible for ambulatory care (akin to the Part B deductible in original Medicare Part B), and another plan had a 20% coinsurance. As discussed earlier, analysts using the RAND Health Insurance data simulated the effects of combined plans, including plans with $50 deductibles and 20% coinsurance, as well as full coverage plans with no deductibles or coinsurance.[25] Thus, one can estimate the relative spending with all copayments removed (as with most Medigap plans) compared with a plan with the same features as Medicare Part B.

The RAND results suggest that complete elimination of deductibles and coinsurance (vis a vis the basic Medicare Plan A+B structure) increases utilization (and hence, by extrapolation to the Medicare population, Medicare program costs) by about 30–50%.

Another comparison looks at the average annual spending of those with and without Medigap insurance. This comparison is subject to potential selection bias, since those who anticipate larger expenses may have a higher propensity to purchase Medigap plans. Nevertheless, the comparisons are revealing. According to a report commissioned by the Medical Payment Advisory Commission (MedPac) using Medicare data from 2003–2008,[26] total annual spending for health care was significantly larger for those with Medigap than for those with Medicare only. The largest increases in total spending (27%) came from those with individually-purchased insurance, the smallest (14%) for those with employer-sponsored insurance. Most of the increases came from non-emergency hospitalization and physician services, and most of it emerged when nearly all copayments had been removed.

In 2013, the Government Accountability Office (GAO) created a separate and very useful analysis of the effect of Medigap plans on overall medical spending.[27]

They separated Medigap plans into two categories—those purchased by individuals after enrolling in Medicare and those who acquired Medigap policies before enrolling in Medicare as a post-retirement benefit (subsidized, of course, by the preferred tax treatment of employer-paid premiums discussed in Part I of our book). The value of this comparison is simple: those who enrolled in the Medigap plans before they became Medicare enrollees are less likely to exhibit self-selection (the situation where sickly people purchase more insurance) than those who made the purchase after enrolling in Medicare. The tax subsidy to the employer-provided post-retirement benefit reinforces our ability to use this distinction to help understand the role of Medigap plans in total spending—it provides an extra incentive for people to acquire the insurance even when they do not consider themselves at high risk for future illness and expenses.

Their data are consistent with this thinking. Those with Medicare only had annual expenses of $8064 (in 2010). Those who had purchased a Medigap plan after enrolling in Medicare had annual expenses of $15,612—94% higher (almost double) than those without supplemental coverage. A third category—those who had supplemental coverage through previous employment (either employer sponsored or union sponsored) had average expenses of $14,363, representing a "mere" 78% increase above those without supplemental insurance.

The difference between the "pure Medigap" and the "employer sponsored" supplemental insurance most likely represents self-selection rather than pure incentive effects of the supplemental insurance on utilization. Indeed, some of the extra 78% spending from those with employer-sponsored supplemental insurance is likely to come from self-selection. Regarding the GAO study, we have no way to know for sure how much is self-selection, but we can be sure that those with Medigap and related employer-based plans cost the Medicare system much more than those without such coverage.

A more detailed analysis by Cabral and Mahoney[28] uses a careful analysis of Medigap plans and state-by-state differences in how these plans are structured to estimate the effects of Medigap plans on overall Medicare spending. They estimate that the average Medigap plan increases overall spending by about 22%. They also estimate the price-sensitivity of Medicare enrollees to Medigap premium levels, and find a high price-responsiveness (elasticity of –1.8).

In his 2013 budget proposal, President Obama proposed at 15% surtax on Medigap plans. Cabral and Mahoney estimated that such a 15% tax on Medigap policies would drive the Medigap market down modestly, a 40% surtax would drive it down to about a third of its current level, and a tax that accounted for the entire costs imposed on the Medicare program would essentially drive Medigap plans from the market and save about 10% per year in Medicare program costs. This estimate shows how large an externality the Medigap system imposes on the rest of the economy—those paying Part B premiums, those paying Medicare payroll taxes, and those paying general revenue taxes that support three-quarters of the Part B program.

Canada has a universal Medicare plan for all citizens. However, they banned the sale of private insurance, which (since their Medicare provides universal coverage) has the primary effect of banning supplemental plans. Thus, Canada has avoided the problem created for Medicare by Medigap plans in the US.

We do not favor the Canadian approach for the US. We favor providing more choice whenever possible. But those choices should not inflict costs on others without proper payment in return. But at least according to the analysis by Cabral and Mahoney, a socially optimal tax that accounted for all of the costs imposed by Medigap plans would essentially drive Medigap plans out of the market (because of the high price-sensitivity of consumers to Medigap premium levels).

However, the widespread availability of good substitutes for Medigap—most notably the ready availability of good risk-limiting MA plans—reduces our concerns about this issue. Any concerns about taxing Medigap plans heavily would be further mitigated by removing the shackles from HDHP plans within the Medicare MA structure as we have proposed earlier.

If taxing Medigap plans sufficiently to account for the extra costs they impose leads to them becoming undesirable in the wider scheme of things, then that is the proper outcome. Continuing to allow these Medigap plans to impose uncompensated costs on others is bad public policy, and should not continue. We do not know the best level to set a tax on Medigap plans and do not propose a specific tax here, but we are convinced from available evidence that a major tax on Medigap plans is economically appropriate and represents sound public policy.[29] The estimates from the GAO and those by Cabral and Mahoney would provide a good starting point for policy development.

Proposal 9: allow Medicare Advantage plans to offer different coverage options

Proposal 7 speaks to the Congressional ban on use of "cost" in Medicare coverage determinations. Whether or not that concept is embraced, a separate pathway exists to remove the monopoly on coverage determinations from CMS—allow MA plans to structure their own coverage rules, separate from those of Medicare A+B as specified by CMS coverage determinations. Under current rules, all MA plans must cover every medical technology that CMS chooses for A+B. They are free to add others, but cannot subtract.

The consequence of this rule is that when Medicare adds coverage for some new diagnostic test or therapy that is very expensive, everybody in the Medicare system will have it available. Particularly since Medicare does not (by rule/custom) consider costs when making such decisions, the risk exists that some very expensive therapies (as measured by cost-effectiveness) will achieve coverage. If Medicare adopts a technology that costs $2 million/QALY, they have added that burden to every enrollee. Allowing MA plans to make independent determinations on such choices will add to the efficiency with which the private insurance market can control costs.

We have good legislative precedent in the Medicare Part D plans that are allowed to specify not only their own formulary (the drugs they will cover) but also the pricing attached to each drug (typically ranging from a small copay for 30 or 90 days of a generic drug in Tier 1 to much higher copays for expensive and rarely used drugs in Tier 4). We simply propose to let MA plans have the same freedom in determining the coverages they offer. Competition between plans (where consumers trade off costs and coverage) will illuminate how consumer preferences sort out.

Proposal 10: experiment with new forms of physician compensation

The basis for compensating physicians remains nearly identical to the way the market looked before health insurance existed. With few exceptions (notably prepaid group practice plans, now generally known as HMOs—Kaiser Permanente and similar groups providing the key example), doctors have long-remained paid in a volume-driven fee for service (FFS) system. The market is shifting now, however, with increasingly large fractions of doctors paid on salary. Salaried arrangements vary hugely from contract to contract, but they offer interesting opportunities to reshape the US health care system. And as with hospital compensation, Medicare can lead the way.

In a critique of the ACA, Gail Wilensky, PhD (who, among other things, served from 1990–1992 as head of the HCFA, predecessor to CMS) has said, "Most troubling, the ACA contains no reform of the way physicians are paid, which is the most dysfunctional part of the Medicare program."[30]

Health economists have long understood that the best compensation for physicians would use a blend of salary and FFS.[31] At one extreme, pure FFS creates financial incentives for doctors to distort the advice they provide to patients, leading to increases in health care utilization known among health economists as "induced demand." For a simple personal example, go look at your shampoo bottle. It probably says something like "Lather, rinse, repeat." If we took that advice literally, of course, we would spend the rest of our lives in the shower, lathering, rinsing, and repeating. But even with a sensible stopping rule, the advice provides a nice example of induced demand. You really do not normally need a second "lathering," but when people do it, they end up buying more shampoo than they would otherwise.

Doctors can do the same thing by offering advice that leads to more use of services than the patient really needs. Some simple and obvious examples include whether or not a patient needs cardiac bypass surgery or implantation of a cardiac stent to open up clogged coronary arteries, surgery to improve a low back injury, or a Caesarian section instead of normal delivery. More subtle variants of demand inducement include recommendations about using physical therapy and imaging, where physician ownership of such services leads to increased profits with increased use. Health economists call this "demand inducement."

Demand inducement can occur even in apparently benign settings such as the office visit for a pediatrician. How often does the doctor recommend a "well care" visit? It turns out that even pediatricians shift their recommendations based upon how they are paid.[32] And obstetricians shift the rate at which they recommend C-sections to patients when economic pressures on their incomes increase.[33] And orthopedic surgeons who own imaging facilities recommend imaging at four times the rate of those who don't,[34] and those who own physical therapy facilities recommend therapy at 1.4 times the rate of those who don't.[35] These are but a handful of the documented examples demonstrating the powerful effect of FFS compensation on treatment recommendations.

The option at the other extreme—flat annual salary compensation—has its own flaws. Doctors, like other humans, have other things they like to do in their lives. Thus, doctors on flat salaries work less—a lot less in large medical practices—than doctors on an FFS system.[36] All of these observations lead us to the belief that a mix of salary and FFS probably works better than either extreme alone.

Many compensation systems adjust salaries for the doctor's effort, almost always measured as the number of patients seen per day (particularly in the primary care setting) or a more finely granulated "relative value units" measure. Many medical groups have some combination of a base salary (which will typically range from 20% up to nearly 100%) and a work-related bonus, sometimes graduated so that extra special effort gets higher additional compensation—sometimes up to three tiers of bonus payments.

However, modern compensation methods take into account a wider array of parameters than a simple visit count. The two key elements that some systems take into account (in addition to patient volume) include quality of care and team-based cooperation. We can examine each in detail.

In the inpatient setting, Medicare already pays hospitals (but not doctors) based on pre-established quality indicators. These include important factors such as readmission rates (a signal that something wasn't done right on the initial admission to the hospital) and infection rates. Hospital-acquired infections are both common and serious, since the widespread use of antibiotics in hospitals often leads to the emergence of bacteria that strongly resist the otherwise potent effect of antibiotics. The worst include Multiply-Resistant Staph Aureus (MRSA), a highly resistant strain of a particularly dangerous bacterial group, and the more recently emerging carbapenem-resistant Enterobacteriaceae (CRE).

Finding useful quality indicators in the outpatient setting has proven elusive, but a number have emerged that seem to have reasonably high value. Some of these are "process" indicators, such as the proportion of patients receiving appropriate vaccinations. But some hinge on patient outcomes, which often translate either directly or indirectly into improved health status. Some examples:

- For diabetics: the proportion with HbA1C under a target level (e.g., 8). HbA1C provides a useful cumulative measure of how well the patient's insulin has been under control. What fraction of patients have had inspection of their feet (for sores) and eyes (for retinal problems associated with diabetes)? Note that the first measure is an actual achievement of a medical goal, not merely a process measure.
- For patients with hypertension, the proportion with blood pressure under a target level (e.g., 140/80). Again, note that this is a real medical outcome, not just a process measure.
- What proportion of patients smoke? What proportion of smokers have quit?
- What proportion are overweight? What proportion have lost meaningful amounts of weight?

These indicators are essentially impossible to measure without electronic health records (EHRs), but good EHRs will show these and other things readily, including indicators relying on lab tests (such as HbA1c for diabetics).

Modern medicine—particularly that involving chronic care conditions (see our separate discussion on these issues in Chapter 10)—involves team-based care. Thus, compensation can involve a third component in addition to volume and quality—"plays well with others." Some medical groups now directly measure these behaviors and include them in annual salary determination, including measures of attendance at medical staff meetings, "360 degree" measures of group compatibility from those working with each doctor (other doctors, nurses, medical assistants, and others) and patient satisfaction surveys.

CMS (Medicare) has a very elaborate quality measurement system that can be used or modified by private insurance plans (either for under-65 or MA). The CMS Patient Quality Reporting System (PQRS—conveniently appearing as four sequential letters in the alphabet) has 44 pages listing 328 quality indicators, many of which only pertain to an inpatient or post-surgical environment, but hundreds of which also pertain to ambulatory care, mostly involving patients with chronic conditions or measuring vaccination rates appropriate to age groups. Some of these measures come only through patient satisfaction surveys (e.g., after cataract surgery) and some will have ready measurement only through EHRs, but some can be measured directly through claims data, since they will involve billable events (where doctors are sure to bill in our volume-driven FFS system). Thus—in concept—most third-party health insurance carriers (both private and public) have a wide array of quality measures that they can introduce into compensation systems.

The easiest way to introduce quality indicators into physician compensation comes through doctors paid on salary, rather than directly in complete FFS mode. An example plan might have the following sort of structure:

- 60% of agreed compensation via base salary;
- 20% on volume-basis, measured as deviation from target load of 20 patients per day seen in primary care setting. (In an eight-hour day, that allows 24 minutes per patient.);
- 10% based on meeting quality criteria (such as the CMS PQRS);
- 10% based on teamwork and participation (attending staff meetings, 360-degree surveys of co-workers, and patient satisfaction surveys).

Obviously, the number of possible variants rapidly approaches infinity. The point is that compensation can easily include formally measured quality and teamwork as well as volume of activity.

In pure FFS environments (which will remain for some doctors in almost any imaginable setting in the US), it is still possible to introduce quality measures into the fee structure, for example, by setting the base compensation at (say) 80% of current levels and then augmenting each FFS payment in proportion to the extent that chosen quality indicators are met.

We do not claim special knowledge about *the* best way to carry out physician compensation. We are persuaded—in agreement with Gail Wilensky (quoted earlier)—that the current system is near-to or completely broken.

CMS should continue to experiment within the context of CMMI with alternative payment plans to find the right measures of and weights applied to various quality indicators. We similarly urge private insurance to use and modify such measures, as appropriate for their settings, including finding ways to incorporate team participation parameters as seems fitting. We discuss these issues further in the context of chronic disease management in Part III of this book.

Notes

1 An "urban legend" among early health services researchers suggests the following: Medicare planners brought the proposed plans for Medicare to then-President Lyndon Johnson, who, after hearing them out—including that there would be no Part A deductible—asked "Do you mean that there is no cost for being hospitalized?" They answered, "Yes sir, that's the plan." And he allegedly said, "Hell, my Daddy would have gotten himself into the hospital every time he had a hangover. Make them pay for the first day." So this—as the legend has it—led to the one-day deductible for hospitalization in Part A. Johnson's father, Sam Ealy Johnson, a cattle rancher and sometime politician in the Texas State Legislature, died in 1937, while his son Lyndon was 29 years old. President Johnson himself never lived to enjoy the fruits of his Medicare legislation—he died at the age of 64, almost exactly four years after leaving the White House.

2 The Appendix to this chapter provides a discussion of the optimal insurance coverage, suggesting that the original Medicare Part A and Part B deductibles were not far off from what one would describe as the optimum level of deductibles.

3 Garber and Phelps, 1997, Chetty, 2012.
4 Analyses of optimal insurance coverage suggests that for hospital care (accounting for the financial risk and the price sensitivity—the intrinsic balancing act in health insurance) the optimal percent paid out of pocket would be about 5%. With a projected average cost for Medicare admissions of about $14,000 in 2017, the "best" deductible would be about $700 per admission. See Phelps (2014) for the approach leading to the 5% coinsurance rate estimate.
5 For simplicity, one might set both of these at an initial level of $400 and index them with the CPI, thus eliminating a potential source of confusion to Medicare enrollees about which amount applied to which plan.
6 This number is a rough estimate of the difference between the free care RAND HIS plan and the $150 deductible plan as shown in Table 1.2. We use the 1/3 ratio because the Part B deductible is about one-third of its proper size.
7 Part B deductibles on average would rise by $192, and Part A deductibles would fall by $185. The net increase is $7 per person. For 57 million Medicare enrollees, the net fiscal effect is $0.4 billion—decimal dust in the Medicare budget.
8 These quotes taken from www.dartmouthatlas.org/keyissues/issue.aspx?con=1338, last accessed February 27, 2015.
9 Newhouse and Garber, 2013, Newhouse et al., 2013.
10 www.cms.gov/Research-Statistics-Data-and-Systems/Computer-Data-and-Systems/MedicaidDataSourcesGenInfo/Downloads/MAX_IB11_PhysicianParticipation.pdf, last accessed August 3, 2017.
11 Healthy Indiana Plan: Lessons for Health Reform, www.mathematica-mpr.com/~/media/publications/PDFs/health/healthyindianaplan_ib1.pdf, last accessed January 11, 2015.
12 www.npr.org/blogs/health/2014/07/22/333745570/states-experiment-with-health-savings-accounts-for-medicaid, last accessed January 11, 2015.
13 See www.medicare.gov/coverage/preventive-and-screening-services.html (last accessed August 3, 2017) for a full list of the screening and preventive services (e.g., vaccines and tobacco use, alcohol use and obesity counseling) covered by Medicare and the copayments required.
14 Roebuck et al., 2011. The sample included 112,757 with hypertension, 16,353 with congestive heart failure, 42,080 with diabetes, and 53,041 with dyslipedemia. Some had multiple conditions, so these add up to more than the total sample size.
15 Phelps et al., 2012.
16 We have personally observed this decision structure within the Department of Veteran's Affairs, HMO organizations, and insurance companies with multiple "managed care" options. The bifurcation of drug-plan management from other coverage decisions seems almost ubiquitous.
17 This is the natural equilibrium state for a non-cooperative game with these features.
18 In fact, the PCORI enabling language does not rule out cost-effectiveness analysis, but (more precisely) the use of quality adjustments when calculating the "health benefit" side of a cost-effectiveness analysis.
19 Neumann et al., 2005.
20 Nelson et al., 2010.
21 Phelps and Reisinger, 1988.
22 Sadanand and Wilde, 1982, Roth, 2015.
23 The most recent survey data available provides 2010 data. See Huang et al., 2013.
24 www.markfarrah.com/press-room/Medicare-Supplement-Enrollment-Reaches-Nearly-12-Million-According-to-Mark-Farrah-Associates.aspx, last accessed June 12, 2017.
25 Keeler et al., 1988.
26 Hogan, 2014.
27 Government Accountability Office, 2013, Figure 6.

28 Cabral and Mahoney, 2014.
29 It is readily feasible to analyze the consequences of the tax in terms of Medicare spending and adjust the taxes to account for the information derived from the first year or two of implementing the Medigap tax. A good conceptual framework would compare the changes in medical spending of those who maintained their Medigap plans, those who dropped them, and those who never had Medigap plans—what is known among health policy analysts as a "difference of differences" model.
30 Wilensky, 2012.
31 Ma and McGuire, 1997.
32 The best example: In a classic randomized trial, pediatricians in training were paid either on flat salary or in an FFS system. The FFS doctors recommended about one more visit per year for the pediatric patients (five instead of four) than the salary-paid doctors. And interestingly, the salary-paid doctors under-shot the well care visit recommendations of the American Academy of Pediatrics, while the FFS doctors overshot those same recommendations. See Hickson et al., 1987.
33 Gruber and Owings, 1996.
34 Hillman et al., 1990.
35 Mitchell and Scott, 1992.
36 Gaynor and Gertler, 1995.

Part III

Things that affect everybody

10 Chronic conditions

Millstones and their costs

Many people have chronic illness or injuries ("conditions") that cause pain and suffering, limit their ability to work effectively either in the market or in the home, and people with multiple chronic conditions have very high health care costs. This leads us to consider three distinct public policy questions, the answers to which are not necessarily obvious (at least to us), but which deserve more complete attention from researchers and policy makers:

- How can we prevent chronic conditions from arising so often?
- How can we best reimburse the treatment of chronic conditions?
- What does an aging society imply in terms of chronic conditions and their resource use and cost consequences?

Chronic conditions are very costly to treat. The rate of health care spending rises exponentially with the number of chronic conditions, and for a given number of chronic conditions, costs also rise with age, but not as dramatically as with the number of chronic conditions. Perhaps most importantly, 83% of all US health care costs occur for persons with at least one chronic condition.

Figure 10.1 shows the total spending in fee for service (FFS) Medicare for people with various numbers of chronic conditions, by age bracket. There is a small age effect for a given number of chronic conditions, but it is swamped by the actual count of chronic conditions itself. Look within the age 65–74 age bracket first. Those with 0–1 chronic conditions spend (on average for the entire FFS Medicare enrollee population) a mere $1648. Increasing the chronic condition count to 2–3 triples the average annual expenditure (to $4839), going to 4–5 chronic conditions more than doubles it again (to $10,563) and those with 6+ chronic conditions spend an average of $31,746—about 20 times the spending rate for those with 0 or 1 chronic conditions. This same pattern repeats itself for each successive age group. The costs for a given number of chronic conditions rises slightly with age (except for the 6+ group, where higher mortality rates reduce the total spending slightly), but the "chronic condition count" swamps the age effect.

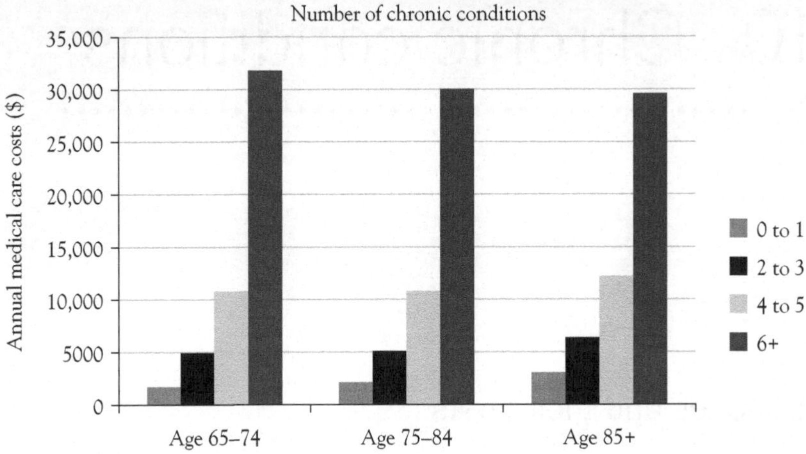

Figure 10.1

Total annual medical spending (vertical axis, in dollars) by number of chronic conditions, by age
Source: CMS Chronic Conditions Data Warehouse

The next step looks at how the number of chronic conditions changes with age. This, it turns out, is how "aging" manifests itself most importantly—greater age increases the number of chronic conditions. As Figure 10.2 shows, the chances of a Medicare enrollee having 0 or 1 chronic conditions plummets as age increases, and the number of chronic conditions not only increases with age but at an increasing rate. For those under 65, a bit under one-half (47%) have 0 or 1 chronic conditions (almost half of that group) and only 9% have 6+ chronic conditions. In the highest age interval (85+), only 17% (about one in six) have 0 or 1 chronic conditions, and over one-quarter of this age group has 6+ chronic conditions. Well over half of this age group has at least 4 chronic conditions, which (see previous figure) implies average medical spending per person per year well in excess of $20,000 for this group.

Dementia deserves special recognition, both because of the consequences for the affected individual and—more so than most other chronic disabling conditions—the demands on the family and caregivers. Recent National Institute of Aging data (see Figure 10.3) show a strong relationship with age, such that one-quarter of those 80–89 years old have some form of dementia, and three-eighths of those aged 90+ have dementia. Overall, this resource estimates that 6 to 10% of the US population of ages 65+ have some form of dementia.

Recent data from the Health Interview Survey tell us both that the rate at which people report chronic conditions increases with age, and within age cohorts, is increasing over time. Compared with similar data from 2002, the risk of having multiple chronic conditions has increased in both the under-65s and

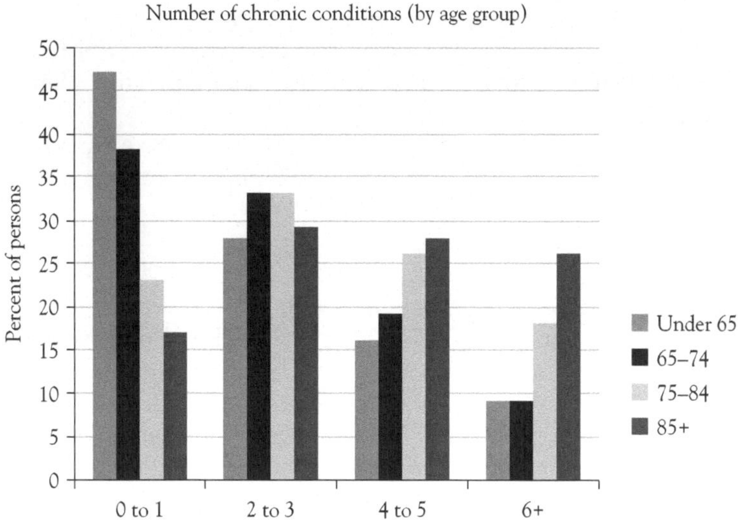

Figure 10.2

Percentage of persons in different age groups with various numbers of chronic conditions
Source: CMS Chronic Conditions Data Warehouse

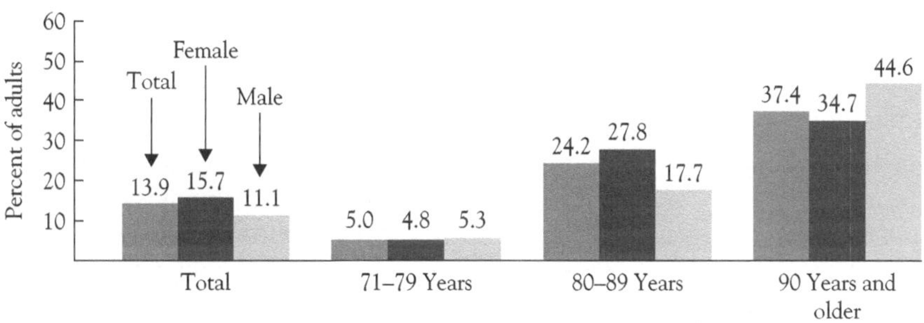

Figure 10.3

Dementia prevalence, by age, for persons aged 71 and above, for males, females, and total
Source: CMS Chronic Conditions Data Warehouse

those over in later estimates for 2010–2014. The rates are highest for blacks, lowest for Hispanics, and in-between for white non-Hispanics.[1]

Not surprisingly, chronic illness conditions are more prevalent with lower family income. This relationship can come from at least two sources. First, chronic conditions reduce one's ability to work productively, hence causing family income to fall. Second, for many reasons, people with lower incomes have worse access to health care, and hence either incur more chronic conditions (due to failures of prevention and lifestyle choices) or have them treated insufficiently (so they remain as chronic conditions rather than returning to normalcy).

The "grey tsunami"—understanding age pyramids

The prevalence of chronic conditions rises with age, and hence will invariably become more important in the US and other developed nations as the age profile changes over time. On this front, the US (along with other developed nations) faces what some have called "the grey tsunami." The best way of showing this uses "population pyramids," which show the distribution of males (left side) and females (right side) in various age groups. The term "pyramid" comes from the shape of these pictures, where the diagram (historically) systematically narrows as age increases.

Figures 10.4a–d show these pyramids for 1950, 2000, and projections for 2025 and 2050. The 1950 diagram has a classical "pyramid" shape with the exception of two age groups affected by World War II—the group aged 20–24 (from combat mortality) and the groups from ages 5–19, reflecting lower fertility during the war (with soldiers overseas) and in the pre-war Depression. The age group 0–4—the beginning of the post-war "baby boom"—appears in the lowest bar of the 1950 chart.

Now shift to the Year 2000 chart—50 years later (Figure 10.4b). The very first cohort of "boomers" are now aged 50–54, and 20 more years of "boomers" follow behind them (ages 30–49). The "population pyramid" has now acquired (perhaps appropriately) a "middle aged spread" around its waistline. Note also the increasing number in the 80+ group, and particularly the number of women in that group. Women outlive men in the US by about five years, partly due to biological differences, but a significant proportion of the difference arising because the men smoked considerably more than the women in earlier years, and the excess deaths from smoking (cancers, heart disease, and other conditions) have caught up with the men.

Shift ahead again 25 years to 2025 (Figure 10.4c) and the "pyramid" has become almost a cylinder. The survivors from those who were 0–4 in 1950 are now 75 years older—aged 75–79—and the 80+ group contains all survivors who were born in 1945 or earlier. This is the population the US will have in less than a decade from this book's publication.

Finally, look into the more distant future of 2050 (Figure 10.4d), when the "X-generation" will have matured. Demographers use this loose term to describe children born between the late 1960s and the late 1980s. For purposes of our reading these graphs, we can use 1970 to 1990. In 2050, that group will be aged 60 to 80. Most of them will be eligible for Social Security and Medicare (under current program structure). Note the wide top layer of those aged 85+,

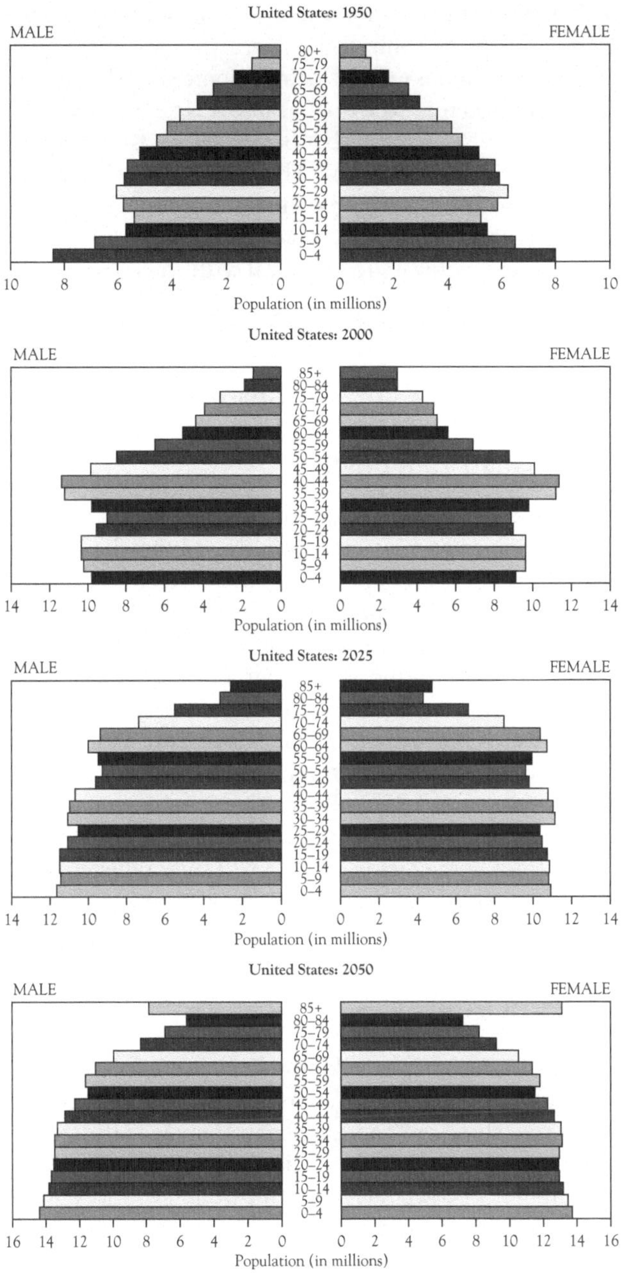

Figure 10.4

Age pyramids for US population, 1950 (panel a), 2000 (panel b), 2025 (panel c), and 2050 (panel d)
Source: US Census Bureau, International Data Base

vastly larger than previous generations have seen, and notably larger than the 80–84 population for the first time in US history.

These population pyramids reflect a demographic shift that is both inevitable and costly. We delve into this issue not because it is new and not because others have not raised the issue previously, but because it leads us to some potentially valuable ways to mitigate the effects. The logical path begins with the way aging mostly manifests itself as increased rates of chronic conditions, and then explores the origins of these chronic conditions, some controllable, some not. We then propose some pathways to help deal with the controllable portions of this risk.

Combining pyramids and millstones

Pyramids and health care costs

While the idea of combining (population) pyramids and millstones (health burdens) sounds somewhat as if one were describing the fate of the slaves in the age of the Pharaohs, it simply combines the two previous sections to make the obvious point—chronic condition burdens increase exponentially with age, and thus also does medical spending (within Medicare, mostly) increase. Those rates of chronic illness burden accelerate as age increases. And as the population projections shown in the previous section reveal, the US is heading towards a population that is not only top-heavy in "retiree" age persons, but increasingly so in the group most burdened by chronic illness conditions—those aged 85 and over. If we do not find a way to reduce the chronic illness burdens in this population and medical costs associated with them, the health care costs in the US will inevitably grow. We can help to deal with this growing problem only if we find new ways to think about chronic conditions.

Pyramids and public finance

One of the implications of these oddly shaped population "pyramids" comes from the way we finance our national retirement program (Social Security) and Part A of Medicare. These programs use payroll taxes as the basis of financing them, and thus in many ways their viability depends on the ratio of workers to retirees. Figure 10.5 shows relevant data from 1900 forward—recall that the Social Security system was created in 1935 and Medicare in 1965. When Social Security was created in 1935, about 6% of the US population fell into the 65+ age bracket, and only 0.25% (one out of every 400 persons) reached ages 85+. At Medicare's creation in 1965 (remember—Medicare is an amendment to the Social Security Act and adopted its age rules), the over-65 group had increased to about 10% of the population, and the over-85 group remained under 1%.

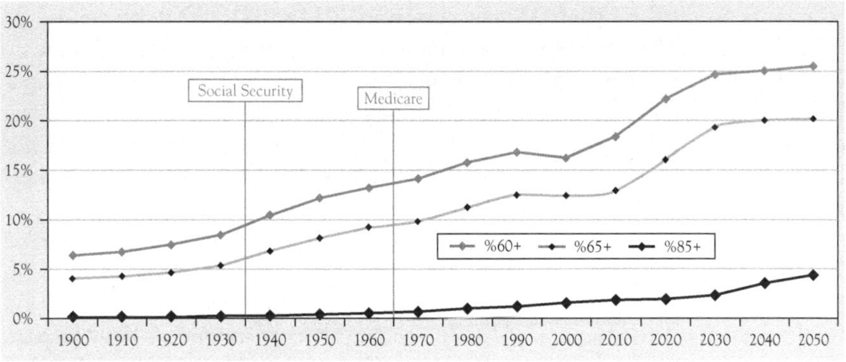

Figure 10.5

Proportion of US population age in age ranges 60+ (top line), 65+ (middle line), and 85+ (lower line) for years 1900 to 2050
Source: US Census Bureau

By 2010, the 65+ population had reached 13% of the population, with just under 2% reaching ages 85+. By 2050, 20% of the US population will have reached ages 65+, and 4.3% will reach ages 85+.

The "working age" population is best characterized in US Census data by the group aged 18–64, although of course many persons outside this age group actually work part or full time. This group will bear the heaviest share of the payroll tax burden to support Social Security and Medicare Part A. In 1970, shortly after Medicare was created, the ratio of "workers" to "retirees" (i.e., ages 18–64 = "workers" and ages 65+ = "retirees") was quite favorable at 5.66:1—there were almost six workers' payroll taxes supporting each retiree's Social Security and Medicare Part A.

By 2010, the "workers" had expanded from 56% (in 1970) to 63% of the US population, but the over-65 population had also expanded from 9.9% of the total to 13.0%, so the ratio became somewhat less favorable at 4.85:1. By 2050, the "workers" age group will have fallen to 57% of the population, and the "retiree" group will have increased to 20.2% according to current Census Bureau projections. This leads to a ratio of "workers" to "retirees" of only 2.82:1—almost exactly half of what it was in 1970 (and at the creation of Medicare in 1965).

To be clear, these ratios are forecasts that depend on predictions of fertility trends, mortality rates, and—perhaps the easiest "lever" to turn—immigration policy, but no matter what happens over the next 35 years, the ratio of "workers" to "retirees" will decline dramatically relative to conditions at Medicare's beginning.

While these ratios are relevant for understanding Social Security obligations, they remain incomplete in terms of forecasting Medicare costs, since medical spending increases more rapidly with age. To put it in simple terms, Medicare recipients over the age of 85 cost more than twice as much as Medicare recipients aged 65–84 ($46,000 per person in 2013 vs. $19,000). So we should "double count" the 85+ Medicare population when thinking about Medicare Part A payroll taxes and Medicare's financing. Instead of an "over 65" population in 2010 of 13%, we should really say that it has become 14.9% (after double-counting the 85+ group of 1.9% of the population). By 2050, it will not be "merely" 20.2% but (for Part A accounting) 24.5%. And the ratio of "worker" to "retiree" with this adjustment falls even further from 2.82:1 to 2.33:1.

A wise policy analyst once said "Things that can't go on forever ... won't." The financing of Social Security and particularly Part A of Medicare through payroll taxes may well not continue into the distant future. The payroll tax burden may have too many undesirable economic consequences. The US population trends are essentially inevitable, unless we somehow dramatically alter either fertility patterns or immigration law.

Expanding the number of tax-paying individuals relative to the number of retirees helps sustain the payroll tax financing of Social Security and the particularly troublesome issue of Part A Medicare financing. One way to alter these "worker" to "retiree" ratios, of course, is to allow substantially greater immigration and pathways to citizenship for currently undocumented workers and to expand the pathways for other legal immigration. These are complex issues in many ways—as the 2016 presidential election cycle emphasized—but a significant number of politicians expend efforts both to limit immigration and to reduce tax burdens. Our point here is simply that payroll tax burdens to finance Part A and Social Security will inevitably rise (more so for the payroll tax financing for Part A) as the population ages, and hence that finding ways to enhance the base of taxpaying workers can help resolve this dilemma. Opening the immigration doors provides one obvious solution.

The Congress could also choose among many other ways to reduce this payroll tax burden, including: (a) shifting from payroll to general income taxes or even other tax sources; (b) altering provider payments to reduce Medicare costs; (c) altering the incentives to use medical care (both demand and supply incentives); or (d) shifting the financial burden to Medicare recipients, e.g., by turning Medicare into a voucher program and then limiting increases in the value of the voucher. We do not presume to offer the best solution to this dilemma here, but merely note the importance of confronting the issue in a focused public policy debate.

One further solution remains that we discuss next—alter the rate at which chronic conditions become manifest. This approach is the only one we can envision that is not in its essence a zero-sum game.

The underlying causes of chronic conditions—a pathway to a solution

We have discussed the relationship between age and medical spending. Here we delve deeper into the issue to illuminate the underlying causes of this relationship.

Of course, in general, it is quite simple: as we get older, our bodies wear out faster. But unraveling the relationships leads to a pathway to think about how to help solve the problem, rather than just bemoaning the fiscal and personal consequences. We have seen in previous figures how medical spending increases exponentially with the number of chronic conditions, and how the number of chronic conditions increases exponentially with age. This raises the inevitable question—what can we do about the cost consequences? The path towards a brighter future is illuminated by four key lamp post ideas:

- Lifestyle choices—particularly tobacco use, obesity, alcohol abuse, and to a lesser degree illicit drug use and unprotected sex—all strongly influence the number of chronic conditions.
- The National Institutes of Health (NIH) research program pays minimal attention to the issues affecting the rate of chronic condition formation, particularly factors affected by individuals' lifestyle choices.
- Treatment of chronic conditions proceeds better when coordinated than uncoordinated. The FFS system is particularly ill-suited to foster coordinated care for chronic conditions.
- With chronic conditions, maintenance drugs can be highly effective both in reducing total cost of care and improving health outcomes. Thus, barriers to adherence to drug regimens in chronic diseases must fall.

With these issues in mind, we now set forth four key proposals to improve the future with regard to chronic conditions, proposals that we will then discuss and defend in more detail:

> **Proposal 1:** *In both private health insurance and Medicare and Medicaid, strengthen rewards for people adopting and maintaining healthy lifestyle choices that reduce the risk of chronic illness, including introducing health insurance discounts for non-smokers and non-obese people.*

> **Proposal 2:** *Shift the NIH research priorities to better reflect the true causes of health burden and premature death—tobacco, obesity, and lack of exercise, with a much stronger emphasis on prevention through medical intervention, education, and provision of information than currently exists.*

> **Proposal 3:** *In both private health insurance and Medicare and Medicaid, shift the financial incentives for providers to emphasize coordinated care for people with chronic conditions, particularly those with multiple chronic conditions.*

> **Proposal 4:** *In both private insurance and Medicare and Medicaid, provide full coverage for maintenance drugs for people with chronic conditions, particularly when generic drugs adequately reduce or eliminate consequences of the condition.*

We elaborate on each of these issues next.

Origins of chronic conditions

The Chronic Condition Data Warehouse of CMS shows the frequency with which we can observe various chronic conditions in the Medicare population—the prevalence rates. These represent only the most common conditions, and hence under-count the actual totals, but it is easy to see that the prevalence rates add up to far more than 100%—as must happen, since most Medicare enrollees have multiple chronic conditions. Thus, these specific conditions add up to a total of 3.83 conditions per enrollee. Figure 10.6 shows those of greatest importance.

Lifestyle effects

By far the most common chronic condition problems are hypertension, hyperlipidemia (high cholesterol), ischemic heart disease (IHD), diabetes, and rheumatoid and osteoarthritis. One single human behavior exacerbates each of these—obesity/lack of exercise. Tobacco smoking contributes to many of these and others as well—hypertension, IHD, heart failure (HF), hip fracture

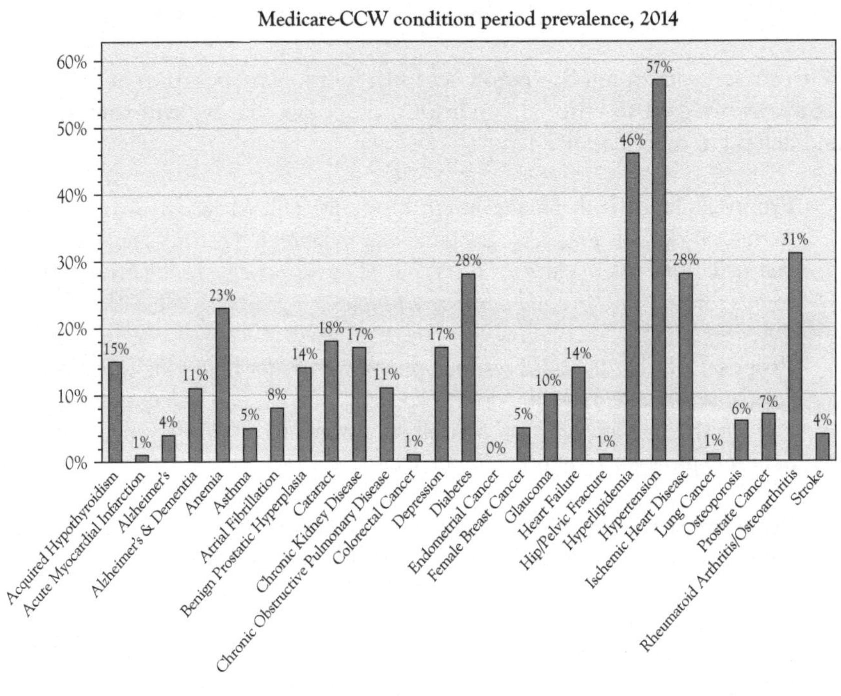

Figure 10.6

Prevalence of chronic conditions, by type, for leading causes of chronic disability, 2014
Source: CMS Chronic Conditions Data Warehouse

(especially for women, due to increased rates of bone depletion), atrial fibrilation (A-Fib), chronic obstructive pulmonary disease (COPD), stroke, lung cancer, cataracts, breast cancer (especially for those who began smoking before their first child), and others. Hypertension is a known precursor to heart disease, stroke, and kidney failure, among other major causes of death. It seems manifestly clear that if we are ever able to reduce the cost consequences of chronic conditions, we need to address head-on their prevalence, which in turn requires addressing head-on the lifestyle choices of tobacco use and obesity, topics to which we return shortly.

Genetic risks

It is not just behavior that leads to these chronic conditions—would that it were that simple. Chronic conditions have multiple origins. Some arise as time bombs lurking within our genes, including many cancers, certain forms of heart disease, hypertension, diabetes, and (as we learn with increasing frequency) degenerative neurologic conditions such as Alzheimer's disease, Parkinson's disease, Huntington's disease, multiple sclerosis, and many others. However, with few exceptions, a simple genetic defect alone does not suffice to cause the disease.

The genetic link can increase the risk, but some other environmental factor (often multiple causes, many still unknown) is often needed to trigger the disease. Alzheimer's disease, for example, has been linked to inflammation processes, chemical exposures, head trauma, insufficient blood supply (heart failure) and other risks. Some lifestyle issues affect the risk of Alzheimer's, most notably obesity, high intake of saturated fats (but "good fats" such as high-density lipoproteins (HDLs) seem protective), and certain foods seem protective—those with high anti-oxidant levels such as green leafy vegetables, berries, and certain other fruits, fish containing omega-3 fatty acids, and some nuts, particularly those high in vitamin E. Some vitamins, including E or E and C together, plus B12 and folate may lower Alzheimer's risk.[2]

This list of potential precursors to Alzheimer's disease stands merely as an example of the complexity of trying to prevent some of the most important chronic conditions. Most of the highly important conditions shown in Figure 10.6 have a similarly complex etiology.

The proverbial "bottom line" is that we still do not have a good grasp on the causes of many chronic conditions (particularly Alzheimer's and other dementia conditions) so focusing basic research on these issues can have high dividends. But in addition, we need to focus on translational research that moves from highly biological and genetic research to research that brings new prevention and treatment to the foreground.

No "silver bullet" program exists to solve this dilemma. It will require continued research into the genetic and biological pathways that lead to these chronic conditions, improved translational research that shifts findings from these basic sciences into practice, and—the greatest missing element—a far deeper understanding of how to modify human behavior to alter or counteract deleterious lifestyle choices. This latter focus will necessarily include information dissemination and other educational programs (most likely focused on specific groups with differing educational, ethic, and belief-structure backgrounds), incentives, regulation of harmful products, and new scientific research to find ways to help people "kick the habit" of deleterious behaviors (most notably, smoking, obesity, alcohol abuse, and other substance abuse).

How to treat chronic conditions

By their very nature, chronic diseases are difficult to treat, particularly when they occur in combinations. Thus, a frontal attack on the chronic disease issue will almost certainly require a shift towards more coordinated care. Little of what we say below is novel, but it deserves discussion even so, and hence we proceed with our review of these issues.

The benefits and curses of specialization

One gerontologist known to both of us had a simple strategy when beginning to treat a new patient. He had patients empty their medicine cabinet into a bag and bring everything into the office. The medications commonly spilled out onto the table like an army of invading ants. Many are costly and many create side effects. Our gerontologist-friend commonly found that some of the drugs have the sole purpose of dealing with the side effects of other drugs, sometimes with side effects of side-effect-reducing drugs. So he commonly stopped all but a few medications, and began with drugs to treat the most important single problem, then slowly and carefully added others as needed. Many of his patients improved rapidly with this approach.

We portray this anecdote to highlight a serious and highly-studied problem. Drugs have side effects, and some drug combinations (drug–drug interactions) are dangerous and possibly lethal. Our system of financing (and hence, providing) health care is particularly poorly suited to dealing with these issues. In the ideal world, patients have a "medical home" where a single primary care provider keeps track of all of this, a person who is often ill-suited to master the complexities of unique drug–drug interactions. In less than ideal situations, patients are left to fend for themselves in figuring this out. (Our later chapter on Electronic Health Records deals with this issue also.)

We also live in a world of medical specialization. Specialization is actually (on net) both a good thing and inevitable. Adam Smith, one of the earliest practitioners of economics, observed the phenomenon correctly in 1776: "Division of Labor is Limited by the Extent of the Market."[3] In a frontier economy, everybody is somewhat good at a lot of things. In an economy (such as ours) characterized by most people living in large population centers, we commonly find specialists available to do almost anything. And they do those single things better than generalists (Jacks and Jills of all trades) can do.

In small towns, one mechanic fixes all types of cars. In large cities, we find companies and mechanics specializing in various specific brands of cars ("dealerships") and often independent specialists in certain sub-sectors (German cars, diesel engines, sports cars, off-road vehicles, etc.) In small towns, one person will repair all sorts of gadgets. In large cities, we can find separate specialists for refrigerators, washers and driers, toasters, television sets, computers, lawn mowers, and the like.

The same holds true for medical care. In small towns, we find family practice doctors, nurse-practitioners, and the occasional internal medicine or pediatrics specialist. In large cities, specialists abound. We not only have orthopedic surgeons, we have them specializing in hand and wrist surgery, foot and ankle surgery, knee surgery, hip surgery, spinal surgery, and surgery for other parts, but sometimes we find even specialized procedures on these specialized parts (e.g., knee replacement surgery or cataract removal or retinal eye surgery).

Fields such as internal medicine and pediatrics have also fractured into pieces, so we can see (within internal medicine) sub-fields such as cardiology, endocrine disease, allergies, infectious diseases, genetics, lung disease, digestive disorders, and the like. Within those, we can find further sub-specialization, so that we commonly find not just cardiologists but "diagnostic" and "interventional" cardiologists (those who insert stents into blood vessels to reduce risks of clogged arteries). What used to be called "radiology" is now "imaging science," with specialists in magnetic resonance imaging (MRI), computed tomography (CT), positron emission tomography (PET), ultrasound, radionucleide imaging, and often sub-fields such as CT angiography.

One might describe this all by paraphrasing the famous poem about fleas, referring instead of fleas to medical "fields" of specialization. The revision would read:

> Big fields have small fields,
> To further sub-divide 'em,
> And small fields still smaller fields,
> *And so, ad infinitum.*

A simple rule tells how much this happens in various parts of the country: Look to see how many people there are in the US compared with the number of specialists in a field.[4] The ratio—potential patients per doctor—tells a lot about where we can expect to find specialists. Table 10.1 lists the ratio of patients to specialists in the US.

Start near the top of the table: There are a bit over 3000 people per family practice doctor (using the entire 2010 US population of 309 million to match the 2010 physician data). On average, any community with at least 3000 people will likely have a family practice doctor (or general internal medicine specialist) available, but not commonly in communities notably smaller. The average family practice doctor "needs" about 3000 people to survive financially, and few such doctors will willingly move to smaller communities.

Table 10.1 Medical specialists relative to population

	Number	Population/Doctor
TOTAL	681,620	453
Primary Care	248,910	942
General and Family	101,520	3041
General Internal Medicine	97,120	2415
General Pediatrics*	50,260	1476
Medical Specialties		
Allergy	3,030	77,414
Cardiovascular Disease	20,310	11,549
Dermatology	10,160	23,087
Gastroenterology	10,620	22,087
Other Subspecialties	30,880	7596
Surgical Specialties	143,780	1631
General Surgery	22,090	10,619
General Surgery Subspecialties	7,000	33,509
Neurosurgery	4,520	51,895
OB/Gyn	42,320	5543
Ophthalmology	17,830	13,156
Orthopedic Surgery	21,980	10,672
Otorhinolaryngology	9,070	25,862
Plastic Surgery	5,900	39,757
Thoracic Surgery	4,110	57,072
Urology	9,050	25,919
Other Specialties		
Anesthesiology	41,570	7427
Diagnostic Radiology	20,820	14,829
Emergency Medicine	22,590	13,667
General Preventive Medicine	1,700	181,615
Neurology	13,150	23,479
Nuclear Medicine	1,320	233,898
Pathology	3,370	91,616
Physical Medicine & Rehabilitation	7,910	39,032
Psychiatry	35,170	8779
Radiation Oncology	4,590	67,265
Radiology	7,580	40,732

Source: The Physician Workforce: Projections and Research into Current Issues Affecting Supply and Demand; US Department of Health and Human Services; Health Resources and Services Administration; Bureau of Health Professions Dec-08

* For pediatrics, denominator is population under age 18

They can always squeeze into larger towns and cities rather than foregoing income by moving to ever-smaller towns.

Drop down now into the section on Surgical Specialties. There are about 52,000 people, on average, per neurosurgeon in the US. Thus, towns with notably less than 50,000 people will not typically have a neurosurgeon available. People seeking this type of specialized care in small towns will have to travel to "the big city" for access to a neurosurgeon. Dropping down into the "Other Specialties" part of the table, we find a range from about 7500 people per anesthesiologist to almost 250,000 people per Nuclear Medicine specialist. The latter will generally practice only in cities of a quarter million and more population.

This specialization brings with it both benefits and curses. The benefits are obvious: when you have a rare and complicated disease, it is normally valuable to have a highly capable specialist treating your disorder. If you happen to have a rare tropical infectious disease (acquired, perhaps, in travel), a specialist in tropical medicine will likely do better for you than your family practice doctor. If you acquire breast or prostate cancer, it is good to have somebody absolutely familiar with the most recent treatment options. And so on... for almost every disorder known to medicine.

Yet with this comes the curse of specialization, particularly when the disorders are chronic, rather than acute disorders. Different specialists treat chronic obstructive lung disease, hypertension, diabetes, rheumatoid arthritis, heart diseases, and other common chronic conditions (see Figure 10.6 for the most common). Many people have a number of these conditions. Thus, they commonly have a parallel number of doctors... at least one for each chronic condition, often more. Sometimes they have doctors who specialize in the treatments of the side effects of the other treatments they receive.

Specialists who focus on chronic diseases commonly include practitioners of cardiology, gastroenterology, neurology, physical medicine and rehabilitation, psychiatry, and rheumatology. The "supportive populations" for these specialties range from about 12,000 persons (cardiology) to 22,000 (Gastro-intestinal (GI) disorders), 23,000 (neurology), almost 40,000 (physical medicine and rehabilitation), and 47,000 for rheumatology. This means that in general, anybody living in or near a city of 50,000 or more people will likely have access to most of the medical specialists treating the most important chronic conditions, and the requisite city size drops down to about 25,000 if the chronic condition set does not include rheumatoid arthritis. About 80% of the US population lives in urban areas, which means that the same 80% generally have access to specialty care to treat numerous chronic conditions. The remaining 20% live in rural areas where medical care will typically come through generalist practitioners—family practice doctors, nurse practitioners, and others. Those who live in the urban areas face the benefit and the curse of specialization—their doctors are more specialized in their skills, but their care is more likely to be fragmented, uncoordinated, and sometimes in conflict.

The coordination task

In a world dominated by FFS medical care, few of these specialists either have the knowledge or incentives to worry much about the treatment received from other doctors. First, it does not fall into their domain of expertise. Second, if they venture into those domains, they may face added legal risks (or at least the perception of the heightened risk). Third, they cannot easily bill the insurance plan for extra time to analyze the full range of issues. Fourth, they may well not know all of the drugs prescribed by the other doctors, or even if they do, they may well not fully understand all of the side effects that these drugs might create. And certainly they cannot always master all of the possible drug–drug interaction risks.

They also seldom coordinate medical testing. Each specialist has a battery (for example) of blood tests routinely used to monitor their patient's condition. So each one regularly orders blood tests, often duplicating at least some of the tests recently done by other doctors treating other disorders. Even if they know the results of such tests, they are likely to re-order the tests, since they can bill a bit extra for the blood draw, and they probably have their favorite laboratory to do their tests as well. Laboratories also differ in the way they calibrate some tests, so an HDL measure from one might differ from that of another. So we regularly see re-testing by numerous doctors. Several things can help solve this problem.

Shared electronic health records

First, shared electronic health records (EHRs) can help. The operative word here is "shared" and that unfortunately does not apply to the situation of many patients with chronic diseases. Even if each of their health care providers uses an EHR, this provides no assurance at all that all of the doctors treating all of their chronic (and acute) medical conditions can "see" all of the pertinent medical records. We discuss these issues more extensively in Chapter 12.

True care coordination

To optimize treatment of chronic disease, sharing of health records is probably not enough. Coordinated treatment offers the greatest promise for solving these issues—doctors, nurses, dieticians, pharmacists, and therapists all coordinating their care with a common plan. This is the promise of a new approach to treating chronic disease, a shared approach, a shared medical record, and almost necessarily, a shared compensation. This can happen in complete managed care organizations (Health Maintenance Organizations (HMOs)) that have full responsibility for treating patients, but only poorly in FFS settings. We discuss these issues more fully in a subsequent section (later) and in a later chapter regarding Accountable Care Organizations (ACOs).

Addressing the labor shortage

The aging in the population and growing prevalence of chronic illnesses to treat begs the question: what if there are not enough doctors to treat these patients in the future? One answer is that incentives should be set to increase the production of physicians. However, the production process duration from college senior accepted into medical school to practicing physician is a minimum of seven years for a primary care physician and over ten years for many specialty physicians. Since the 1960s, health care education has permitted another option: nurse practitioners and physicians assistants who can substitute for many of the same tasks performed by physicians today. Furthermore, changes to state-specific scope of practice laws now allow nurse practitioners to perform services once relegated exclusively to physicians such as the prescription of medications. We envision that expansion of non-physician providers—particularly nurse practitioners—can help fill the gap between supply of and need for primary care providers treating patients with multiple chronic conditions.

The best way to address a potential labor shortage in the future of health professionals to treat chronic illness is to encourage new physician and as well as nurse practitioner production as long as they can complement each other through coordinated treatment. This is the best long-term strategy to avoid a scope-of-practice war between physicians and nurse practitioners. In addition, taking advantage of new treatment locations such as retail clinics where nurse practitioners and physicians can cooperate to produce an equivalent quality and lower cost treatment option than physician-only care offers an approach to make chronic care management less expensive and more coordinated.[5] Many retail clinics are linked to stores with pharmacies that have excellent multi-year patient history of patient past pharmacy use as well as adherence to prescriptions for chronic conditions. A further advantage of retail clinics is that they are very easy to deploy compared to a new clinic or hospital urgent care center since their construction is generally tied to a retail store's scale and scope in construction and management.

New payment concepts

The Affordable Care Act (ACA) provided incentives for Medicare program innovations such as bundled payment and full-risk bearing ACOs. We discuss ACOs more fully in a subsequent chapter. However, the challenges of treating a chronically ill population deserve special attention. Currently, Medicare does have Special Needs Plan (SNP) options within Medicare Advantage (MA) plans that address some of these concerns, but to reach the next level, we feel that Medicare must create incentives for a market of MA plans focused on treating the chronically ill. Existing Medicare FFS claims can help identify high multi-comorbid prevalence counties where such an MA population would be offered to give insurers incentives to enter a set of markets.

Furthermore, Medicare could establish a different and likely higher benchmark payment for MA plans focused on chronically ill seniors. These chronically ill focused MA plans must use health information technology (IT) systems that link EHRs, e-prescribing, and their claims data in real time to qualify for payment. Such an advance in MA program design would likely accelerate the spread of MA plans and create an opportunity for health plans and medical providers to jointly deploy a modern health care system that truly seeks to keep the chronically ill as healthy as possible and hopefully stem the pace of incidence of additional comorbidities for a patient. These chronic-illness-focused MA plans would be capitated for an annual period and be benchmarked with linked FFS claims for performance bonuses.

Innovative new managed care plans that focus on patients with chronic conditions need not be limited to Medicare alone. In the under-65 market, the ACA permits states to make experiments to treatment population more effectively and also gives them some control of resources collected by federal penalties for the law after 2018. To be effective, risk adjustment technologies should utilize the combined data stream of pharmacy, EHR, and claims data. Such a required data stream would best be achieved by Medicare setting the example of the value of combined data resources to pave the way for commercial carriers to adopt similar data integration practices. We discuss these combined issues more fully in subsequent chapters.

Medicare's future expenditures might be more efficient with a coordinate and capitated care model. An added bonus would be the adoption of this plan design by commercial carriers to slow the onset of avoidable chronic conditions through treatment and lifestyle intervention from coordinated care models.

Prescription drug adherence, costs, and financing

Many chronic conditions can be controlled well, and their rate of progress slowed considerably, through the use of appropriate prescription and non-prescription drugs. In some cases, simple anti-inflammatory drugs significantly help the patient (non-steroidal anti-inflammatory drugs, aka NSAIDs). Many of the most useful prescription drugs are low-cost generic drugs, often with more high-powered (and much more expensive) non-generic alternatives. For many people with chronic conditions, the costs of these drugs—particularly for those with multiple chronic conditions—creates a large financial burden. Prescription drug coverage emerged over the last few decades from "almost never covered" to a high-priority insurance coverage as the costs and health benefits of drugs increased over time. The creation of Medicare Part D (which began in 2006) signaled a major change in drug coverage for the elderly (who have the greatest burden from chronic conditions), shifting it from the realm of Medigap plans into a new specialized insurance market. Medicare Part D had some major issues (see our discussion in Part II), but even with the new "fixes" in the ACA, the issue of maintenance drugs for chronic conditions still looms large for many people.

Because of this, we discussed in more detail in Chapter 9 a proposal to alter the structure of health insurance plans—with Medicare leading the way—to bypass all deductibles and coinsurance for a subset of chronic-condition maintenance drugs that are either proven to save total costs (which many do) or create health gains at very low cost relative to other alternatives. The key here is to reduce financial barriers to patients' adherence to prescription drug plans. For many important chronic conditions, adherence to prescription plans (mostly involving generic drugs) has high payoff in terms of improving patient health *and* lowering total health care costs, as we discussed previously.[6] The concept has high payoff in the over-65 population, but can readily improve the care of chronic conditions for people of all ages, and, thus, we urge its adoption in the under-65 population as well.

How to reduce the frequency of chronic conditions

It would be unrealistic to believe that we have within our grasp the ability to eliminate chronic conditions, but we can and should take steps to reduce the rates at which they appear. Three approaches seem most useful from our perspective: (1) creation and dissemination of information about the risks and consequences of various lifestyle choices; (2) creating proper incentives for healthy behavior; and (3) creating new ways to help people change their behavior when they wish to do so. In some cases, public policy has assisted in these areas, yet in other cases, it has worked against the desirable outcome of reducing lifestyle behavioral choices that adversely affect health.

Information as prevention

One of the most dramatic changes in the entire realm of public health and lifestyle choices was ignited (a word we choose deliberately) by the Surgeon General's Report on Tobacco in 1965, demonstrating how information, public policy, and private choice all interact. The Surgeon General at the time—Luther Terry, MD—probably did more to save lives and reduce health care costs than any other physician in human history by commissioning the committee's work that created this report. As Figure 10.7 shows, smoking rates plummeted dramatically beginning the year following this report's appearance, and have continued to drop year after year for nearly half a century. The cumulative illness burden saved by this report—and the subsequent changes in public policy and private choices—have been a remarkable public health success story.

What happened, of course, was half a century of change in public laws, business rules, societal attitudes, creation of smoking-cessation aides, a continued program of information provision, and changes in the financial consequences of smoking, including directly the cost of cigarettes, as affected by tax policies and indirectly by changes in such things as the pricing of life insurance, disability insurance, homeowners, insurance, and, in some cases, health insurance.

The first steps came with laws about smoking in public indoor spaces, where state and local bans on smoking led some smokers to quit. Many private

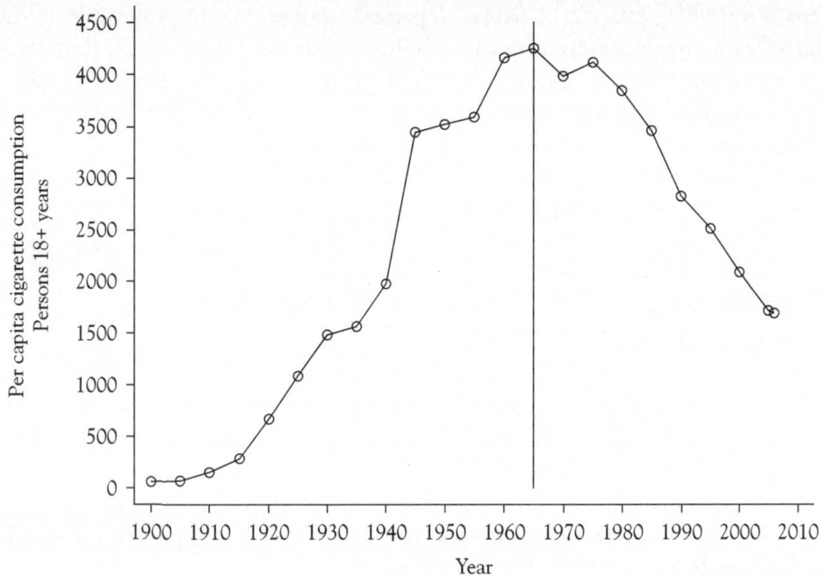

Figure 10.7

Per capita cigarette consumption, United States, years 1900 to 2010
Source: Phelps, 2010

institutions followed suit even when not required by law, expanding the "no smoking" from the indoor environment to wider areas of the surrounding outdoors. Hospitals led this movement in many important ways. Original exemptions from indoor smoking bans for bars and bowling alleys gradually eroded, and smoking bans extended to outdoor settings such as sports arenas. Federal laws limited and then eliminated smoking on airplane flights.

Societal attitudes about smoking also shifted. Smoking was once considered a sign of sophistication. Movies up to the late 1960s almost always put smoking in a positive light in character portrayals of both male and female leads. Writers of all political persuasion and social background glorified smoking. That has all changed.[7] One seldom sees smoking portrayed in such ways now in any art form, and private attitudes have similarly changed. People formerly would routinely smoke when guests in other people's homes, often without asking. Such behavior is now very rare and would generally be seen as wholly inappropriate—indeed, rude—in modern America.

Federal laws about advertising and package labeling of cigarettes have had important effects as well.[8] These laws not only eliminated on-air (and later, cable television) cigarette advertising but also created the counter-smoking ads that are now so familiar, including large-scale support from the advertising industry. State and local laws limited access to cigarettes by minors through such things as "behind the counter" sales rules and elimination of the once-ubiquitous cigarette vending machines, with heavy fines for businesses selling cigarettes to minors. Independent businesses have continued to change policy on their own, including (in early 2014) the startling announcement by the CVS Pharmacy chain that they would no longer sell tobacco products.

We detail this history because it helps illuminate the powerful role of information and its role both in creating public policy and altering private choices. But even with tobacco use, the war is far from won, and with obesity, alcohol and substance abuse, and other behaviors (e.g., impaired or distracted driving) much remains to be done. Here follows a partial catalog of opportunities to help.

Fix the incentives

Our society faces an uncomfortable dilemma, and we do not have a precise solution to resolve it, but we do believe it needs to be discussed and debated—beginning soon. The problem centers on what kinds of incentives we create for people to engage in healthy lifestyles (or conversely, to discourage unhealthy lifestyles). We do not approach this as a question of morality (i.e., are these unhealthy lifestyles somehow sinful or immoral, or even signs of character weakness) but rather (as our book focuses on in general) the importance of setting incentives right.

We begin this discussion with some observations:

- Aside from health insurance, much private insurance builds lifestyle choices into the premiums, generally known as "experience rating." This happens regularly in life insurance, auto insurance, homeowners' insurance, disability insurance, and long-term care insurance.
- Much of the private health insurance market (employer-paid insurance) is generally precluded from using any meaningful experience rating in allocating the costs of employer-paid insurance to employees. Thus, for example, employers treat all employees the same no matter what their age, smoking status, body mass index, and other pertinent personal characteristics. Some of these are precluded directly by labor law (using age, for example, in premium pricing) and others by law, custom, or both. Employers are allowed to use screening for illegal drug use even as a condition of employment, but cannot use body-mass index as a determinant of how much health insurance will cost each employee. Such an act would be construed as discrimination.
- The ACA, while permitting up to a 50% surcharge for smoking in the health insurance exchanges, specifically precludes the use of obesity in the pricing of insurance. Some of these restrictions are desirable—such as the presence of pre-existing conditions (see our discussion in Chapter 6), but others get in the way of moving to a healthier population. The pricing of Medicare Part B, for example, contains no lifestyle incentive structures. It seems inconsistent, for example, to allow smoking surcharges in the

under-65 health insurance exchange market but not to use them in Medicare Part B pricing.
- We know with assurance that prices affect behavior in these issues. Higher prices reduce tobacco, alcohol, and even illicit drug use.[9] Thus increasing the economic incentives to engage in healthier lifestyles can have positive effects on reducing the nation's future chronic disease burden, and hence its health care costs.
- However... and this is a big however... many of these same lifestyle choices have an important genetic component (see discussion in Chapter 6). If a behavior is genetically "hard wired" then it seems wrong to make people pay for the consequences of that "hard wiring."

From all of this, we draw the following observation: there is some appropriate degree to which people pay for the health care consequences of their lifestyle choices, both in private health insurance and in the amounts they pay for Medicare. The correct choice almost surely does not involve 100% recoupment of the cost of lifestyle choices, but similarly, the correct choice almost surely does not involve ignoring the behavior either.

The proper solution to this dilemma will require the research and thinking of people from many disciplines and ways of thinking—economics, genetics, actuarial science, behavioral psychology, pharmacology, history, and most certainly ethics, law, and philosophy. We cannot pretend to know the outcome of this discussion, but we do know that it should begin soon.

Restructure the research engine

Nicotine is one of the most powerful addictive substances known to scientists; quitting smoking is difficult, despite the old quip "It's easy to quit smoking—I've done it many times." But we also know that even the most useful smoking cessation products (e.g., nicotine substitutes such as patches, lozenges, and e-cigarettes) have limited success in helping people quit.

Dieting to lose weight has a similar rate of failure. It is not nearly so hard to lose weight as it is to keep the weight off once it is lost. The most obvious proof of this point is that ads for hundreds (perhaps thousands) of weight-loss pills, programs, and supplements bombard us regularly. An old joke about economists portrays this issue: Two economists are walking down the street together. One reaches over to pick up a $100 bill he sees in the gutter. The other touches his elbow and chides him gently, saying "Tsk. If it were a real $100 bill, somebody would have picked it up already." The same is true of dieting aides. If one approach really dominated the others, we would have only a few offerings, not the multiplicity that we actually see. Somebody would have "picked up" the market.

Smoking and obesity are the most important lifestyle choices at issue, followed next by alcohol abuse, but we should not attribute these issues to moral failure. The choice to smoke, for example, is affected by genetic predisposition, the price of cigarettes (and other tobacco products), the availability of substitutes such as e-cigarettes, public laws and private regulation of indoor smoking, regulation of tobacco advertising, product labeling, peer pressure (both in favor of and against smoking), parental guidance to children, the pricing of various forms of insurance (e.g., discounts for non-smokers for life, health, and homeowners' insurance) and—yes—individual choice. Thus, public policy can have important effects on the rate of smoking participation and total cigarette consumption.

There still remain about 40 million smokers in the US, many of whom wish to but cannot quit. Population survey data show that the proportion of the population overweight and obese is increasing over time and shifting from "overweight" into the more dangerous realms of "obese" and "morbidly obese." They need help, and public policy can provide this help. A new focus within the NIH on research to help resolve these issues will likely yield high dividends in terms of new commercial products and counseling strategies that help people quit smoking permanently.

We have had great success in reducing the ravages of heart disease, cancer and stroke following major investment in NIH research into the fundamental biology of these diseases. We need a similar strategy regarding tobacco addiction and obesity and the lack of exercise. The ongoing (but still incomplete) success of the campaign to reduce smoking gives hope that similar success can be found in other important lifestyle choices, most notably obesity (and lack of exercise) and alcohol abuse.

President Richard Nixon (in 1971) signed the legislation that declared a War on Cancer, the declaration of which reshaped the NIH research strategy and budgeting. In 2015, Vice President Joseph Biden reinforced this idea with a call in late 2015 for a "moon shot" effort to cure cancer. Without denigrating the value of these efforts, we suggest the need for two new similar wars: The War on Tobacco and the War on Obesity. These new "wars" would require reshaping of the strategies of the NIH in their research funding profiles just as Nixon's War on Cancer reshaped the NIH budget and functions in 1971.

The National Institutes of Health (plural) are actually a collection of institutes that focus on different disease areas. The most prominent of these focus on heart disease, cancer, and stroke, the three leading killers of US citizens, first identified in Lyndon Johnson's 1965 effort that created "Regional Medical Programs" and enhanced NIH research to defeat these diseases. Of the approximately $30 billion per year NIH budget, nearly one-third is devoted to these three diseases via the National Cancer Institute (NCI), the National Institute for Heart, Blood and Lung Disease (NIHBL), and the National Institute for Neurological Diseases and Stroke (NINDS), and the total rises to nearly half when we include the National Institute for Allergy and Infectious Diseases (NIAIDS), which is primarily devoted to finding a cure for HIV.

We suggest here that these priorities need substantial realignment. They focus heavily on disease labels—the same ones used in classifying patients when hospitalized or treated by doctors or other practitioners—rather than the true underlying causes of morbidity, mortality, and death. They particularly pay insufficient attention to underlying human behavior that leads to high rates of chronic conditions that in turn carry with them high morbidity, mortality, and death.

The most dramatic way to illustrate this comes from research shown in the path-breaking work of McGinnis and Foege (1993), replicated with more recent data by Mokdad et al. (2004) relating to the "real causes of death." They approached their task in a unique and important way. First, they combed the medical literature to determine the best estimates of excess deaths for some particular human behavior (tobacco smoking, use of illicit drugs, exposure to toxic chemicals, etc.) across all known diseases. Tobacco, for example, creates excess deaths in many forms of cancer, heart disease, hypertension and its sequellae (including kidney disease and heart disease), COPD, and many others. Then they add up the excess deaths compared with non-smokers, and attribute them all to tobacco. They did the same for many other human behaviors. Their "top ten" list accounts for almost half of all deaths in the US in 2000 (Figure 10.8).

How does the NIH budget match up to these "real causes of death"? The answer, unfortunately, is "very poorly." Figure 10.9 shows the percent of all deaths by these types of causes and the proportion of the NIH budget devoted to these issues.[10]

The linkages between NIH spending and the "actual causes of death" categories are not perfect, but the stark message stands out: The NIH budget is aligned in completely different ways than the actual causes of death.[11] To be sure, causes of death are not "everything," but they will almost certainly link closely to morbidity and medical spending as well.

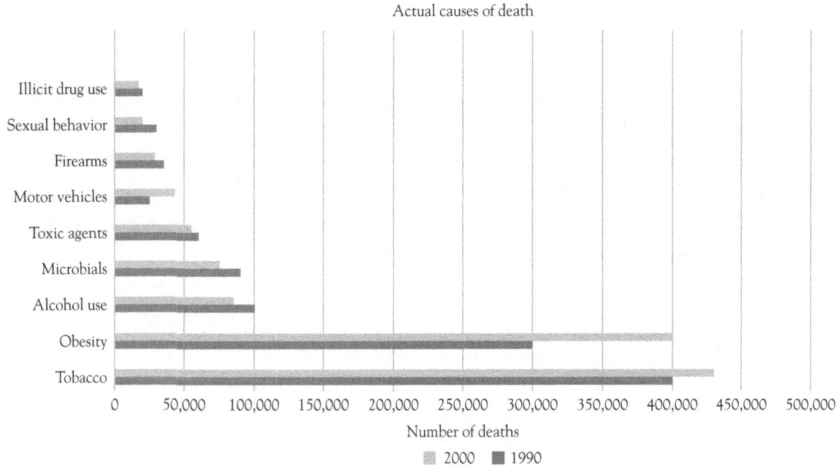

Figure 10.8

Actual causes of death, 1990 and 2000
Source: Derived from data in Mokdad et al., 2004

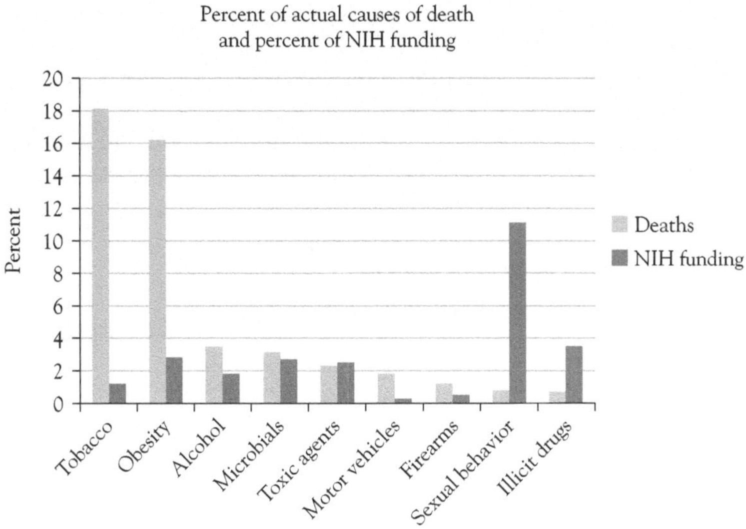

Figure 10.9

NIH funding and percentages of deaths, by actual causes of death
Source: Calculation by authors; actual causes of death data from Mokdad et al., 2004; NIH Budget amounts drawn from Estimates of Funding for Various Research, Condition, and Disease Categories, https://report.nih.gov/categorical_spending.aspx, last accessed February 15, 2015.

The NIH funding strategy aims at understanding the biology of and curing diseases. A more fruitful long-run approach would much more actively aim at preventing them. The NIH spent $5.5 billion on cancer research in 2015, where much of that cancer is caused by tobacco use. On its own website, the NIH has identified $362 million (6.6% of the cancer total) for "tobacco" research. It identifies $1.623 billion for "substance abuse" and a mere $44 million for "substance abuse prevention." It identifies only $156 million for violence research and $1 million for homicide prevention, the two categories most closely linked to firearms deaths. And it identifies only $830 million for obesity research, significant portions of which seem unrelated to the causes or prevention of obesity.

Obesity research deserves particular attention. The NIH has an approach to dealing with obesity that is doomed to failure—they spread the responsibility for obesity issues across the entire NIH without providing any related budget authority. The 2011 Strategic Plan for NIH Obesity Research—its most recent version—devotes 30 pages to describing the NIH efforts to deal with obesity.[12] The entire report contains not a single dollar sign or mention of budgetary authority. Instead of real budgets, we find sections on "crosscutting" and "multifaceted" research.

In this NIH plan, everybody is responsible, which means that nobody is responsible. An old saying goes, "if you assign two people to feed a dog, it will starve to death." Thus it is within the NIH regarding obesity research. The problem goes to the heart of the way the NIH is organized. Each Institute has its own disease focus. The scientific prestige and hence research allocations aim primarily at "fundamental" science that will cure (or occasionally will prevent) the disease of focus to each institute. But tobacco and obesity have consequences that do not occur in single organ systems or disease categories. Their effects are ubiquitous. Hence the current NIH approach is doomed to failure. Focused research requires focused budgetary authority. This cannot happen with the current NIH budgeting strategy.

To fix this problem, the NIH must either re-organize to create *major* institutes focused on disease prevention or (more plausibly) have legislation sequester funds from the existing institutes (or add new funds, or some combination thereof) that get into the hands of a prevention "czar" who can direct research towards disease prevention. This need not be done instantly (that would overly disrupt ongoing research teams) but can and should occur as a major shift in the way the NIH budget priorities are set over time.

Conclusions

To reiterate our message on chronic diseases, we provide the following summary:

- The changing age profile of the US population inevitably leads to increasing disease burden and treatment costs from the rapid growth in chronic conditions.
- Reducing the rate of chronic disease incidence and prevalence requires major changes in public policy that: (a) increase the incentives to avoid deleterious lifestyle choices; (b) provide more and better information to help inform consumer decisions; (c) increase biomedical research to help understand the genetic and biological pathways to chronic disorders; and (d) develop new ways to help people alter their lifestyles when they wish to do so (medications, devices, educational programs, etc.)
- We must shift the ways we treat chronic diseases to encompass integrated medical records and enhanced collaboration among health care providers of all types. Achieving this goal will almost certainly require shifts away from current FFS financing. Medicare and Medicaid can and should take the lead in finding new approaches for treating chronic conditions and implementing these approaches rapidly. As with other important health care financing changes in the past half century (e.g., hospital and physician reimbursement) the private sector will rapidly follow useful changes made in Medicare.
- Restructure Medicare insurance coverage (Parts B, C, and D) to provide free access to prescription drugs and other secondary prevention interventions that deal effectively with chronic conditions, either by delaying their onset or reversing their consequences.

Notes

1 *Health*, 2015, Table 39. Available at www.cdc.gov/nchs/data/hus/hus15.pdf, last accessed August 7, 2017.
2 Source: www.alz.org/alzheimers_disease_causes_risk_factors.asp, last accessed August 7, 2017.
3 Economist and Nobel Laureate George Stigler published an extensive economic analysis of this single sentence from Adam Smith. See Stigler, 1951.
4 This analysis follows a concept originally developed by Hotelling (1929) described as spatial competition. This approach was applied specifically to analyze physician location by Newhouse et al., 1982a, 1982b.
5 Spetz et al., 2013.
6 Roebuck et al., 2011.
7 A similar shift took place with regard to drunk driving and public drunkenness. The "happy drunk" of the Red Skelton era has vanished. Drunk driving seldom if ever now appears in a humorous way in movies, television, or literature. These shifts in attitude both follow public sentiment and sometimes create it.
8 The most important law was the Public Health Cigarette Smoking Act, signed into law by President Nixon in 1970.
9 Regarding tobacco, Becker et al., 1991, 1994, Chaloupka, 1991, Baltagi and Griffin, 2001, Gruber and Kosegi, 2001. Regarding alcohol, Cook and Tauchen, 1982, Chaloupka et al., 1998, 2002. Regarding illicit drugs, Becker et al., 1991, van Ours, 1995.
10 The NIH budget data are approximations that assign NIH spending to "actual causes" categories as close as NIH data classifications in their budget documents permit. The NIH data come from http://report.nih.gov/categorical_spending.aspx, last accessed February 20, 2015. Details of assignment available from authors upon request.
11 The spending patterns for these "actual causes" (tobacco and obesity most importantly) have a common theme: They greatly under-spend on substances that are legal (tobacco and alcohol and food) and overspend on things that one would normally consider illegal (notably illicit drugs). The unusually high rate of spending (relative to deaths) for sexual activity appears because the original Mokdad et al. (2004) study classified AIDS deaths as relating to sexual behavior, not microbial agents, so we classified AIDS-related research similarly. The disparity between funding on tobacco and alcohol vs. that on illicit drugs (compared with the deaths attributable to these behaviors) leads us to conclude that we are fighting the wrong drug war.
12 www.niddk.nih.gov/about-niddk/strategic-plans-reports/Pages/strategic-plan-NIH-obesity-research.aspx, last accessed June 16, 2017.

11 Bringing health care waste, fraud, and abuse technology into the 21st century

The possible magnitude of health care fraud and abuse (F&A) staggers the imagination. Industry experts' estimates of the costs for F&A range from tens to hundreds of billions of dollars yearly. In 2002, a study by the (now-named) Government Accountability Office (GAO) estimated that one out of every seven dollars paid to Medicare is lost to fraud.[1] Health policy experts Berwick and Hackbarth provide a *lower bound* estimate for waste, fraud, and abuse of 20% of health care spending.[2] While fraud can be committed by patients, analysis suggests that the vast majority is perpetrated by health care providers.[3]

In testimony before the United States Senate Committee on the Judiciary, on May 20, 2009, Malcolm K. Sparrow, a prominent expert on fraud, said that health care fraud and abuse costs hundreds of billions of dollars per year, with the actual figure anywhere from $100 billion to $400 or $500 billion.[4] That year, total health care spending in the United States was about $2.5 trillion, so Sparrow's estimates span a range from 4% to 20% of total spending, with a midpoint of about one out of every eight dollars. Thus—without quibbling about which estimate is better—we have reasonable evidence that the problem is huge. These estimates converge to something like one out of every seven or eight dollars arising from fraud and abuse. To put it in a different perspective, Sparrow's midpoint estimate of $300 billion represents about $1000 for every man, woman, and child in the United States. Each of us is being robbed of $1000 a year, and the efforts to fix the problem are archaic and (demonstrably) ineffective.

The next generation waste, fraud, and abuse solution for health care needs to be implemented for the entire health insurance market. The Centers for Medicare and Medicaid Services (CMS) can and should lead the way with Medicare and Medicaid, but the best solution involves all health insurance companies working together. Separate, piecemeal approaches cannot fully succeed; collaboration can work.

The current approach—using edits on a post-payment basis—catches mostly policy errors and not fraud-rings or providers or consumers who are exploiting the health care system for their own gain. The ideal prevention system needs to be transaction-based and must assess claims on a real-time basis and before a payment is made. This will dissuade perpetrators and abusers from committing acts in the first place and significantly reduce and even eliminate some of the expensive recovery efforts. The basis for moving into the 21st century simply requires the use of proven technology from Financial Services that can be leveraged and effectively utilized in health care for cost-effective waste, fraud, and abuse identification and prevention.

The ideal system

The ideal waste, fraud, and abuse system must be holistic. It must be able to view all the provider and patient activities across multiple payers. It has to integrate into the existing health care claims flow with minimal effort, time, and cost. The system can and should be modeled after what is used in the Financial Services industry. That system utilizes integrated real-time transaction risk scoring and referral strategy capabilities to identify claims that are statistically unusual.

An Appendix to this chapter sets out in more detail the structure of an ideal waste, fraud, and abuse detection system. In brief, it must involve a modularized architecture that is accessed from a common resource (vs. requiring all users to regularly install and coordinate upgrades). The data bank must contain records from all insurers—both public and private—in a common format that will allow analysis of provider behavior across all payment systems. The common data resource must be a third party trusted by health care providers, insurers, and patients alike.

The fraud detection system must work in real time—just as the credit card fraud detection system does now in the Financial Services sector—with predictive algorithms developed to help classify transactions as legitimate or fraudulent. And it must not interfere with the standard delivery of health care, any more than the Financial Services sector's fraud detection systems limit legitimate financial transactions.

The task list

The set of requirements summarized here and detailed in the Appendix to this chapter may seem daunting, but the mechanisms to do this—as we have noted already—exist in abundance in the Financial Services sector, where credit card companies came together on their own to solve a mutually-shared problem.

One might ask why the same "coming together" has not happened in the world of health care to solve the waste, fraud, and abuse problem. The answer is simple: although authorized (and indeed, required) to fix the problem, CMS has made little to no meaningful movement to fix its own waste, fraud, and abuse problem, and has taken no action at all (and it is not authorized to do so) to work with the private sector to find mutually supportive solutions. The Financial Services sector did not have a large component of the transactions residing in a federal government program, and hence did not have to wait for the government to come to the table. The health care sector has just the opposite situation, where Medicare is the largest gorilla in the forest. Nothing can happen until CMS gets actively involved.

The Affordable Care Act (ACA) did include some provisions to reduce fraud. For example, section 6402 of the ACA allows CMS's Office of the Inspector General (OIG) greater access to and uses of data for conducting oversight and law enforcement activities, exempting OIG from the prohibitions against matching data across programs in the Computer Matching and Privacy Protection Act, and it authorizes OIG to enter into data sharing agreements with the Social Security Administration (SSA). Section 6401 of the ACA requires the Secretary to establish procedures for screening providers and suppliers participating in Medicare, Medicaid, and the Children's Health Insurance Program (CHIP).

While the ACA provided some resources for fraud mitigation, the real key to potential future success could come from the Small Business Jobs Act of 2010.[5] Section 4241 of that Act authorizes the Secretary of the Department of Health and Human Services (DHHS) to use predictive modeling and other analytics technologies to identify improper claims for reimbursement and to prevent the payment of such claims under the Medicare fee for service program. The statute provides that the predictive modeling program should capture Medicare provider and beneficiary activities across the Medicare program to provide a comprehensive view of all providers, beneficiaries, and geographies within the program. The goal is to identify and analyze provider networks, provider billing patterns, and beneficiary utilization patterns, and to use that information to detect patterns and networks that represent a high risk of fraudulent activity.

The statute specifically requires DHHS to: (1) analyze large data sets for unusual or suspicious patterns or anomalies or contain other factors that are linked to the occurrence of waste, fraud, or abuse and undertake such analysis before payment is made; (2) prioritize such identified transactions for additional review before payment is made in terms of the likelihood of potential waste, fraud, and abuse to more efficiently utilize investigative resources; (3) capture outcome information on adjudicated claims for reimbursement to allow for refinement and enhancement of the predictive analytics technologies on the basis of such outcome information, including post-payment information about the eventual status of a claim; and (4) prevent the payment of claims for reimbursement that have been identified as potentially wasteful, fraudulent, or abusive until such time as the claims have been verified as valid. The statute also requires that the predictive modeling program be integrated into the existing Medicare fee for service program claims flow with minimal effort and maximum efficiency.[6]

Congress appropriated $100 million for the program, beginning January 1, 2011, until expended.[7] Further, the statute permits the Secretary of DHHS to waive such provisions of titles XI, XVIII, XIX, and XXI of the Social Security Act, including applicable prompt payment requirements under titles XVIII and XIX of the Act, as the Secretary determines to be appropriate to carry out the program.[8]

Much of what we urge could take place within the context of this already-extant guidance from the Congress. We do not know the best way to bring CMS into compliance with the current law. Perhaps it requires more direct Congressional oversight. Perhaps a "whistleblower" could initiate action from within, claiming that CMS has wasted billions of taxpayer dollars by not following through on the current Congressional mandate. But the mechanisms to solve the problem both appear to exist and seem to have lain fallow.

Almost certainly, the one new step required to get to a fully integrated fraud detection system would be legislation that both authorizes and requires CMS and TRICARE (the health insurance plan for armed forces active duty and retirees) *and* all private health insurers of all types (group, non-group, Medicare Advantage, Medigap, and any other) to submit common-format claims for central analysis. Thus, we offer a specific proposal:

> **Proposal 5:** *Create new legislation requiring CMS and all private insurers to place all claims data (in a common format) into a central data bank that can be used for active detection of fraud and abuse, following the model of the Financial Services sector in detecting credit card fraud. In the same legislation, strengthen the existing requirements for CMS to follow through on currently enabled fraud detection efforts.*

Once the legislative mandate exists requiring every insurer to cooperate, we can anticipate that competing organizations will emerge to carry out the tasks of the "ideal system" as specified in this chapter's Appendix. Only one "data pool" is necessary, but from that reservoir of data, we can readily envision multiple companies or consortia attacking the problem with different algorithms and approaches. Competition will be our friend here.

Algorithms in this system are essentially diagnostic tests designed to classify transactions into "good" or "needs action," just as diagnostic medical tests seek to sort patients into categories of "healthy" and "sick." And just as with all diagnostic tests, classification errors will happen. A long literature exists to determine the best way to "operate" such tests, balancing the anticipated costs of false positive and false-negative classifications.[9] The same can be applied to detection of fraud and abuse.

All of the fraud-detection algorithms will improve over time. They will not drive fraudulent and wasteful behavior to zero—indeed, it is not optimal to do so[10]—but when done properly, hopefully approaching the attributes of our "ideal system," it will go a long way towards reducing waste, fraud, and abuse, and thereby lowering the health care bills and taxes to support Medicare and Medicaid.

Notes

1 General Accounting Office ("GAO"), Report to Congressional Committees, Medicare Fraud and Abuse: DOJ Continues to Promote Compliance with False Claims Act Guidance, April 2002.
2 Berwick and Hackbarth, 2012.
3 Coalition Against Insurance Fraud. "Go Figure: fraud data." www.insurancefraud.org/stats.htm, last accessed July 27, 2009.
4 Sparrow, May 20, 2009.
5 42 U.S.C. 1320a-7m. Available at www.gpo.gov/fdsys/pkg/USCODE-2010-title42/pdf/USCODE-2010-title42-chap7-subchapXI-partA-sec1320a-7m.pdf, last accessed August 7, 2017.
6 42 U.S.C. 1320a-7m(b)(3).
7 42 U.S.C 1320a-7m(h)(1).
8 These titles of the Social Security Act cover General Provisions, Peer Review, and Administrative Simplification; Health Insurance for the Aged and Disabled; Grants to States for Medical Assistance Programs; State Children's Health Insurance Program; respectively.
9 See, for example, Phelps and Mushlin, 1988 and references therein.
10 Darby and Karni, 1973.

12 Towards a functional electronic health record—soon

The way we were ... and are

One of the most common statements about the health of the US health economy is "the system is broken." Whether stated by the President of the Mayo Clinic or the chief executive officer (CEO) of United Health Group, we hear this common refrain often. And just as the doom and gloom of our current state of affairs is articulated, a shaft of brilliant, bright wonderful light breaks through the darkness to lead the health care system to salvation. It is the salvation of tomorrow made available through health information technology (IT). When might we expect to actually have a usable system?

Past discussions of the Electronic Health Record (EHR) have tended to blur two important but different goals. One goal seeks to create a unified and comprehensive patient record—spanning all provider and other potentially useful data sources—to improve individual patient care outcomes. The second goal seeks to grade providers on their quality of care—focused (at least currently) on using within-organization data, with the goal of adjusting provider payments based on quality outcomes. CMS had moved extensively in this direction in recent years. While these goals are not mutually exclusive, and indeed, reinforce one another, they are separate goals with their own distinct requirements.

Since 2004, the US government has invested billions to spur the growth of health IT, mostly with a focus towards the second goal—grading provider performance for payment adjustment. The largest outlay of expenditure occurred in 2009 with the federal stimulus Bill. Federal resources have created a new agency, the Office of the National Coordinator of Health Information Technology (ONC) to further advance the direction of the nascent health IT industry.

The good news is that the industry has responded. American hospitals and clinics are adopting EHR systems very rapidly. For one reason, as part of the American Recovery and Reinvestment Act (ARRA) of 2009, the US government tied financial incentives to "Meaningful Use." As the overall changes in the Affordable Care Act (ACA) grow, pressure will continue to grow for health care care providers to adopt EHR systems with the intention of improving quality and patient outcomes and reducing cost. This effort from providers, albeit fragmented and largely uncoordinated, has illuminated some of the true potential in nation-wide interconnected health IT systems, but also exposed the gaps in the existing processes and pathways.

"Meaningful use" does not necessarily equate to "shared use." At present, the "meaningful use" guidelines are not sufficiently assertive either in advancing full data sharing (more about this issue follows) or in use of evidence-based care through proven features like computer-assisted support to help find the right medical intervention for a patient. And progress towards the "better patient care" goal has done little to help in achieving the other—universally available EHRs spanning all providers for all patients.

By early 2017, 93% of all doctors actively used an EHR, and 77% had demonstrated meaningful use of government-certified EHR technology.[1] Unfortunately, the current pathway focuses most intensively on ways to use EHR for grading providers' performance (and hence adjusting payments with quality outcomes). The other goal—providing a unified and comprehensive EHR to improve patient outcomes with full data sharing—remains elusive.

Towards a better solution—today

Is it possible to build a comprehensive health IT infrastructure in just a few years—not decades—a system that patients could access *and* payers could use to reward high quality care? We believe that the answer to this question is at least a tentative "yes." To make the case, we set forth some assumptions about the existing state of the health IT world and we then describe how systems can be taken off the shelf and combined to create a genuinely useful health IT solution that gets much if not most of what patients want: a solution that can make a real difference in their care. We can start right now.

Five assumptions are required to support the thesis that health IT is ready for widespread application today, both for treating patients and adjusting provider payments to reflect quality outcomes.

The first assumption is that much of the necessary clinical and financing data are already present in our health care provider and health care financing systems.

The second assumption is that available data can be connected by patients (or their surrogates) by formally requesting that their data be aggregated for their own purposes and benefit. This step has not yet happened in health care, but (as we discuss later) seems to be a relatively straightforward step using proven methods from the financial services sector.

The third assumption is that third-party data aggregators exist today who can take on tasks independent of insurers and providers. These third-party data aggregating entities take disparate information about any person and are "trusted" with linking data elements (e.g., name, social security number, address) to merge the information to create a comprehensive set of information on a patient or consumer. As with the second assumption, this step has not yet happened, but seems to be a relatively straightforward step from existing systems in other service sectors (financial services, internet providers, social media).

A comprehensive EHR would include not only medical records from providers (doctors, nurse practitioners, therapists) but also from pharmacy purchases, and perhaps even data from newly emerging health and activity monitoring systems that are now readily available, sensing data such as heart rate, sleep activity, exercise effort, and more. Other sources can add fruitfully to a person's EHR even if they do not immediately refer to the individual in question. For example, social media feeds have become a source of information for tracking down the progress of emerging infectious disease outbreaks, a concept highlighted at a February 2012 international conference at Harvard University.[2]

Outside of the health care industry, data aggregation like this already occurs in the financial services industry in several settings. Credit bureaus act as trusted third parties to aggregate summarize information used for underwriting consumer and commercial loans. Financial planners aggregate data across people's entire financial portfolios to plan retirement strategies. These are but a few of the available illustrations of non-health care firms playing a critical third-party aggregator role.

This brings us to the fourth assumption—that the data and systems actually exist today and can be used to generate metrics of health care quality—for use in Goal #2 (grading health outcomes to adjust provider payments). One of the central goals of both Democratic and Republication initiatives within CMS is to pay providers based on high quality care. And yet one of the central arguments to invest in health IT is that we don't have the data to create quality of care metrics.

Which one is right? After two decades of calls for better health IT, we believe that there has been sufficient infrastructure development to move forward and use what has been built today to measure quality. Indeed, CMS is doing it regularly to pay for an increasing fraction of Medicare claims.

Thus, we believe, achieving Goal #2 (providers paid on quality of care outcomes) is well on the way to being met. Continuous improvement will make these metrics better and extend them to more and more of the medical care rendered in US hospitals, clinics, and eventually in outpatient physician office settings. Goal #1—a unified medical record at the individual patient level—remains more elusive. We turn our attention next to ways to achieve this goal as well.

How far have we come?

The fifth necessary assumption to create a fully functional medical records system is that methods exist to allow full data access by patients. We turn to these issues next.

Provider-based systems

The health IT industry today is made up of a set of vendors who create products for clinical and non-clinical users of the systems. The products are mostly designed to aid data entry for later analysis or treatment or facilitate billing. The vendors in the health IT industry represent some of the largest publicly-traded firms in the nation, including McKesson and General Electric. Each vendor has a premiere branded system that they sell to medical providers.[3]

The key role of each of these vendors is to provide software for medical providers to record their interactions with patients, and in turn to guide clinical care. The data are then stored on site at the institution or ported to a secure cloud-based data repository. They all have regular backups. Many of the vendors have preferred to not use the cloud in the past in order to maximize equipment installation revenue at customer institutions. However, price competition among the vendors is forcing a reorientation towards the cloud. This reorientation presents a valuable opportunity for data aggregators to create far more comprehensive patient histories for cloud-based computing platforms, versus the current model where all the data are held in a proprietary fashion by the vendors or the provider.

Non-traditional data streams

Once the health IT systems are installed, there are both traditional and non-traditional sources of existing data that can help improve patients' health—reaching towards the elusive Goal #1. The traditional data sources are pharmacies, hospitals, and physicians/clinics. The large retail pharmacy chains and providers today all use a common data system developed in the 1990s. All have supported access to real-time data on patients' e-prescribing history for half a decade or more.

Outside of group health or salaried managed care organization combining clinical and administrative data on a real-time basis, the state of the world for an overwhelming majority of the health insurance private and public contracts is less encouraging: incomplete and unconnected medical and health records.[4]

Even those data systems that exist deal poorly (if at all) with other opportunities to incorporate data that could improve patient well-being. None of these "outside source" data feeds are essential to build the first-stage comprehensive medical record, but all can be fruitfully added at later dates.

Social media websites such as Facebook and Google+ could provide conduits for data from three avenues. The first are mobile data applications that could provide real-time data to a personal health record that could be shared with a provider or insurer, data ranging from personal location and movement to regular feeds from implantable medical devices with limited-field wireless transmission.

The second avenue for data creation is personal entry of data for fine-tuning diagnoses and treatment responses. Although many concerns regarding data privacy come to mind, this could be a generational concern, particularly given the willingness (indeed, eagerness) for many individuals within the millennial generation to share personal information.

The third option could use data feeds from social media to track emerging health risks facing individuals, e.g., food poisoning outbreaks at restaurants, influenza, or other outbreaks spread at large public gatherings (sports events, concerts, conferences...), perhaps combined with active data from smartphones and other devices as to an individual's location.

Many internet-based services exist that already use personal location fruitfully, mostly aimed at enhancing the individuals' dining, transportation, or shopping options. We see no reason why these could not also extend to health-improving applications (such as noting that a person had been at a concert where an outbreak had emerged or dined at a restaurant that had become a known source of food poisoning).

The role of Clinical Decision Support (CDS) systems

Fully featured EHR systems can do more than move medical records, images, and data rapidly. They can also provide immediate decision support to health care providers and patients. Good steps have been made to identify the key features of such systems.[5] As long as a decade ago, Clinical Decision Support (CDS) was moving into real-time clinical practice.[6] These systems can protect against drug errors, guide providers towards better and less wasteful uses of medical technologies, and assist providers and patients in working through complex treatment options.[7] The interoperability standards to make this work are essentially in place, and can readily extend from the hospital into the ambulatory setting.[8] Nothing stands in the way of our making better use of these systems to improve patient care and reduce cost, perhaps except for our own inertia. We turn to this issue next.

What stands in the way? Barriers to success

Privacy issues

Several significant barricades arise to *using* data available today for health care system improvements. First on the list is consumer privacy. Consumers may feel their right to health data privacy is paramount even if that comes at a cost of their data not being adequately shared between providers/patient. If so, consumers must realize that they are taking a personal health risk as data become more connected and treatment protocols are customized with an array of interconnected data.

A similar privacy issue is the medical provider's desire for privacy. This is a very real concern, especially for mental health providers. What we see emerging here is a risk–risk tradeoff. Health risks can be lowered but only at the expense of increased privacy risks. The proper adjustment point on that teeter-totter will almost surely be individually defined, so we argue that individual consumers should control those decisions.

Data ownership

Providers/hospitals feel they own the data and do not want to share the information to reveal how their performance would compare to others, and could easily see wider sharing of medical record data as a source of increasing medical malpractice suits. This concern is mostly misplaced—if a consumer has a problem leading to a lawsuit, the medical records are fully discoverable anyway.

Of course, just the reverse may also be true—patients may find (after reading a record) that their care was within normal bounds, and decide not to sue, when otherwise they might have had to sue to gain access to the records. Or they may feel the need to launch a lawsuit just to be able to see their records, in which case the secrecy is self-defeating. We suspect that defense attorneys working for health care providers will opt for secrecy in general, but they may well be wrong. The only way to tell is to change behavior and see what happens, and few providers will want to be the first-mover on that issue.

Another set of data owners are insurers. These companies also may not want to share the data so that consumers or providers could see what care truly costs relative to peer institutions as well as compared to premium expense. Furthermore, some private insurers commoditize the data for sale as part of a profitable market research activity serving medical product and pharmaceuticals' development and marketing.

Technical issues

A third concern is technical, but is slowly being overcome. The issue is that the technology platforms are not fully compatible for data sharing. However, as more data move to a secure cloud-based environment—either within a firm's "walls" or through leased third-party data centers outside of the firm—this barrier will fall.

As with other health care innovations, Medicare is often the key to moving adoption across the industry. The ACA requires standardized extracts of all "Medicare claims under parts A, B, and D be made available to 'qualified entities' for the evaluation of the performance of providers of services and suppliers." As of 2017, only 17 organizations had been identified by CMS as Qualified Entities who will be able to create publicly-available quality and efficiency reporting, six of which are qualified to operate nationally. The most recent addition to the list came in March 2017.[9] Unfortunately, while the ACA is creating new initiatives that will provide for the sharing of data, it falls short in not providing any assurance that the resulting analytics will be anything different than what is currently available.

Financing

The final barrier is financing. Ideally, consumers should have the ability to see without restriction at a small fee or possibly even own their data. Payment for the data operational costs could readily be funded through the health insurance premium structure, or through separate fees to third parties, treated similarly to fees for mobile smartphone use or satellite or cable television service. The data could be available on a demand basis like a credit report service or financial services reports. No single approach need be adopted universally; we expect to see experimentation and evolution on this front in much the same way that competition has created different (and evolving) models of telephone and internet access, both stationary, mobile, and combined. We need not specify the best models; they will emerge on their own.

A bridge to rapid deployment

The key to a rapid transition to a health IT world of substantial and immediate value is to bridge the multiple existing data sources together to see how much of the complete patient picture already exists. For example, if all of the data sources mentioned—including the hospital providers—were all combined, it is likely a patient's data might be far more complete than any one single source, including even what best-in-practice systems such as Kaiser Permanente and Intermountain health systems could provide. Multiple sources can help make something possible and fill in gaps—where one hole is present, another source can fill. This approach will never achieve perfection, but it is better than what we have now, which has been documented to kill many people (statistically speaking).[10]

The connection of multiple data sources will require willful cooperation. Cooperation will only be possible with common interest in the value of complete data for the business of health among patient, provider, insurer and vendor interests. To date, major health care providers have driven the clinical dimension of health IT investment in search of a perfect system for use within their own organizational boundaries.

Two key activities will accelerate the journey to a functional health IT network that meets Goal #1, both with prior precedents. First, there need to emerge Trusted Third Parties (TTPs) that allow consumers to own or have at least unrestricted access to their health IT data in all its forms and from all its sources. Credit bureaus already link and tie data to people without their knowledge, and it is legal. Financial planners link data from numerous financial resources for individuals to provide a comprehensive overall view of their financial status. The key is to extend the data stream to medical data as well. The data-aggregators that will emerge in the waste-fraud-abuse fight (see Chapter 11) may become active players in the health IT world as well.

Second, we also must consider the incentives for participation by consumers. It is plausible that privacy may have a price: If the willingness to share personal data leads to a reduction in health insurance premiums, the market may accelerate the shift towards shared data. The key question is whether providers' access to the information lowers health care costs sufficiently to lead to a reduced premium—a question that cannot be answered without "running the experiment." In effect, if shared data systems do reduce health care costs, then a willingness to share data will become a consumer attribute in the setting of health insurance premiums, just as age, type of car, and past driving record are factors in the pricing of automobile insurance.

A few key steps necessary will help make this happen. Patients must own or at least have full access to their own data through TTPs. Next, the cloud needs to be used to connect the data through trusted-third-party technologies. Consumer access to data must be made simple through existing consumer platforms that consumers actually use like social media websites.

We think it unlikely that any system will emerge that requires compulsory data sharing for all patients. Our nation's history is so firmly tied to freedom and privacy that we cannot envision mandatory linkage of medical records—at least in our lifetimes. Thus (we presume) participation by patients (consumers) will be voluntary (either an opt-in or opt-out system). There remains a separate question as to whether providers and insurers can remain out, or if their participation must ultimately be mandatory. We believe at this point that mandating provider participation (when patients so request) may be essential.

The central issues are more political than technical. Three political tasks remain to get to fully integrated EHRs that help fulfill Goal #1 (integrated individual patient records with ubiquitous access as determined by the individual patient): (1) defining property rights and digital management rights so everybody in the system knows what to expect; (2) providing legal assurance that participants in this endeavor will not be unduly harmed for good-faith efforts, just as we have provided legal protection for people performing emergency medical assistance to those in dire need; (3) setting the incentives properly to get all parties involved—health care providers, health insurers, and patients (consumers).

How does record sharing occur now?

To think about getting to a widely shared EHR, let us first consider how medical information gets shared currently. The first answer is "slowly, incompletely, and seldom—if ever—do patients see their entire medical record." Medical records are often held by providers as closely as are corporate strategic documents, political campaign strategy plans, and game plans for the Super Bowl.

How does this "slow" system work? This discussion implicitly assumes a Primary Care Provider (PCP)—things are worse for people without a PCP. Currently, PCPs in essence serve as the data-aggregators for their patients. Before the emergence of electronic records, their paper-based files were the closest thing available to a comprehensive medical record. They are not "trusted third parties" since they are in fact "agents" in the direct doctor–patient (principal–agent) relationship, but they are at least generally "trusted."

In this paper-based environment (and even in an EHR environment with provider-specific systems), when a patient sees a specialist, the knowledge gained during the specialty visit may or may not get back into the PCP's records. If the PCP made the referral in the first place, the specialist will typically send a *summary* report to the PCP with the specialist's findings. Historically, these were transmitted by mail, then by fax, later perhaps as a PDF attached to an email (with higher resolution than a fax permits), and now the possibility emerges of electronic trading of information. But by whatever physical system, the PCP's records commonly serve as the "trusted party" repository of medical information.

PCPs—who are increasingly salaried or exclusively contracted to hospitals or clinics with EHR systems—should have better access to patient data than their state of affairs in a world exclusively composed of paper. However, with the rare exception of large multi-hospital chains such as Hospital Corporation of America or Health Maintenance Organizations (HMOs) such as Kaiser Permanente or Intermountain, the data usually remain primarily on the PCP's hospital's system and do not easily interconnect with another hospital, patient by patient.

If the patient has gone to the specialist without a direct PCP referral, the report will still often get back to the PCP, since specialists routinely ask who a patient's PCP is, and routinely send reports. Since most diagnostic imaging studies are now recorded digitally, not just the report of the study (the imaging specialist's interpretation of the images) but the images themselves can *in concept* follow the patients, either back to the PCP or even in the hands of the patients themselves. Many diagnostic imaging centers now routinely provide patients with CD or DVD disks containing not only the full array of diagnostic images but also built-in software to view these images.

With a few counter-examples, the information flow in this model is essentially one-way. The referring PCP may give a brief indication of the reason for the referral (e.g., "low back pain," or "persistent acid reflux," or "chest pain upon exertion") but essentially never does the specialist have available the entire medical history of the patient. So the specialist does not know for sure what medications the patient takes regularly (although many ask, and sometimes may receive a complete and correct answer). The specialist may also not know much about the full array of chronic conditions that each patient brings to the encounter, some of the treatments of which may interact with the disease focus of the specialist to whom the patient is being referred. The operative presumption should be that medical records are incomplete, often badly so.

What happens when a patient moves to a new location (or otherwise changes PCP)? In the world of paper records (or with proprietary, non-connected EHRs), if the patient so requests, the previous PCP (usually for a fee) will send a paper *copy* of the medical records to the new PCP. The original PCP will normally retain the original (e.g., for medical–legal reasons), and may well send that original version to some TTP such as Iron Mountain, RecordNations, or Access (or many others that exist) for permanent storage (and retrieval, as necessary). In concept, the new PCP then has access to all of the patient's past history—at least as recorded by the original PCP, and the previous PCP has access to the records via retrieval from the TTP storage facility.

Of course, unless the patient requests the record transfer, the new PCP has no previous history of the patient (and will probably conduct and bill an extensive visit to create an initial "history and physical exam" record). We need not dwell upon the obvious fact that the fee for service payment system encourages such behavior.

But holes probably have already appeared in the record. Some of the handwritten material—barely legible to the doctor who wrote it—will be illegible to any other mortal, including the new PCP. Perhaps only portions of the record were sent along, rather than the entire file. Perhaps only written records, but not imaging films, were sent along. Gaps happen.

In almost no cases will doctors turn over even a copy of the medical records directly to their patients. By current standards, the doctor (or hospital, or whomever) "owns" the record. For example, the code of ethics of the American Medical Association (AMA) states the following about patient access to records:

> E . 7.02. Notes made in treating a patient are primarily for the physician's own use *and constitute his or her personal property*. However, on request of the patient, a physician should provide a copy *or a summary* of the record to the patient or to another physician, an attorney, or other person designated by the patient. Most states have enacted statutes that authorize patient access to medical records. These statutes vary in scope and mechanism for permitting patients to review or copy medical records... The record is a confidential document involving the patient–physician relationship and should not be communicated to a third party without the patient's prior written consent, unless required by law or to protect the welfare of the individual or the community... Physicians may charge a reasonable fee for copying medical records. ... Updated June 1994. *[italics indicate our emphasis]*

Note the emphasis in the AMA's statement on property rights. The AMA says that the doctor owns the records, but also admits that the patient has at least a partial property right to obtain copies (or summaries) of the records, and also control over how these records are to be shared. But the discussion properly focuses the issue on the definition and enforcement of property rights.

This sets the stage for thinking about a world with completely shared EHRs. It involves (as the AMA's statement discusses) several components: (a) who owns the record; (b) under what conditions may/must the doctor share it; (c) what laws govern patients' rights to see the record; and (d) that the doctor has the right to a reasonable fee for making copies. All of what we have now in paper record systems can carry forward to the digital world with little modification.

How would this happen in an EHR world?

The simple answer is "much the same, except much faster, more completely, more legibly, and with assured patient access to the data." In the world we envision, patients would have full control over where their medical record went and who could see it. One major difference would emerge: instead of PCPs (where they exist) serving as the central aggregators of medical information, we envision the emergence of multiple TTP firms in this new IT space, competing on price, reliability, data security, and ease of patients' access to their own records. This provides an excellent example of the benefits of specialization: doctors practice medicine but leave IT operations to those trained in that field. You should not want your physician to be your IT specialist, and you should not want your TTP practicing medicine on you or your family.

In this new world, consumers would specify their own health data TTP, which they could change at will, to maintain current copies of the medical records of all health care providers whom they notify. Patients could specify this access selectively, if they wished, e.g., if they had a particular provider that they did not wish the others to know about. Patients would specify a set of providers and other individuals (e.g., family members, health proxy decision makers, attorneys) who would have permission to "read" the record, and this access could be limited to some subset of the records for any person given access. Thus the consumer would have total control over the access rights. Only health care providers and others specified by the patient could add to the record; others would be permitted to read it, but not alter it.

The fastest growing segment of the health insurance world is the High-Deductible Health Plan, known widely also as the Consumer Directed Health Plan. What we propose here is simply the Consumer Directed Electronic Health Record (CD-EHR).

One other major distinction would appear: TTPs would also compete in the services they offered to help consumers review and understand their own records. This would partly include the selection and presentation of records in visual display—a portal to "MyMedicalVita" provided by the TTP. It might include written notes, lists of prescriptions (amalgamated across providers), reports from specialist referrals, or it might also include presentation of diagnostic imaging results. It could also include information estimating caloric use, caloric burn during the week, alcohol consumption, and adherence to desirable health habits (exercise, tooth brushing, and the like).

We can also envision a fee-based activity where the TTP providers or independent experts would help people understand their records, serving a similar role to professionals who help people manage their financial portfolios.

These "advisory" roles could be connected to the TTP or wholly independent—the market would probably offer both alternatives.

This latter function—full consumer access to records—involves a major shift in the mentality of health care providers about ownership of the record. As the AMA ethics quote suggests, current thinking views the record as the property of the provider, but with (legislatively defined) rights for patients to read that record. As the record-holding and access shifts, the medical records essentially become the property of the patient—*work made for hire*—just as the report of an economist-expert witness in a legal case is the property of the law firm hiring the economist.[11] Whether the ownership literally shifted to the patient or not, the effect would be the same—the patient would control the access to the record.

One major impediment exists today that limits our ability to bring this reality into existence: provider reluctance to share complete medical records. While most states have laws controlling patients' access to their own records, they create a mixed story about access, and do not deal well with the world of EHRs. This leads to our next proposal:

> **Proposal 6:** *Create new legislation requiring (within appropriate time lines) that all health care providers with sufficient EHRs provide and keep current a copy of all of the records to the TTP named by any patient to assemble and maintain a complete EHR for that patient.*

A second law may also prove important (but we cannot determine that yet): a law limiting liability for data breaches and a national compensation plan created (and funded by taxes on the TTP industry) to pay for losses associated with security breaches. Such a plan could follow the pathway of the Vaccine Injury Compensation Program created by the Congress in 1986.

The cost of actually providing the copy from the health care provider to the TTP will be small: electronic record systems regularly create mirrored copies—backups—on a daily basis. This proposed law requires nothing more than the creation of a second current copy at the TTP designated by the patient. The real costs will come in the operation of the TTPs, with their IT systems and processes to assure proper security, correctly control access to the records (according to the patients' wishes), and provide a portal through which patients (and those they permit) can view the records. We presume that these costs would appear directly as fees charged by the TTPs to the patients (their customers).

Who will become the trusted third parties?

From where might the TTPs arise? Some obvious choices come to mind easily. First, the companies providing the medical record service (and routine backup capability) to the providers are an obvious alternative. They will have the record in place already, they will fully understand the formatting issues associated with their record, and the process of receiving the copy would be trivially simple.

An alternative might be a health care system—an Accountable Care Organization (ACO), or large teaching hospital, or an HMO, for example—serving the same sort of role that PCPs have for decades served with paper records.

Yet another alternative might be some outside entity that had great expertise in large data file management and interface mechanisms—Google, Facebook, and other similar organizations come to mind. Or it may be a major consumer technology firm like Apple with its new collateral of health data from wearable technology.

Or it might be a major health insurance carrier. Or it might be companies providing similar aggregation of and access to financial records through highly secure portals. Many major financial institutions have such capabilities now, updated daily, with carefully constructed graphs and tables for data presentation.

Our task here is not to define the market, but rather to enable it. Furthermore, we envision that the wiring or plumbing (we are agnostic as to whether electricians or plumbers are the appropriate metaphorical agents) to link and aggregate already exists. Security, as needed, can be enhanced by use of virtual private network (VPN) connections and encryption. Once data collection and sharing becomes perfunctory at the point of all care (by habit or by law), it will evolve and grow.

Incentives for individuals to participate

Many people familiar with the possibilities of EHRs have concluded that health care costs will fall—perhaps considerably—for those who have fully shared health care records. To the extent that this promise is fulfilled, competition among health insurance companies should recognize the financial savings and reward those who participate in a fully shared EHR system with lower health insurance premiums. This would happen readily in the under-65 market and in Medicare Advantage plans within Medicare, but to make the system fully incentive-compatible, Medicare would also need to alter the Part B premium structure to account for savings created by enrollment in fully shared EHR systems by those continuing to use Regular Medicare (Parts A and B). Similar incentives to enroll should be put in place in Medicaid programs as well.

Conclusion

This approach will not instantly lead to perfect EHRs. It will, however, make a significant improvement in just a few years and perhaps even save many patients' lives. The key step will likely be the legal requirement that all providers participate with copies of their records for all patients who request such participation. Such a law would enable the TTP market to emerge, and the rest would follow.

Notes

1 http://dashboard.healthit.gov/quickstats/pages/FIG-REC-Physicians-Live-MU-Speciality.php, last accessed August 7, 2017.
2 www.nature.com/news/epidemiologists-put-social-media-in-the-spotlight-1.10012, last accessed August 7, 2017.
3 The vendors include the following: Cerner Millennium PowerChart with Discern Expert; Eclipsys Sunrise Clinical Manager 5.0; Epic Systems EpicCare Ambulatory; GE Centricity Practice Solution; GE Centricity/Carecast v5.1.8 (formerly IDX); MEDITECH MAGIC 5.4 SR3; McKesson Horizon Expert Orders 7.6 SP1; McKesson Practice Partner v9.2.2; NextGen EMR 5.5.
4 Parente, 2010.
5 Kawamoto et al., 2005, Wright et al., 2007.
6 Fonkych and Taylor, 2005.
7 Haynes and Walker, 1987, Institute of Medicine, 2000, Berwick and Hackbarth, 2012.
8 DHHS, 2008.
9 www.cms.gov/Research-Statistics-Data-and-Systems/Monitoring-Programs/QEMedicareData/index.html, last accessed September 2, 2017. The last update of the list occurred on March 22, 2017.
10 Institute of Medicine, 2000.
11 For an extensive discussion of the legal issues, see http://copyright.gov/circs/circ09.pdf, last accessed August 7, 2017.

13 Maximizing the promise of Accountable Care Organizations

Financial restructuring of the health care system is inevitable given the $500 billion in cuts to the Medicare program proposed by the Affordable Care Act (ACA), perhaps to be replaced by even more ambitious cost-reduction targets in any Republican "replace" legislation. Cuts will go deeper based on the fact that almost $300 billion in governmental program payments to physicians were not addressed in the fiscal impact statement of the Congressional Budget Office (CBO) on the legislation. One possible "assist" comes from a new way of delivering care—the Accountable Care Organization (ACO).

Defining Accountable Care Organizations

The ACA defines a new type of organization to deliver health care—the ACO, which is held out as a beacon of hope, providing ways to improve quality and reduce costs.

Proponents (and designers) of the ACO concept define it as having three crucial aspects:

- provider-led organizations with a strong base of primary care that are collectively accountable for quality and total per capita costs across the full continuum of care for a population of patients;
- payments linked to quality improvements that also reduce overall costs; and,
- reliable and progressively more sophisticated performance measurement, to support improvement and provide confidence that savings are achieved through improvements in care.[1]

The ACA proposed a set of service delivery ACO pilots for Medicare patients to pay providers for successful patient outcomes, not just services rendered. The model is so new that testing of its effects has just begun. One study published in early 2015 provides the first evidence, comparing Standard Medicare (A+B) beneficiaries enrolled in one of 332 ACOs using the Pioneer ACO model with regionally-matched "controls." The analysis used a two-year baseline period and a two-year "experimental treatment" period. The new ACO model produced reductions of about $425 per year, the largest differences occurring in inpatient spending.[2] As modest as this might seem, that represents approximately a 4% reduction in per capita spending in Medicare, and would save $2 billion per year if similar reductions occurred across the entire Medicare enrolled population.[3]

Whether these gains can be replicated elsewhere, or whether they are actually smaller than the future will reveal (as ACOs work their way up the learning curve) remains to be seen. A more recent Centers for Medicare and Medicaid Services (CMS) report says that annual savings from the initial set of ACOs rose from $88 million in year 1 to $96 million in year 2 to $120 million in year 3 (with essentially the same total enrollments), suggesting that these organizations learn "on the job" and improve over time.[4] Note also that these were not actual reductions in costs from the baseline period, but slower rates of increase than were observed in comparable control patients. We return to this issue of "learning on the job" shortly.

One of the principle charges made by ACO advocates states that "the health care system is broken due to fee for service (FFS) reimbursement." In contrast to the physician fixed salary approach of a Kaiser Permanente model, FFS has been the dominant growing form of provider reimbursement because it is relatively easy for an insurance company to operate and it does not put any fixed constraints on an insurer to pay for services not rendered. Even the newest form of health insurance such as High-Deductible Health Plans (HDHPs) rely on FFS reimbursement systems.

To elaborate, we can conceptualize a spectrum of payment systems. One polar extreme is the widespread FFS system. The other polar extreme is what we once called prepaid group practices, and now call Health Maintenance Organizations (HMOs), where a single organization assumes all of the financial risk for treating patients, owns the hospital network, and contracts with groups of physicians to provide all necessary medical care for enrollees. In these plans, the doctors are almost always paid on a flat salary per year rather than on the FFS system common elsewhere in the system. These plans are commonly described as *capitation* models, since the health care providers are paid on a *per capita* basis rather than on an FFS basis.

Only a few alternatives exist along this spectrum anchored at one end by the FFS model and at the other end by the HMO capitation model. Some physician groups have a mixed payment plan for doctors blending a base salary and bonus payments to encourage productivity (number of patients seen per day) and, more recently, even bonus payments hinging on service quality. But these groups are almost always limited to single specialty groups where every doctor deals with similar types of patients. Only the HMO model spans the entire array of patient types (with different acute and chronic conditions).

The most prominent method to pay for health care that lies somewhere between FFS and capitation arose with Medicare Part A's shift to a Prospective Payment System (PPS) for hospitalizations. Rather than paying hospitals (as was initially the case) on an FFS basis, the PPS system now pays a lump sum to the hospital for each hospitalization, using a method to cluster patients into similar groups (called Diagnosis-Related Groups, or DRGS) that each have a fixed payment associated with them. The PPS system works easily for hospitalizations because the time frame is fixed—starting with the hospital admission and ending with the hospital discharge—and only one health care provider is involved (the hospital). Doctors treating the patients within the hospital are still paid on an FFS basis under Medicare Part B.

Finding ways to extend the "prospective payment" concept beyond the hospitalization event has proven difficult. The only experiments underway currently within Medicare merely expand the concept to post-hospitalization care. The next step involves finding ways to treat chronic care patients outside of the hospital in a world with no fixed time frame (no specific beginning or ending) and multiple providers involved. Therein lies the challenge to ACOs.

The issues are myriad. Who bears the risk for unseen complications? How does the ACO allocate funds among the various providers? What happens at the "boundary" between the responsibilities of various providers as the clinical condition of the patient blurs normal definitions of specialization? Solving these issues will require new thinking about payment protocols, team (vs. individual provider) treatment strategies, and the complete sharing of medical records (as discussed in the previous chapter). The record-sharing will in a sense be easier in the ACO concept, because when a patient chooses an ACO as a provider, record sharing should occur automatically.

One of the clear goals of the ACA is to encourage greater value for resources expended on health care within the Medicare program. Section P.L. 111–148 of ACA (Title VII)—Improving Access to Innovative Medical Therapies—provides several important clues as to how Medicare will lead the way in reforming payment systems for health care organizations that provide health care services in this type of environment.[5]

An important new model of health care payment reform is known interchangeably as bundling episodes of care or service bundles (SBs). SBs are thought to be particularly important in chronic care patients treated in the hospital but whose complications lead to significant hospital and end-of-life costs. This is the territory that ACOs must explore, and it currently is *terra incognita*.

As previously noted, ACOs receive and distribute all payments to providers. When a patient presents at any care setting—most importantly in the outpatient clinic—the ACO with whom a primary care doctor is affiliated will become that patient's medical provider. All members of the ACO, starting with the primary care physician or nurse practitioner, will be required by law to demonstrate progress in a set of quality measures to receive payment, initially including:

- functional status improvement;
- reduction in avoidable hospital readmissions;
- rates of discharge to the community;
- rates of admission to the emergency room after hospitalization;
- incidence of health care acquired infections;
- efficiency measures;
- patient perception of care;
- clinical outcomes.

Health care, whether delivered in a hospital, a physician's office, or in a nursing home, is a complex process involving multiple parties and challenges. Today, the strategies of health care providers are designed to maximize patient flow and provider reimbursement for all patient treatments. The new quality-focused ACO payment mechanisms will reward organizations (and hence individual providers) not only for treating patients but also for making measurable strides to improve quality of care. Introducing quality specifically into the payment methodology is a novel part of ACOs.

As a next step, the ACO model creates the possibility of a shared savings model for hospitals. Specifically, the ACO sets up a shared savings program that directs all Medicare Part A and Part B payments through it, in exchange for improved coordination of patient services, medical supplies, medical equipment, and drug utilization among FFS Medicare recipients. A typical Medicare ACO will likely include a hospital, primary care physicians, specialists, and allied medical professionals. Experts expect that quality improvements will account for much of the observed reductions in cost of care, hence leading to the savings that the ACOs and Medicare will share.

In theory, any provider such as a hospital, a clinic, or a home health agency may become an ACO but only if it is willing and financially able to accept certain forms of risk for a minimum of 5000 Medicare beneficiaries. Under these arrangements the ACO will be responsible for receiving and distributing all monetary reimbursement and "gain share" payments to medical providers that are owned or have contracted with the ACO.

However, according to a 2009 analysis, 37% of all standard Medicare patients who are admitted to a hospital utilize some form of post-acute medical care, including long-term care hospitals, inpatient rehabilitation facilities, skilled nursing facilities, and home health agencies.[6] This situation creates considerable financial risk for hospitals, since hospitals currently have little or no control over post-acute health care settings. As a result, hospitals everywhere are now engaged in a thorough review of service lines in terms of quality and cost. Health care policy makers argue that major cuts in hospital reimbursement will incentivize the formation of hospital-based ACOs and that the financial structure of the ACO will enable hospitals to minimize financial penalties while allowing them to capture new sources of revenue. In the most plausible outcome, hospitals and post-hospital care organizations will either merge or become meaningful partners to bring about the shared savings that ACOs and the ACA anticipate.

The focus on post-hospital treatment may be a key to the problem. In an extensive analysis of regional variations in health care costs (as we discussed in one of our proposed Medicare reforms), a major study by the Institute of Medicine found that much of the regional variation in costs of treating Medicare patients came from substantial differences in the ways post-acute hospital care was used.[7] Regions with high total costs of care were high in the use of post-acute services (nursing homes, rehab facilities, and the like), and regions that were low in total cost of care used such services sparingly. These results suggest that the post-hospital care territory may be the key to success for ACOs. The Chinese character for "crisis" blends the separate characters for "danger" and "opportunity." So it may well be for ACOs with post-hospital care.

Outside of the ACO structure (but with a similar intent), CMS initiated quality-based reform for health care providers by shifting the risk for preventable readmissions for certain conditions—initially acute myocardial infarction, pneumonia, and congestive heart failure (CHF). In 2014, they added acute readmissions for chronic obstructive pulmonary disease (COPD), and total hip and total knee replacements. In 2015, they added readmissions for coronary artery bypass grafts (CABG) surgery, and in 2016 finalized the rules for several more types of pneumonia hospitalizations. More are scheduled to follow throughout 2017 and beyond.

As CMS develops methods for predicting achievable rates of treatment without readmission (and hence estimating rates of preventable readmissions), we expect that these rules will apply to increasingly large fractions of all Medicare hospitalizations.

Beyond fantasy—making real the elusive risk-taking "unicorn" ACO

When ACOs started to gain popularity following the passage of the ACA, of the two parties involved in their deployment—payers and providers—the providers had greater interest. In particular, providers and hospitals saw ACOs as an opportunity to gain leadership of the provision of health care without heavy oversight of health insurers and to deal with the concerns they had with the incentives of the FFS reimbursement system.

In 2011, Mark Smith, MD, MBA, president and chief executive officer (CEO) of the California Healthcare Foundation stated that "the ACO is like a unicorn, a fantastic creature that is vested with mythical powers. But no one has actually seen one."[8] One way to make the ACO real is be clear about the key question: "Who is accepting the financial risk for patient population seen?"

Payers are particularly skilled at accepting risk. They are not very skilled at managing health care, despite being called managed care organizations, the exception being if the payer also owns a disease management company the way United Health Group owns Optum Health. So to make the unicorn real, we must: (a) clearly identify who is accepting risk; and (b) have confidence that they can manage that risk successfully.

For example, if a hospital system is to call itself an ACO because it structured a deal with an insurer to hold its risk, then that hospital will be in a weak position. If, on the other hand, the hospital buys the insurer and it has risk-holding intellectual property and expertise, then it is in a strong position—but then it is also an insurer.

Legacy HMOs like Kaiser Permanente, Emblem Health (GHI), or Health Partners, already take on and manage risk. The capitation model is well suited to do this. Exactly how ACOs can accomplish this when dealing with less than the full spectrum of care for patients becomes a central issue. Nobody knows how this will work yet, but if we are to see ACOs operating in a world that is partially FFS and partially SBs (a limited form of capitation), then they will need to figure this out.

In summary, the ACA is a $1 trillion attempt to "fix" the problems in the US health care system. Embedded within this legislation is payment reform, which is acknowledged both by the bill's detractors and supporters as a crucial catalyst towards a system that is economically sustainable. A fundamental building block of payment reform may well be SBs that, through innovation and economic realities, lead to better value and measurable improvement of the patient condition.

The ACO concept can be best understood as a decentralized bundled payment system. In Medicare's Part A payment reform, one central government agency (at that time, the Health Care Finance Administration (HCFA), now CMS) dictates the entire structure of a new bundled hospital payment mechanism. The ACO concept in some ways is similar—it moves toward bundled payments—but in another important way, it differs immensely. Rather than CMS specifying how the bundled payment would be distributed among cooperating organizations that make up the ACO, the process lets each ACO decide how to divide up the bundled revenues.

A parallel issue emerges when paying for prescription drugs. Currently we pay "by the pill," exactly in parallel with an FFS provider payment. One could also consider paying "by the treatment" for some diseases, or even "by the cure" for others (a true "pay for results" model). At present, we know almost nothing about how such alternative models might work.

The "decentralized bundling" aspect of ACOs has great merit. It creates the opportunity for widespread experimentation in ways to manage risk in the SB domain. The approach will have far greater value if CMS adds sufficient funds to evaluate the many different models of ACOs that emerge, so that quality-improving and cost-saving "regularities" in structure and internal incentive models can be shared more rapidly among all participants. That way, the health care system will evolve more rapidly to the frontier of most-efficient production, in this case not only efficiency in terms of lower cost but also in higher patient quality.

Capturing the full value of the experiments

There is an important data need to allow our nation to gain the fullest possible value from the ACO experiments. Recall (from earlier) the recent CMS report that the initial set of ACOs seems to increase their costs savings year by year with more experience. The value of ACOs will rise faster and further to the extent that this "learning while doing" can be measured and disseminated.

To do this, the Center for Medicare and Medicaid Innovation (CMMI) must require that the data used for the evaluation of the various ACO experiments have a common structure so that generalizability can get a proper test. Many successful innovations in health care cannot be replicated; they may depend on special circumstances or key leaders, for example. To make sure an ACO actually advances the science of risk management and medical care, it must create verifiable and reproducible results with common metrics from insurer claims and electronic health records. CMMI is best placed to standardize the language to allow these comparisons. Thus, we offer the following specific proposal:

> **Proposal 7:** CMS *should establish specific (and well-funded) programs to analyze the outcomes in various* ACOs, *including the early creation of a common vocabulary to describe* ACO *structures and mandating that* ACOs *(as a condition of operation) gather common information about not only their outcomes but also the organizational structures and financial incentives they employ to achieve those outcomes*.

And finally, we note that all the innovative features of ACOs should not be seen as competing objectives, but rather mutually reinforcing. For example, bundled payment will work best with full risk contracts where the institutions taking the greatest gamble get the biggest rewards when they are successful. When quality improves in health care, total system costs often decline. Thus we can all hope that it will be with ACOs.

Notes

1 McClellan et al., 2010.
2 Nyweide et al., 2015.
3 Average Medicare spending for the US was about $10,000 per enrollee in this period—$500 billion spending for 50 million enrollees, in round numbers.

4 www.cms.gov/Newsroom/MediaReleaseDatabase/Fact-sheets/2015-Fact-sheets-items/2015-08-25.html, last accessed August 7, 2017.
5 Grier, 2010.
6 Jencks et al., 2009.
7 Newhouse and Garber, 2013, Newhouse et al., 2013.
8 www.hhnmag.com/articles/4329-chasing-unicorns-the-future-of-acos, last accessed August 4, 2017.

14 Getting rid of overstated medical bills

Near tax day in 2013, Steven Brill published in *Time Magazine* a dramatic *exposé* of the difference between medical bills (those from hospitals, doctors, drugs,... everything) and the amounts these providers actually receive as payment for their services.[1] While this may sound like it deals with a mere annoyance, the problem of highly-inflated medical bills is real, and has important economic consequences. Perhaps most importantly, absurdly high medical bills that have no basis in reality lead people who receive them to do things that are bad for them and for the economy: their credit standings degrade, they undergo emotional distress, they have difficulty in accessing medical care, they sometimes file for bankruptcy, and—although good data are lacking—they may even sometimes commit suicide as a consequence of the apparent financial cliff they face. So Brill's exposé has more than casual meaning, and it is not new. This issue has existed since before Medicare's introduction in 1965.

As it emerged in 1965–1966, Medicare had to find a way to pay hospitals and doctors for care they provided to Medicare enrollees, and they did not want to pay billed charges, understanding full-well that if they offered to pay billed charges, the fees charged would skyrocket. For Part B, they created a set of administered-price rates for various physician services (using a Relative Value Schedule approach from commercial insurance)—the basis for which was altered in fundamental ways in 1989 with the Resource-Based Relative Value Schedule (as part of the Omnibus Budget Reconciliation Act of 1989).

Hospital payments originally followed a different path. Hospitals were required to calculate their overall costs of operation—a standard cost-accounting process—and their total charges, and then to calculate an overall Ratio of Costs to Charges (RCC). Hospitals were then paid for each service rendered using the Ratio of Costs to Charges Applied to Charges (RCCAC). One consequence was that a hospital could actually receive higher payments from Medicare by adding to its costs—not a recipe that would normally lead to efficient production of health care. Among other things, this helped fuel a medical arms race between hospitals that rapidly drove up health care costs, a problem solved in major part by the later modification to a hospital prospective payment system using Diagnosis-Related Groups (DRGs)—but that remains a different story for a different discussion.

As time progressed, the gap between charges (the absurd numbers that appear on your medical bills) and actual amounts paid by insurers and most patients has increased.[2] Since we focus on incentives in this book, we were drawn to ask, "why do hospitals and doctors and other providers want to list these absurdly high prices?" Perhaps the only people who actually ever pay them are wealthy members of various Middle Eastern Royal Families who come to the US for exotic medical care. But they frighten many uninsured individuals, and cascade into a multitude of bankruptcies based on the premise that the hospitals (and doctors) will at least try to collect some significant portion of the "list price" bill. Put simply, if you are uninsured and you receive a bill for (say) $100,000 from a hospital for a four-day simple surgery, the simplest and most likely response is to file for bankruptcy.

One study that sampled individuals throughout the United States who had filed for bankruptcy found that 60% of bankruptcy filings were because of medical debt (according to the filers' declaration).[3] Almost all of them (92%) had medical debt exceeding either $5000 or 10% of pretax income. A separate analysis in 2013 by a price-comparison survey company found a similar result—1.7 million medically-related bankruptcy filings per year, accounting for three in five of all filings, and also found that 17 million people had their credit ratings adversely affected by medical debt.[4]

Hospitals and other providers actually have a logical reason to do this—it raises the apparent amount of charity care they provide. To understand why this is important, we need to take a small excursion into the tax law of the United States.

Section 501(c) of the Internal Revenue Service (IRS) tax code defines the types of institutions that automatically qualify as recipients of charitable deductions. The pertinent portion is subsection 3, which lists the following criteria for automatic eligibility:

> 501(c)(3) Corporations, and any community chest, fund, or foundation, organized and operated exclusively for religious, charitable, scientific, testing for public safety, literary, or educational purposes, or to foster national or international amateur sports competition... or for the prevention of cruelty to children or animals...

This list does not include organizations providing health care—hospitals, clinics, nursing homes, pharmacies, doctors, therapists, diagnostic facilities, etc.

Section 501 further describes in subsection 501(r) that hospitals particularly do not qualify for tax-exempt treatment under 501(c)(3) unless they meet a series of requirements detailed in the section that relate to:

- community health needs assessment requirements... (described in paragraph (3));
- financial assistance policy requirements (described in paragraph (4));

- requirements on charges (described in paragraph (5)) and;
- billing and collection requirements (described in paragraph (6)).

Paragraphs 4 through 6 of this section of IRS code create the problem. In brief, they require that hospitals:

- have a written policy about who is eligible for financial assistance;
- require that for people covered by that eligibility policy, they do not charge those people more than they would normally charge to insured individuals for emergency and other medically necessary care;
- have a billing policy that does not use onerous means to collect bills from people identified as eligible for financial assistance.

None of this specifies how much they can "write off" as charitable care, nor does it say anything about the nature of the eligibility policy. It simply says that hospitals must have such a policy. The policy could be very broad or very narrow, and the IRS rules would not distinguish one from the other.

Health economists have known for decades that the boundary between bad debt and charity care is very fluid, so they essentially always discuss "bad debt and charity care" as a single entity. But the current tax code provides only minimal limitation as to how hospitals calculate that amount. Thus, they have strong incentives to create "list prices" that seldom get paid by individuals but—crucially—are regularly written off as bad debt or charity care.

The same issues apply to for-profit organizations of any sort (some hospitals, nursing homes, pharmacies, therapists, diagnostic services, home health providers, etc.) who claim bad debts as an offset against their profits. To the extent that they can over-inflate the amount of bad debt claimed in their tax returns, they can reduce their income tax liability and hence increase after-tax profits.

In both the For Profit and Not for Profit worlds, these incentives to create false and absurdly high list prices have predictable consequences:

- They over-inflate the apparent amount of charity care given by the providers.
- They create incentives for individuals to declare bankruptcy to avoid the hassle of dealing with the hospital (or other provider)—even though that provider might readily negotiate the amounts downward or remove the charges if asked.
- They create significant confusion about the actual costs of our health care system.

We propose a simple solution to all of this: Modify Section 501(c) of the IRS tax code to specify that the amount claimed by any health care provider (whether operating as not for profit, for profit, partnership, or any other legal form of organization) as charitable services provided or bad debts claimed is limited to the greater of: (a) the amount that Medicare would pay for the same service; or (b) the amount that their state Medicaid program would pay. If the IRS made this simple change, the incentives to keep the "list price" books would diminish hugely. It would not go away—there is always the prospect of the random Saudi Royal Family member having an auto accident right in front of the hospital's emergency department (ED) who might actually pay these charges. But most of the adverse incentive would disappear, an outcome of which we would approve.

> **Proposal 8:** *Pass legislation specifying that the charitable deduction or bad debt expense claimed by any health care provider is limited to the greater of: (a) the amount that Medicare would pay for the same service; or (b) the amount that their state's Medicaid program would pay.*

This may all sound a bit trivial in the grand scheme of things, but our purpose in this book was to find and correct perverse incentives, and this issue surely falls into that category. It rose to sufficient prominence in our thinking that we decided to add this short chapter in our book to deal with it. We suspect there are some—those who find these outrageously high medical bills annoying at a minimum and perhaps preposterous as well—who may think that this chapter and its recommendation is the most important we have written, while others may feel that it is trivial. We believe that it falls somewhere in between, but is nevertheless worth doing.

Notes

1 Brill, 2013.
2 In early 2017, one of us (Phelps) had abdominal surgery with a five-day hospitalization that followed. The surgery was successful and without incident at a major teaching hospital. The subsequent bill for the five days was $140,000, $21,500 of which was "allowed" by the relevant insurance plan (a Medicare Advantage plan) with a $1150 copayment due from the patient. The point is that the original bill was (in round numbers) 6.5 times the actual amount received by the hospital.
3 Himmelstein et al., 2009.
4 www.nerdwallet.com/blog/health/2014/03/26/medical-bankruptcy/, last accessed August 4, 2017.

15 Concluding comments

In many ways, the US has the best health care system in the world, but it can and must be made better. It costs too much for what we receive. Our health outcomes are far worse than many other nations with lower standards of living and lower medical spending (either in actual amounts or as a percentage of gross domestic product). We deserve better.

Our analysis traces back to the root causes of many of these issues. We find repeated instances where past laws and rulemaking have left the system riddled with distorted incentives. As economists, we know that people respond to incentives. Rather than blaming people and organizations for responding as they do, we urge that the incentives get fixed.

Much of this will involve legislative action. We have not attempted to craft exact legislative language, but rather to indicate the key components of necessary legislation. Major legal confusion was spawned by what some call a simple drafting error in the Affordable Care Act (ACA) that led to a challenge (King vs. Burwell) to a key portion of the regulations following that Act, specifically those in Treasury Department code 26 C.F.R. § 1.36B-2(a)(1). We have chosen to leave the drafting of exact legislative language to those specializing in that activity, and instead have laid out the basic economic issues that the legislation should deal with. Think of these as architectural drawings, not construction blueprints.

The most important change that we see resides in the tax law. We must remove the favorable treatment of employer-paid health insurance, and we believe that we have crafted a way to accomplish that task that is politically feasible *and* that will permanently stimulate the economy. And with that change, we would eliminate both the ACA's employer mandate and the "Cadillac tax" on high-cost health plans.

We also see a series of changes in Medicare and Medicaid—none earth-shattering, none of which change the fundamental premise of Medicare and Medicaid—but which (when taken together) will make these programs less costly, more valuable to their enrollees, and less of a tax burden into the future. It is essential to reduce this future tax burden, since the ratio of retirees to workers will shift very unfavorably over the coming decades.

We discuss a series of ways to help improve health outcomes, lower costs of care, and hence reduce the future burden on taxpayers. A series of these center around the ways we confront chronic conditions. We discuss changes in the way chronic care is done and paid for, changes in the incentives to engage in healthy lifestyles that will reduce chronic care burdens in the future, and urge a refocusing of National Institutes of Health (NIH) research to better match the true causes of chronic conditions and help prevent them, rather than the current intensive focus on cures.

We also present pathways to improving health care outcomes and costs by enhancing the shift to electronic health records, and finding stronger ways to combat fraud and abuse in health care. Both of these arenas need the leadership of the Centers for Medicare and Medicaid Services (CMS), but require the participation of all health insurers and providers. We see useful and powerful tools already in widespread use in various parts of the financial services sectors that can serve as templates and guideposts in this important endeavor.

And finally, we scratch an itch that we believe has bothered many people: How can a health bill go from "Charges = $140,000" to "Adjusted Charges = $21,500" to "Due from Patient = $1,150?"[1] We present a simple change in the Internal Revenue Service (IRS) code to remove the incentive for health care providers to post these artificially high "charges" and hopefully to see their rapid demise.

The time has come to change the basic paradigms in thinking about health care finance and organization. Getting the incentive right is an essential step to successful change in behavior. The time is now.

Note

1 This is an actual example from a bill for a five-day abdominal surgery event—wholly successful—for the senior of the two authors of this book.

Appendix to Chapter 3

The labor supply (partial equilibrium) estimate

In a simple partial equilibrium exercise, we calculated the percentage change in after-tax wages associated with our proposed change in the tax structure, and combined that with estimates of the elasticity of labor supply found in the literature. This work uses two separate estimates of the elasticity of labor supply, and makes two separate assumptions about the shifting of payroll taxes. One estimate assumes that payroll taxes are not shifted from the employer to the worker (the "short run" outcome), yielding the smallest estimate of the increase in after-tax marginal wage rates, and the other estimate assumes that payroll taxes have been shifted 100% to the worker (the "long-run" outcome), and hence the reductions in the employer's payroll taxes (as included in our proposal) are passed to employees on a one-for-one basis. This leads to the largest increase in after-tax marginal wages, and hence the largest equilibrium increase in labor supply. The two estimates of labor supply elasticity we use are 0.3 from a major literature survey[1] and from a newer synthesis of microeconomic and macroeconomic estimates of 0.5.[2] Table 3A summarizes these results.

As an example of these calculations, with current tax law and no shift of payroll taxes, for a worker in the 22% marginal income tax bracket but below the FICA cutoff and assuming an average state income tax marginal rate of 4.55%, after-tax pay for an incremental $100 of wages would be $65.80. The reduction in individual income and payroll taxes would increase that by $2.16 to $67.96, an increase in after-tax income of 3.3%. Combining that with a labor supply elasticity of 0.3 gives the increase in labor supply (and hence economic activity

Table 3A (Appendix) Percent change in labor supply from proposed tax law changes

		Employers' share of payroll taxes	
		No shift	Full shift
Elasticity of labor supply	0.3	1.0	1.5
	0.5	1.6	2.4

and tax revenues) of 1%, and the 1.6% estimate when using a labor supply elasticity of 0.5. Similar calculations are done with the assumption that all employer payroll taxes (and savings thereon) are passed to employees in terms of wage changes.

Adapting the Congressional Budget Office macro model general equilibrium estimates

In 2004, the Congressional Budget Office (CBO) was asked to analyze the effects of an across-the-board reduction in marginal income tax rates as the only change in the tax structure.[3] They were asked both to understand the consequences on the size of the economy and the effect on the national debt. To accomplish the latter task, they had to make various assumptions as to how any reductions in tax revenue would be dealt with. Their scenario differs considerably from the one we propose, because we would simultaneously increase the base of taxable income, and reductions in the marginal tax rate would be designed to exactly offset the newly created tax revenue if nothing else changed in the economy. Our interest, of course, is how much the economy would grow with the reduced marginal income taxes.

The CBO estimates only looked at a 10% reduction in federal personal income taxes, ignoring both state income taxes and payroll taxes (FICA and Medicare). Thus, they conclude that "the effective tax on labor, which includes those [payroll and state] taxes, would drop by only 5 percent to 6 percent, not 10 percent." Since our proposal would reduce income tax rates by approximately 5.7% and payroll taxes by approximately 8.6% for a weighted total of approximately 6.5%, the gross domestic product (GDP) effects of the 2004 CBO study would understate the consequences of our proposed change in taxation of employer-paid health insurance premiums. To account for this difference, we increase all CBO estimates of GDP effects by 20% (rounding slightly, the ratio of our 6.5% to the midpoint of their 5–6% range).

The CBO models tax changes such as these using two commercially available Keynesian macroeconomic models, those of Macroeconomic Advisors (MA) and Global Insight (GI). They also constructed general equilibrium (GE) models that account for consumers' responses to the way the federal government deals with the deficit. Their GE analyses, upon which we focus, used two assumptions about the deficit—either that it would be offset by reduced government spending or by later income tax increases, these increases being anticipated by consumers in their current decisions. They estimated these models in open and closed economy, and two distinct modeling approaches (which they call Ramsey and overlapping generations (OLG)). The closest model in their work to our proposed tax change (none exactly match) would be the models in which the reduced tax revenue is offset by reduced government spending, but that will lead to an understatement in the increase in GDP if any Keynesian multiplier effect of government spending occurs. Nevertheless, these estimates more closely approximate the world we propose than any of their other estimates, understanding that they will likely understate the increases in GDP arising from our proposed tax change.

In these GE models with reduced government spending to balance the budget, labor input rose from 0.8 to 1.4%, depending on the assumptions, and GDP rose by 0.7 to 1.4% in the pertinent models and time periods. Because their simulated change in marginal tax rates is lower than what we propose, as discussed earlier, we inflate these estimates by 20%, giving labor supply changes ranging from 0.8% to 1.7%.

Direct simulation analysis in a two-good general equilibrium framework

Chari and Eslami undertook a direct analysis of our proposal with several simplifying assumptions.[4] The key difference is that their two-good general equilibrium model (health care and other goods) introduced an increase in the price of one of the goods (health care) that offsets the decrease in the tax on labor income. This new model structure generally reduces the estimated effects on labor supply in equilibrium because of the substitution away from consumption (and hence towards leisure) created by the increased cost of health care.

To use their model directly, one needs to estimate the effect of increases in health care prices (as faced by the consumer) in response to our proposed tax change. They used a summary measure of the price elasticity of demand for health care from the RAND Health Insurance Experiment (a summary elasticity of –0.2) in their simulations. But a second demand parameter intervenes, about which much less is known—the elasticity of demand for insurance coverage in response to changes in its own price.

At one extreme, if the demand for health insurance has zero price responsiveness (elasticity = 0) then the tax change would have no effect on demand, and hence their model would essentially match the CBO's modeling work. Of course, we do not believe that is the case, else we would not consider the tax subsidy to health insurance as an important issue. If one assumes that the demand for health insurance coverage has unitary price elasticity (elasticity = –1) then changes in the tax treatment of health insurance pass one-for-one to become changes in the price of health care. If demand for insurance has more than unitary price sensitivity, the effect becomes magnified, and if demand is "inelastic" (elasticity less than 1 in absolute value) the effect shrinks. Thus, Chari and Eslami's work requires assumptions about the elasticity of demand for insurance, about which there remains considerable uncertainty.

Pauly's 1986 review of the literature gave a wide swath of estimates for this key demand parameter. A more recent analysis summarized the literature on an extensive range of demand parameters in health care.[5] They concluded that the elasticity of demand for health insurance coverage in employer-group markets (their Table III.C) was almost certainly price-inelastic, with a range found in their surveyed literature from –0.1 at the low end to –0.55 and –0.6 at the high end. In what follows, we use an estimate of –0.5. In the model of Chari and Eslami, this is equivalent to using an estimate of the price sensitivity of demand for medical care itself to be –0.1 (not the –0.2 from the RAND Health Insurance Experiment data).

With that assumption, the Chari and Eslami model estimates the increase in output (and labor supply, in equilibrium) of 0.3%. This estimate is smaller than the partial equilibrium result and also smaller than our adjusted estimates from the CBO model. Chari and Eslami also modeled a situation in a one-good consumption model (just as the CBO estimate did) and provided two estimates of the macro-effect. One estimate essentially matched the CBO approach by assuming that revenue decreases arising from the tax cut were made up with changes in lump sum transfers, thus introducing no change in the relative prices of labor and leisure. Their estimate in that setting showed a growth of 0.8%—smaller than but close to the estimates from the CBO analysis. They also estimated a world where there had been a subsidy to consumption overall (but in a one-good model) that was removed to offset the revenue reduction. In that estimate, the economy grows only by 0.3%, essentially the same as in their analysis of our proposal. Thus, the key difference in their work from other approaches is the effect of removing the distorting consumption subsidy.

Chari and Eslami's work emphasizes how sensitive macroeconomic models are as apparently simple assumptions change. They explain the major difference between their work and the CBO general equilibrium estimate as follows:

> In our setting (by removing the subsidy to health insurance and hence to health care), we increase the price of consumption relative to the price of leisure (i.e., not working). As those relative prices change, people reduce their overall work effort compared to a situation with no change in those relative prices. This causes the reduced estimate of the magnitude of the labor supply effect in response to our proposal.

However, they re-created the CBO model in their format (and its general results) but could not find parameter estimates that allowed the two models to converge, even assuming minimal change in total consumption (the key explanation of why their approach differs from the CBO approach). Thus, differences in the basic model specification may lead to the differing results, hence our presentation of these multiple approaches to estimating the aggregate macroeconomic effect of our proposal.

Notes

1 Keane, 2011.
2 Chetty, 2012.
3 CBO, 2004.
4 Chari and Eslami, 2016.
5 Liu and Chollet, 2006.

Appendix to Chapter 5

The Hewitt Health insurance auctions[1]

In March 1999, Hewitt Associates LLC, a Chicago-based global management consulting and employee benefits delivery firm, introduced an auction market for health insurance, where health plans competed directly against each other for securing health insurance contracts from corporate clients. The three primary stakeholders in these auctions were: (i) Employers (e.g., IBM, Morgan Stanley), who were the buyers; (ii) Health Plans (e.g., Humana, Kaiser), who were the sellers; and (iii) Hewitt Associates, who hosted the auctions and also played the role of benefits negotiator.

The purpose of the auctions was to stimulate more direct competition among plans, without sacrificing clinical quality, in a fair and dynamic environment. The goal was to help the buying firms by: (i) screening auction participants based on employer specified criteria; (ii) saving money through real-time negotiations; and (iii) offering employees the best health care option for the best cost. It also helped the health plans by: (a) simplifying the negotiation process; and (b) attracting more clients. Through the intermediation of Hewitt, the auctions allowed the employers to select only high-performing health plans in terms of clinical quality, administrative effectiveness ratings, and employee satisfaction. Interested providers were pre-screened by Hewitt, with only the health plans that met certain minimum standards of quality allowed to participate in the auctions. The use of the web-enabled environment allowed companies to save time and effort in negotiating with the providers online rather than over the telephone or in person. The cycle time to complete the negotiation process was reduced from five weeks to one week.

The pre-auction phase consisted of five steps: (i) Hewitt and the employers developed a Request for Proposals (RFP) and sent it to the desired health plans; (ii) interested plans responded to the RFP; (iii) employers selected the plans they wanted to proceed into the auction, based on review criteria; (iv) selected plans were informed and educated regarding the auction mechanism; and (v) dates for the auctions were set and communicated to all the parties.

Each auction took place over the course of a week in a secured website administered by Hewitt. The auctions were client and market-specific, i.e., a health plan could bid in several auctions for the same employer, each meant for different markets. The markets were defined by the clients; the name of each market roughly correlated with a metropolitan statistical area. Each competing plan was asked to submit initial rates in advance of the online auction. To avoid "shadow pricing" concerns (plans raising bids when they found themselves to be the low bidder), plans were not allowed to increase their rates during the auction; only reductions by coverage category were allowed. Further, unlike the Medicare auctions, where bids are non-binding (i.e., suppliers are not bound by their bids), the bids in the auctions were binding on the health plans.

Participating insurers were required to bid for three to four (depending on the buyer) coverage tiers: employee, employee+spouse, employee+child(ren), and employee+family. The buying firms specified the number of tiers (either three or four) as well as the projected number of employees expected to be covered in each tier. Based on this expected demand, a composite score, i.e., a weighted average of the bids submitted by each provider for each of the three tiers, was calculated. Since the price quotes submitted by the bidders were required to be per-employee-per-month (PMPP), the composite score was referred to as the cost-per-employee.

A potential problem with using a composite score to evaluate bids is that it creates strong incentives for bid skewing. The Affordable Care Act (ACA) health insurance exchange (HIX) has this problem for composite bids wherein bidders distort their bids away from their costs. That is, plans may bid lower on tiers where the buyer has overestimated demand and higher on tiers where the buyer has underestimated demand, resulting in prices for individual tiers that may not align with costs. To mitigate this problem, Hewitt Associates reserved the right to "re-slope the tiers" (i.e., modify the weights of the individual tiers that resulted in the composite score) for pricing purposes if a health plan submitted a bid that displayed (in the opinion of Hewitt Associates) an inappropriate relation of prices in tiers, e.g., a price of $100 for employee+family and $600 for employee.

After three years, the Hewitt experiment ended. One of the biggest problems was the design, like much of e-commerce in the early 2000s, which was ahead of its time. Many of the employers and insurers refused to stay strictly with their bids and would seek to communicate outside the auction mechanism. By the last year, the communication resembled collusion and the experiment was discontinued. Over ten years later, many changes have occurred in e-commerce and business has become far more comfortable with information technology (IT)-only messaging and transactions.

Note

1 This appendix draws from Gupta et al., 2012.

Appendix to Chapter 6

Comment regarding the constitutionality of the individual mandate

by
Thomas H. Jackson and Charles E. Phelps

The US Supreme Court concluded in 2012 that the Individual Mandate was constitutional, using a path that many legal scholars found convoluted (using the tax imposed on non-compliers as the basis for the logic). A separate and clearer path to the constitutionality also exists.

Beginning with the idea that the individual mandate is fundamentally an issue of a "required purchase" leads the analysis down the wrong path. The correct path contains three questions: (1) Does Congress have the power to regulate insurance? (2) If so, does it have the right to preclude using pre-existing health conditions to determine access to or the cost of insurance? (3) If so, is the mandate necessary to allow the market to function properly—and therefore within the power of Congress? We believe that the proper answer to each of these questions is clearly "yes."

First, may Congress regulate insurance? The key issue is whether or not the health insurance market is "commerce," which the federal government may regulate under its constitutional powers granted by Article I, Section 8. None of the legal challenges to the individual mandate question that the regulation of insurance is justified under the commerce clause; indeed, the Supreme Court clearly held in United States v. South-Eastern Underwriters Ass'n in 1944 that the "business of insurance" could be regulated by Congress using that power.

Once past this point, the remaining questions, at least constitutionally, seem easy downhill sledding. Given that Congress may regulate health insurance, the specific form of regulation surely may fall within a wide range of parameters. The most important here—that insurance companies not discriminate either in access or costs based on individuals' "pre-existing conditions"—follows without any real controversy. How could one imagine that the federal government may regulate health insurance, but then say that this power does not extend to such a key issue involving access and price?

Finally, if the federal government has the power to preclude use of pre-existing conditions to set price or control access to insurance, can the market then function without the further step of mandating that all persons purchase insurance?

Consider the alternative: how would the market for health insurance behave if the government prohibited using pre-existing conditions but imposed no individual mandate? If people could wait until they became sick or injured before purchasing insurance, and could then purchase it as if they were completely healthy (i.e., no additional premium for their pre-existing condition), the market would collapse. The very notion that insurance spreads risk across individuals would vanish. Rational healthy people would never buy insurance until they became sick. Thus, once the use of pre-existing conditions is prohibited, it becomes "necessary and proper" for the government to also require that individuals maintain insurance coverage. Without the mandate, adverse selection dooms health insurance markets.

Thus, the individual mandate is justified, not as a direct application of the commerce clause—the wholly wrong place to start—but under the independent provision in Article I, Section 8 of the Constitution, giving Congress the power to "make all Laws which shall be necessary and proper for carrying into Execution the foregoing Powers..." Since McCulloch v. Maryland in 1819, it has been clear that the "necessary and proper" clause independently grants power to Congress; thus, the analysis is complete. The special nature of insurance markets, combined with the specific regulation banning the use of pre-existing conditions, leads to the need for mandatory participation, a circumstance unlikely to repeat itself in other regulated markets, such as those for food.

If one starts with the proposition that the federal government can regulate health care insurance under the commerce clause, then the individual mandate is constitutional, not because the government can compel people to purchase insurance, but because, in the market for health care insurance, the mandate is "necessary" to prevent the regulation from destroying the market that it regulates. Once the Congress enacts the pre-existing condition ban, the legal issue isn't desirability but constitutionality, and the foregoing argument provides a clear path to an understanding that the Individual Mandate is constitutionally valid.

Appendix to Chapter 9

Assessing optimal insurance

To help understand what the best insurance plan might look like, one early analysis showed how health insurance involves a tradeoff between risk-spreading and the creation of adverse incentives.[1] Full coverage eliminates financial risk, but creates importantly large adverse incentives to over-spend on medical care, since people rationally choose health care as if it cost nothing (which is true for them, but not for society). At the other extreme, no coverage (or very large deductibles and coinsurance) minimize the adverse incentives, but create large financial risk.

An analysis using data from the RAND Health Insurance Experiment, simulated a large variety of insurance plans (in 1984 dollars) with different deductible and coinsurance arrangements.[2] The traditional "major medical" plan of that era stood out as one of the leaders in terms of doing this balancing-act well with coinsurance rates of 25% and annual deductibles of $100 to $300 all near the "best" with $200 the "best of the best." The comparable policy in 2015 would have an individual deductible of about $450 for an insurance plan covering all health care services. Medicare Part B's original deductible of $50 in 1965 would be about $375 in 2015, so the original Medicare design for Part B was actually not far from what an "optimal" plan might look like.

Finally, Phelps derived a measure for the optimal coinsurance rate for health insurance plans, balancing the financial risk from health care expenses with the economic loss from increased utilization.[3] This analysis shows that the optimal coinsurance for hospitalization should be in the realm of 5–10% (appropriate for Part A) and for physician services (appropriate for Part B) should be about 40%—higher than the original Medicare's 20% coinsurance rate. The Phelps model does not include a separate deductible in the analysis, so a coinsurance rate above the deductible would be lower than the 40% estimate.

Notes

1 Zeckhauser, 1970.
2 Keeler et al., 1988.
3 Phelps, 2014.

Appendix to Chapter 11

Components of a comprehensive fraud detection system

Modularized Architecture—The solution must be designed from an end-to-end modularized perspective to allow for ease of integration into multiple points along a health care transaction/claim flow (pre- or post-adjudication). The modular approach needs a single entity to host, support, manage and maintain software-based services, predictive models and solutions from a central location for the customers who access it.

It must allow access via a secure private data connection rather than installing the software in multiple IT infrastructures (and data facilities). This design must provide access to the best and latest software without worrying about upgrades, data security and costly installations. All technology and decision components must reside within the module. The third-party host of the modular solution cannot be a direct competitor to any government or private payer or stakeholder who integrates into the system.

Processing, Scoring and Storage—The platform must be a high volume, fast, real-time IT solution, which includes data pooling, data storage, and scoring capabilities to quickly and accurately capture and evaluate data from millions of claims per day. The system must be secure and must have Health Insurance Portability and Accountability Act (HIPAA), Payment Card Industry (PCI), Federal Information Securities Management Act (FISMA) and Statement on Audited Standards Number 70 (SAS 70) compliant data processing centers.

Data Consortium—A centralized data file (consortium) that pools (accumulates) data from all government and private medical claims data sources must be created. Specifically, the Congress must mandate that health care payers are authorized to and must provide existing claims data, such as Medicare's "Common Working File," Medicaid files, and Private Insurance claims data, to consortium data files for the purpose of fraud and abuse detection. Pooled data should be transmitted and stored in an industry-standard secure data environment (see previous requirement) for use in building medical fraud detection models that have a comprehensive view of provider activity across all payers.

Market View—Claims data from all markets must flow through a central source so the waste, fraud and abuse system can "look across" all markets and geographies in health care to identify fraud and abuse in Medicare, Medicaid, TRICARE, and private payers holistically. Cross-market visibility is necessary to identify unusual provider and patient behavior patterns and fraud schemes that may not be identified by looking independently at just one payer's transactions.

Behavior Engine—The system must provide, in real-time, the ability to identify high-risk behavior patterns across markets, geographies and specialty group providers to detect waste, fraud, and abuse, and to identify providers that unknowingly exhibit unusual behavior patterns. Behavior pattern technology that provides the capability to compare a provider's current behavior to their own past behavior and to compare a provider's current behavior to that of other providers in the same specialty group and geographic location is required in order to provide a comprehensive fraud prevention solution.

Predictive Model—The fraud detection and prevention system must implement a statistically sound, empirically derived predictive modeling technology that is designed to prevent (versus post-payment detect) waste, fraud, and abuse. This system must use historical transaction data, from across all markets, to build and re-develop scoring models. It must have the capability to incorporate external data and external models from other sources into a health care predictive waste, fraud, and abuse model. It must also provide for a "feedback loop" to provide outcome information on adjudicated claims so future system enhancements can "learn" from previous claims experiences.

Change-Control—The Platform must have the infrastructure to implement new models and attributes in a test environment prior to moving into a production environment. Capabilities must exist to quickly make changes to models, attributes, or strategies to react to changing patterns in fraud.

Scoring Engine—Must be able to identify high-risk claims by scoring them on a real-time capacity prior to payment. The scores must then be communicated to a Fraud Management System.

Fraud Management System—A Fraud Management system, which contains workflow management and workstation tools, must provide the ability to systematically present scores, reason codes, and treatment actions for high-risk scored transactions. Analysts must have the capability to access, review, and research claims efficiently, as well as decline or approve claims (payments) in an automated manner.

Workflow management must be combined with the ability to utilize principles of experimental design to provide the capability to compare and measure detection rates between test and control strategies. Strategy testing must allow for continuous improvement and maximum effectiveness in keeping up with ever changing fraud and abuse patterns.

The system must provide the capability to test different treatments or actions randomly (typically through use of random digit assignments). The system must allow for tiered approaches for different types of treatments and actions such as:

- Having flexibility, based upon configuration, to identify and queue the smallest percentage of transactions with the highest probability of fraud.
- Payment intervention—decline or partial pay.
- Soft-gloves approach when interacting with providers who are less risky.
- Capability to interact in an automated and efficient manner such as systematically or telephonically to verify claim or provider identity information.

Decision Technology—A critical component in preventing waste, fraud, and abuse is the ability to review and score all claims across all providers in all health care segments systematically, prior to edits or filters. It is necessary to capture the full consumer claim and associated history to incorporate into the fraud system a solution to minimize unwarranted interventions with a provider. The system must have the capability to monitor consumer transactions in real-time and monitor provider behavior at different stages within the transaction flow based upon provider, transaction, and consumer trends. This approach must provide for the identification of provider and claims excessive usage patterns and trends that differ from similar peer groups. The ideal fraud prevention solution must have the capability to trigger on multiple criteria, such as predictive model scores or proprietary attributes. It must be able to segment transaction waste, fraud, and abuse into multiple types for health care categories and business types that occur today.

Feedback Loop—A "Feedback Loop" is mandatory, where all payers provide post payment information about the eventual status of a claim as "Normal," "Waste," "Fraud," "Abuse," or "Education Required." The transactions feedback loop will enable health care agencies to measure the actual amount of waste, fraud, and abuse as well as the savings in the system. This "feedback loop" will also provide the ability to retrain future, enhanced models. It must also create an industry file that contains information on previous fraud and abuse claims as well as abuse perpetrated by consumers, providers, and fraud rings. It will be used to alert other payers, as well as for subsequent fraud solution development.

Tracking and Reporting—Infrastructure must exist to ascertain system, strategy, and predictive model Return on Investment. Dynamic model validation analysis and reporting must be made available to ensure a strategy or predictive model has not degraded over time or is no longer effective. Queue reporting must be created and made available for population estimates of what claims were flagged, what claims received treatment and ultimately what results occurred—fraud identification or normal claim (by segment or decile). The capability must also exist to complete tracking and reporting for prevention strategies and actions residing farther upstream in the health care payment flow. A reliable metric to measure the dollars that are never paid due to identification of fraud and abuse, as well as a capability to effectively test and estimate the impact from different actions and treatments utilized to detect and prevent fraud and abuse must be created and agreed upon by health care leadership. Measuring results must not only include fraud identified, but also waste and abuse too—to capture the full picture of costs mitigated.

In the end, the central operating principle of a next generation of advanced fraud detection must not deny health care services. It must not negatively impact prompt-pay laws because assessments are late. In fact, it must speed up the payment process. Constant and consistent test/control strategies must be implemented by stakeholders, with results shared on a quarterly basis to validate improving progress in identifying and preventing waste, fraud, and abuse. With this advanced technology, health care payers must use standard industry waste/fraud/abuse measures of success.

Bibliography

American Council of Life Insurers, *Life Insurers Fact Book 2012*, Washington, DC: American Council of Life Insurers, 2012.

Anderson G, Chronic Care: Making the Case for Ongoing Care, Robert Wood Johnson Foundation, 2010, www.rwjf.org/files/research/50968chronic.care, accessed August 7, 2017.

Anderson OW, *Blue Cross Since 1929: Accountability and the Public Trust*, Cambridge, MA: Ballinger Publishing Company, 1975.

Arrow KJ, "Uncertainty and the Welfare Economics of Medical Care," *American Economic Review* 1963; 53(5):941–973.

Baicker K, Finkelstein A, "Effects of Medicaid on Clinical Outcomes," *New England Journal of Medicine* 2013 August; 369:581–583, DOI: 10.1056/NEJMc1306867

Baicker K, Taubman S, Allen H, Bernstein M, Gruber J, Newhouse JP, Schneider E, Wright B, Zaslavsky A, Finkelstein A, the Oregon Health Study Group, "The Oregon Experiment – Effects of Medicaid on Clinical Outcomes," *New England Journal of Medicine* 2013 May; 368(18):1713–1722.

Baltagi BH, Griffin JM, "The Econometrics of Rational Addiction: The Case of Cigarettes," *Journal of Business & Economic Statistics* 2001 October; 19(4):449–454.

Becker GS, Grossman M, Murphy KM, "An Empirical Analysis of Cigarette Addition," *American Economic Review* 1994; 84(3):396–418.

Becker GS, Grossman M, Murphy KM, "Rational Addiction and the Effect of Price on Consumption," *American Economic Review* 1991; 81(2):237–241.

Benko LB, "Pitching Plans to the Uninsured. Insurers Increasingly See Viable Market in Growing Pool of Middle-Class Workers Who Don't Have Health Insurance," *Modern Healthcare* 2003; 33(8):8–9.

Berwick DM, Hackbarth A, "Eliminating Waste in U.S. Health Care" [published online ahead of print March 14, 2012]. *Journal of the American Medical Association*, DOI: 10.1001/jama.2012.362

Black B, Espin-Sanchez J-A, French E, Litvak K, "The Long-Term Effect of Health Insurance on Near-Elderly Health and Mortality," *American Journal of Health Economics* 2017; 3(3):281–311.

Brill S, "Bitter Pill: Why Medical Bills Are Killing Us," *Time Magazine*, April 3, 2013.

Cabral M, Mahoney M, "Externalities and Taxation of Supplemental Insurance: A Study of Medicare and Medigap," *NBER Working Paper* No. 19787, January 2014.

Chaloupka F, "Rational Addictive Behavior and Cigarette Smoking," *Journal of Political Economy* 1991 August; 99(4):722–742.

Chaloupka FJ, Grossman M, Saffer H, "The Effects of Price on Alcohol Consumption and Alcohol-Related Problems," *Alcohol Research and Health* 2002; 26(1):22–34.

Chaloupka FJ, Grossman M, Saffer H, "The Effects of Price on the Consequences of Alcohol Use and Abuse," *Recent Developments in Alcohol* 1998; 14:331–346.

Chari VV, Eslami K, "Evaluating the Phelps-Parente Policy Proposal," Department of Economics, University of Minnesota, 2016.

Chernew M, Newhouse J, "Health Care Spending Growth," in Pauly MV, McGuire TG, Barros PP, eds., *Handbook of Health Economics, Volume 2*, 1–43, Amsterdam: North Holland, 2012.

Chetty R, "Bounds on Elasticities with Optimization Frictions: A Synthesis of Micro and Macro Evidence on Labor Supply," *Econometrica* 2012 May; 80(3):969–1019.

Chockley N, Chung A, Findlay S, Kotis L, *The Uninsured: A Study of Health Plan Initiatives and the Lessons Learned*, Washington, DC: National Institute for Health Care, 2003.

Coalition Against Insurance Fraud, Go Figure: fraud data, www.insurancefraud.org/stats.htm, accessed July 27, 2009.

Congressional Budget Office, *The Distribution of Major Tax Expenditures in the Individual Income Tax System*, Washington, DC: CBO, May 2013.

Congressional Budget Office, *Macroeconomic Analysis of a 10 Percent Cut in Income Tax Rates*, Technical Paper Series, Washington, DC: CBO, May 2004.

Congressional Budget Office, "Trends in Federal Tax Revenues and Rates," Statement of Douglas W. Elmendorf, Director, before the Committee on Finance, United States Senate, December 2, 2010.

Congressional Research Service *CRS Report to the Congress: US Health Care Spending: Comparison with Other OECD Countries*, CRS, September 17, 2007.

Cook PJ, Tauchen G, "The Effect of Liquor Taxes on Heavy Drinking," *Bell Journal of Economics* 1982; 13(2):379–390.

Coughlin TA, Holahan J, Caswell K, McGrath M, *Uncompensated Care for Uninsured in 2013: A Detailed Examination*, Menlo Park, CA: Kaiser Family Foundation, May 2014.

Darby MR, Karni E, "Competition and the Optimal Amount of Fraud," *Journal of Law and Economics* 1973 April; 16(1):67–88.

Daschle T, Domenici P, Frist W, Rivlin A, "Prescription for Patient-Centered Care and Cost Containment," *New England Journal of Medicine* 2013 August 1; 69(5):471–474.

Department of Health and Human Services, "Notice of Availability: Secretarial Recognition of Certain Healthcare Information Technology Standards Panel (HITSP) Interoperability Specifications as Interoperability Standards for Health Information Technology," *Federal Register* 2008; 73(15):3973–3977.

Dowd M, "I'm President, So No More Broccoli," *New York Times*, March 23, 1990.

Enthoven AC, "The Competition Strategy – Status and Prospects," *New England Journal of Medicine* 1981 January 8; 304:109–112.

Enthoven AC, "A New Proposal to Reform the Tax Treatment of Health Insurance," *Health Affairs* 1984 Spring; 3:21–39.

Fairlie RW, Kapur K, Gates S, "Is Employer-Based Health Insurance a Barrier to Entrepreneurship?" *Journal of Health Economics* 2011 January; 30(1):146–162.

Falk J, "Comparing Benefits and Total Compensation in the Federal Government and the Private Sector," Congressional Budget Office, January 2012; *Working Paper* 2012-4.

Fisher ES, Wennberg DE, Stukel TA, et al., "The Implications of Regional Variations in Medicare Spending. Part 1: The Content, Quality, and Accessibility of Care," *Annals of Internal Medicine* 2003a; 138(4):273–287.

Fisher ES, Wennberg DE, Stukel TA, et al., "The Implications of Regional Variations in Medicare Spending. Part 2: Health Outcomes and Satisfaction with Care," *Annals of Internal Medicine* 2003b; 138(4):288–298.

Fonkych K, Taylor R, *The State and Pattern of Health Information Technology Adoption*, Santa Monica, CA: The RAND Corporation, 2005.

Frayling TM, Timpson NJ, Weedon N, et al., "A Common Variant in the FTO Gene Is Associated with Body Mass Index and Predisposes to Childhood and Adult Obesity," *Science* 2007; 316:889–894.

Gabel J, Pickreign J, McDevitt R, Briggs T, "Taxing Cadillac Health Plans May Produce Chevy Results," *Health Affairs* 2009; 29:174.

Garber AM, Phelps CE, "The Economic Foundations of Cost-Effectiveness Analysis," *Journal of Health Economics* 1997; 16(1):1–31.

Gaynor M, Gertler P, "Moral Hazard and Risk Spreading in Partnerships," *RAND Journal of Economics* 1995; 26(4):591–613.

General Accounting Office, *Report to Congressional Committees, Medicare Fraud and Abuse: DOJ Continues to Promote Compliance with False Claims Act Guidance*, April 2002.

Gold MR, Siegel JE, Russell LB, Weinstein MC, eds., *Cost Effectiveness in Health and Medicine*, New York: Oxford University Press, 1996.

Goldstein GS, Pauly MV, "Group Health Insurance as a Local Public Good," in Rosett RN, ed., *The Role of Health Insurance in the Health Services Sector*, 73–110, Cambridge, MA: National Bureau of Economic Research, 1976.

Government Accountability Office, *Medicare Supplemental Coverage: Medigap and Other Factors Are Associated with Higher Estimate Health Care Expenditures*, GAO-13-811, September, 2013.

Grier P, "Health Care Reform Bill 101: What Does it Mean For Seniors?" *Christian Science Monitor*, March 22, 2010.

Grossman M, Chaloupka F, "The Demand for Cocaine by Young Adults: A Rational Addiction Approach," *Journal of Health Economics* 1998; 17(4):472–474.

Gruber J, "The Incidence of Payroll Taxation: Evidence from Chile," *Journal of Labor Economics* 1997; 15(3):S72–S101.

Gruber J, Kosegi B, "Is Addiction 'Rational'? Theory and Evidence," *Quarterly Journal of Economics* 2001 November; 116(4):1261–1303.

Gruber J, Owings M, "Physician Financial Incentives and Caesarian Sections Delivery," *RAND Journal of Economics* 1996; 27(1):99–123.

Gruber J, Simon K, "Crowd-out 10 Years Later: Have Recent Public Insurance Expansions Crowded Out Private Health Insurance?" *Journal of Health Economics* 2008; 27:201–217.

Gupta A, Parente S, Sanyal P, "Future of Health Insurance Procurement: Lessons from the Online HMO Auctions," *International Journal of Health Care Finance and Economics* 2012 December; 12(4):303–322.

Hadley J, Waidmann T, Zuckerman S, Berenson RA, "Medical Spending and the Health of the Elderly," *Health Services Research* 2011 October; 46(5):1333–1361.

Haynes RB, Walker CJ, "Computer-Aided Quality Assurance," *Archives of Internal Medicine* 1987; 147:1297–1301.

Helms RB, "Tax Policy and the History of the Health Insurance Industry," in Aaron HJ, Berman LE, eds., *Using Taxes to Reform Health Insurance*, 13–35, Washington, DC: Brookings Institution, 2008.

Hickson GB, Altmeier WA, Perrin JM, "Physician Reimbursement by Salary or Fee For Service: Effects on Physician Practice Behavior in a Randomized Controlled Prospective Study," *Pediatrics* 1987; 80(3):3344–3350.

Hillman BJ, Joseph CA, Mabry MR, et al., "Frequency and Cost of Diagnostic Imaging in Office Practice: A Comparison of Self-Referring and Radiologist-Referring Physicians," *New England Journal of Medicine* 1990; 323:1604–1608.

Himmelstein DU, Thorne D, Warren E, Woolhandler S, "Medical Bankruptcy in the United States, 2007: Results of a National Study," *American Journal of Medicine* 2009; 122(8):741–746.

Hogan C, *Exploring the Effects of Secondary Coverage on Medicare Spending of the Elderly*, Washington, DC: MedPAC, 2014.

Hotelling H, "Stability in Competition," *Economic Journal* 1929; 39:41–57.

Huang JT, Jacobson GA, Neuman T, et al., *Medigap: Spotlight on Enrollment, Premiums, and Recent Trends*, Menlo Park, CA: Kaiser Family Foundation, April 2013.

Institute of Medicine, *To Err is Human: Building a Safer Health System*, Washington, DC: National Academy Press, 2000.

Jackson TH, *The Logic and Limits of Bankruptcy Law*, Cambridge, MA: Harvard University Press, 1986.

Jacobsen G, Damico A, Neuman T, Gold M, "Medicare Advantage 2015 Data Spotlight: Overview of Plan Changes," Menlo Park, CA: Kaiser Family Foundation, December 10, 2014.

Jacobson GA, Neuman P, Damico A, "At Least Half of New Medicare Advantage Enrollees Had Switched from Traditional Medicare During 2006–2011," *Health Affairs* 2015; 34(1):48–55.

Jencks SJ, Williams MV, Coleman EA, "Rehospitalizations Among Patients in the Medicare Fee-For-Service Program," *New England Journal of Medicine* 2009 April 2; 360:1418–1428.

Joint Committee on Taxation, *Estimates of Federal Tax Expenditures for Fiscal Years 2012–2017*, Washington, DC: US Government Printing Office, February 1, 2013. JCS-1-13.

Karaca-Mandic P, Abraham J, Phelps CE, "How Do Health Insurance Loading Fees Vary by Group Size?: Implications for Healthcare Reform," *International Journal of Health Care Finance and Economics* 2011; 11(3):181–207.

Kawamoto K, Houlihan CA, Balas EA, Lobach DF, "Improving Clinical Practice using Clinical Decision Support Systems: A Systematic Review of Trials to Identify Features Critical to Success," *British Medical Journal* 2005; 330:765–768.

Keane MP, "Labor Supply and Taxes: A Survey," *Journal of Economic Literature* 2011; 49(4):961–1075.

Keeler EB, Buchanan JL, Rolph JE, et al., *The Demand for Episodes of Treatment in the Health Insurance Experiment*, Santa Monica, CA: The RAND Corporation Report R-3454-HHS, March 1988.

Keynes JM, *A Tract on Monetary Reform*, London: Macmillan, 1924.

Kotlikoff LJ, Summers LH, "Tax Incidence in a Life Cycle Model with Variable Labor Supply," *Quarterly Journal of Economics* 1979; 93(4):702–718.

Kronich R, "Health Insurance Coverage and Mortality Revisited," *Health Affairs* 2009 August; 44(4):1211–1231.

Laugesen MJ, Glied SA, "Higher Fees Paid to US Physicians Drive Higher Spending for Physician Services Compared to Other Countries," *Health Affairs* 2011; 30(9):1647–1656.

Liu S, Chollet D, *Price and Income Elasticity of Demand for Health Insurance and Health Care Services: A Critical Review of the Literature*, Washington, DC: Mathematica Policy Research, March 24, 2006.

Ma CT, McGuire T, "Optimal Health Insurance and Provider Payment," *American Economic Review* 1997; 87(4):685–704.

McClellan M, McKethan AN, Lewis JL, Roski J, Fisher ES, "A National Strategy to Put Accountable Care into Practice," *Health Affairs* 2010; 29(5):982–990.

McGinnis JM, Foege WH, "Actual Causes of Death in the United States," *Journal of the American Medical Association* 1993 November 10; 270(18):2207–2212.

Madrian B, "Employment-Based Health Insurance and Job Mobility: Is There Evidence of Job-Lock?" *Quarterly Journal of Economics* 1994; 109(1):27–54.

Manning WG, Newhouse JP, Duan N, et al., "Health Insurance and the Demand for Medical Care: Evidence from a Randomized Experiment," *American Economic Review* 1987; 77(3):251–277.

Mitchell BM, Phelps CE, "National Health Insurance: Some Costs and Effects of Mandated Employee Coverage," *Journal of Political Economy* 1976 June; 84:3.

Mitchell JM, Scott E, "Physician Ownership of Physical Therapy Services: Effects on Charges, Utilization, Profits and Service Characteristics," *Journal of the American Medical Association* 1992; 268(15):2055–2059.

Mokdad AH, Marks JS, Stroup DF, Gerberding JL, "Actual Causes of Death in the United States, 2000," *Journal of the American Medical Association* 2004 March 10; 291(10):1238–1245.

Mushkin S, "The Internal Revenue Code of 1954 and Health Programs," *Public Health Reports* August 1955; 70(58):791–800.

Nelson EA, Gessner BD, DeRoeck D, Duclos P, "The Role of National Advisory Committees in Supporting Evidence-based Decision Making for National Immunization Programs," *Vaccine* 2010; 28(Suppl. 1):S/A1–A110.

Neumann PJ, Rosen AB, Weinstein MC, "Medicare and Cost-Effectiveness," *New England Journal of Medicine* 2005 October 6; 353(14):1516–1522.

Neumann PJ, Sanders GD, Russell LB, Siegel JE, Ganiats TG, eds., *Cost Effectiveness in Health and Medicine, Second Edition*, Oxford: Oxford University Press, 2017.

Newhouse JP, *The Erosion of the Medical Marketplace*, Santa Monica, CA: The RAND Corporation, R-2141-1-DHEW, December 1978.

Newhouse JP, "Has the Erosion of the Medical Marketplace Stopped?" *Journal of Health, Politics, Policy and Law* 1988 Summer; 13(2):263–278.

Newhouse JP, Garber AM, "Geographic Variation in Medicare Services," *New England Journal of Medicine* 2013 April 13; 368(16):1465–1468.

Newhouse JP, Garber AM, Graham RP, et al., *Variations in Health Care Spending: Target Decision Making, not Geography*, Washington, DC: National Academy of Sciences, 2013.

Newhouse JP, the RAND Health Insurance Experiment Group, *Free for All? Lessons from the RAND Health Insurance Experiment*, Cambridge, MA: Harvard University Press, 1993.

Newhouse JP, Williams AP, Bennet BW, Schwartz WB, "Does the Geographic Distribution of Physicians Reflect Market Failure?" *Bell Journal of Economics* 1982a; 13:493–505.

Newhouse JP, Williams AP, Bennet BW, Schwartz WB, "Where Have All the Doctors Gone?" *Journal of the American Medical Association* 1982b; 247(17):2392–2396.

Nyweide DJ, Woolton L, Cuerdon TT, Pham HH, Cox M, Rajkumar R, Conway PH, "Association of Pioneer Accountable Care Organizations vs Traditional Medicare Fee for Service With Spending, Utilization, and Patient Experience," *Journal of the American Medical Association* 2015; 313(21):2152–2161.

Parente ST, "Harnessing Health Information in Real Time: Back to the Future for a More Practical and Effective Infrastructure," in the Series: *Beyond Repeal and Replace: Ideas for Real Health Reform*, Washington, DC: American Enterprise Institute, December 8, 2010.

Pauly MV, *Health Reform without Side Effects: Making Markets Work for Individual Health Insurance*, Stanford, CA: The Hoover Institution Press, 2010.

Pauly MV, "Taxation, Health Insurance, and Market Failure in the Medical Economy," *Journal of Economic Literature* 1986; 24(2):629–675.

Phelps CE, *The Demand for Health Insurance: A Theoretical and Empirical Investigation*, Santa Monica, CA: RAND Corporation, R-1054-OEO, July 1973.

Phelps CE, "The Demand for Reimbursement Insurance," in Rosett RN, ed., *The Role of Health Insurance in the Health Services Sector*, 115–155, New York: The National Bureau of Economic Research, 1976.

Phelps CE, *Eight Questions You Should Ask About Our Health Care System (Even if the Answers Make You Sick)*, Stanford, CA: Hoover Institution Press, 2010.

Phelps CE, *Health Economics* (5th ed.), Boston, MA: Pearson Press, 2012.

Phelps CE, "The Inter-Related Markets for Medical Care and Health Insurance," February 17, 1996, https://urresearch.rochester.edu/institutionalPublicationPublicView.action;jsessionid=C214EA518440B61EE2AEE9149F8E3977?institutionalItemId=2376, last accessed August 7, 2017.

Phelps CE, "Medical Insurance: Risk Spreading vs. Moral Hazard Revisited," *Working Paper*, November 23, 2014.

Phelps CE, Buysman E, Gomez-Rey G, "Costs and Clinical Outcomes Associated with Use of Ranolazine for Treatment of Angina," *Clinical Therapeutics* 2012; 34(6):1395–1407.

Phelps CE, Mushlin AI, "Focusing Medical Technology Assessment Using Medical Decision Theory," *Medical Decision Making* 1988 October; 8(3):279–289.

Phelps CE, Reisinger AL, "Unresolved Risk Under Medicare," in Pauly MV, Kissick WL, eds., *Lessons from the First Twenty Years of Medicare: Research Implications for Public and Private Sector Policy*, 117–150, Philadelphia, PA: University of Pennsylvania Press, 1988.

Prudential Insurance Company, *Sixth Annual Study of Employee Benefits: Today and Beyond*, Newark, NJ: The Prudential Insurance Company of America, 2011.

Roebuck MC, Liberman JN, Gemmil-Toyama M, Brennan TA, "Medication Adherence Leads To Lower Health Care Use and Costs Despite Increased Drug Spending," *Health Affairs* 2011; 30(1):91–99.

Roth AE, *Who Gets What—and Why: The New Economics of Matchmaking and Market Design*, New York: Houghton Mifflin Harcourt, 2015.

Rothschild M, Stiglitz J, "Equilibrium in Competitive Insurance Markets: An Essay on the Economics of Incomplete Information," *Quarterly Journal of Economics* 1976; 90(4):629–649.

Royal College of Physicians of London, *Purchasers' Guidelines to Genetic Services in the NHS. An Aid to Assessing the Genetic Services Required by the Resident Population of an Average Health District*, London: Royal College of Physicians, 1991.

Saccone SF, Hindrichs AL, Saccone L, et al., "Cholinergic Nicotinic Receptor Genes Implicated in a Nicotine Dependence Association Study Targeting 348 Candidate Genes with 3713 SNPs," *Human Molecular Genetics* 2007 January 1; 16(1):36–49.

Sadanand A, Wilde LL, "A Generalized Model of Pricing for Homogeneous Goods Under Imperfect Information," *Review of Economic Studies* 1982; 49:229–240.

Schwartz A, Wilde LL, "Competitive Equilibria in Markets for Heterogeneous Goods Under Imperfect Information: A Theoretical Analysis with Policy Implications," *Bell Journal of Economics* 1982a; 13(1):181–193.

Schwartz A, Wilde LL, "Imperfect Information, Monopolistic Competition, and Public Policy," *American Economic Review* 1982b May; 72(2):18–23.

Schwartz A, Wilde LL, "Intervening in Markets on the Basis of Imperfect Information," *Pennsylvania Law Review* 1979; 127:630–682.

Skinner J, "Causes and Consequences of Regional Variations in Health Care," in Pauly MV, McGuire TG, Barros PP, eds., *Handbook of Health Economics, Volume 2*, 1–43, 45–92, Amsterdam: North Holland, 2012.

Skinner J, Fisher ES, "Reflections on Geographic Variations in U.S. Health Care, Dartmouth Institute for Health Policy and Clinical Practice," May 12, 2010, www.dartmouthatlas.org/downloads/press/Skinner_Fisher_DA_05_10.pdf, last accessed August 7, 2017.

Sommers BD, Gawande AA, Baicker K, "Health Insurance Coverage and Health – What Recent Evidence Tells Us," *New England Journal of Medicine* 2017 June 21, DOI: 10.1056/NEJMsb1706645

Sommers BD, Long SK, Baicker K, "Changes in Mortality after Massachusetts Health Care Reform: A Quasi-Experimental Study," *Annals of Internal Medicine* 2014 May 6; 160(9):585–593.

Sparrow MK, "Criminal Prosecution as a Deterrent to Health Care Fraud": Testimony before the Senate Judiciary Subcommittee on Crime and Drugs, Washington, DC, May 20, 2009.

Spetz J, Parente ST, Town RJ, Bazarko D, "Scope-Of-Practice Laws For Nurse Practitioners Limit Cost Savings That Can Be Achieved in Retail Clinics," *Health Affairs* 2013 November; 32(11):1977–1984.

Stigler G, "The Division of Labor Is Limited by the Extent of the Market," *Journal of Political Economy* 1951; 59:185–193.

Stroupe KT, Kinney ED, Kniesner TJ, "Does Chronic Illness Affect the Adequacy of Health Insurance Coverage?" *Journal of Health, Politics, Policy and Law* 2000 April; 25(2):309–341.

van Ours JC, "The Price Elasticity of Hard Drugs: The Case of Opium in the Dutch East Indies, 1923–1938," *Journal of Political Economy* 1995 April; 103(2):261–279.

Wilensky GR, "The Shortfalls of 'Obamacare'," *New England Journal of Medicine* 2012; 367(16):1479–1481.

Wright A, Goldberg H, Hongsermeier T, et al., "A Description and Functional Taxonomy of Rule-Based Decision Support Content at a Large Integrated Delivery Network," *Journal of the American Medical Informatics Association* 2007 July–August; 14(4):489–496.

Zaccagnino MJ, "International Health Care and Physician Remuneration," Senior honors thesis, University of Rochester, Department of Economics, 1994.

Zeckhauser RJ, "Medical Insurance: A Case Study of the Trade-off Between Risk Spreading and Appropriate Incentives," *Journal of Economic Theory* 1970; 2(1):10–26.

Index

Diagrams and graphs are given in italics.